WORKING
THE PIVOT
POINTS

TO MAKE AMERICA WORK AGAIN

Frank Islam • Ed Crego

12/17/13

Jay,

Thanks for your good work.

Hope you enjoy this book and
its Education chapter.

— Ed Crego

IMC Publishing
Potomac, MD

Table of Contents

Foreword

This is a book about American pivot points. We define pivot point as *an area that must be leveraged and addressed effectively in order to effectuate change and achieve positive outcomes.*

Pivot points define the character and shape the destiny of a nation and its people. They establish the rules of the game and influence the attitude of the public. They create an upward or downward trajectory and accelerate or decelerate forward movement and progress.

The debt ceiling debate in the summer of 2011 and the manner in which it was handled was a critical pivot point. Although the debate centered on what in the past had been a minor issue, the nature of the process and the discourse and disgust that it engendered elevated this from a symbolic or ritualistic act in a minor pivot point area to one with significant short-term and long-term ramifications.

Pivot points can be major, moderate or minor in nature. How we manage our current major pivot points will determine the country's future success and that of our citizens.

In our opinion, the major pivot point areas for the United States today include:

- The deficit and debt crisis
- Revenue deficits
- Congressional dysfunction
- Citizenship dysfunction
- Individual economic well-being
- Global competition
- Manufacturing
- Entrepreneurs
- Immigration
- Education
- Innovation

We devote a chapter to each of these pivot points. In each chapter, we describe the nature and status of the pivot point at the time the book went to the publisher, chronicle the progress made or lack thereof on the point over the past two years and present ideas for "working" the pivot point area going forward.

The central elements for working a pivot point are:

- Pivot persons—citizens and leaders from the private and public sectors who commit to working together to create shared solutions to problems and to advocate for their implementation
- Pivot policy—a mutually agreed upon agenda for action on the shared solution
- Pivot programs—well-defined, controlled and results-oriented methods for rolling out the policy in as cost-effective and efficient manner as possible

We discuss these elements throughout the book as we review each pivot point.

We begin the book in the preface and the first chapter by examining why pivot points matter today and in American history. We end the book in the epilogue by providing our summary judgment regarding where the United States stands in addressing all of these major pivot points and with some prognostications regarding the future.

We decided to write this book in mid-2011 and we said "pens down" on July 4, 2013. So, essentially it covers a two-year time period. During that period, in many of these key pivot point areas, positive progress has either been painfully slow in coming or nonexistent.

We expected that to be the case given the tone and tenor of these times. And, as we point out in the first chapter and epilogue of the book, it is not atypical for key pivot points throughout American history.

That is why we have written *Working the Pivot Points* as a work in process and designed it to be a living document. We end each pivot point area chapter with a section called "Pivot Point Report Card." We have structured that section to enable the reader to reflect on the status of that area at the time he or she is completing the chapter.

We will be posting our own assessments on progress in these pivot point areas on an occasional basis. To see those assessments and to provide your own input and feedback on an area, visit *http://www. workingthepivotpoints.com.*

While at that site, you can also sign up to subscribe to our *Pivot Points Newsletter,* which we will be issuing on a monthly basis. We will address these current and other emerging pivot point areas in the newsletter.

In conclusion, pivot points treated properly should not be about endings or beginnings but about being and becoming. They should be about listening and learning. They should be about realizing the full potential and possibilities for America and Americans. We hope this book makes a small contribution to achieving those ends.

Preface: Pivot Points in Perspective

I want to talk to you tonight about a fundamental threat to American Democracy . . .

The threat is nearly invisible in ordinary ways. It is a crisis of confidence. It is a crisis that strikes at the very heart and soul and spirit of our national will . . .

Confidence has defined our course and served as a link between generations. We've always believed in something called progress. We've always had a faith that the days of our children would be better than our own.

Our people are losing that faith, not only in government itself but in the ability as citizens to serve as the ultimate rulers and shapers of the democracy.

President Jimmy Carter spoke those words in his "Crisis of Confidence" speech—later labeled his "malaise" speech—delivered from the Oval Office on July 15, 1979, at the height of the country's energy crisis and with inflation spiraling out of control.[1]

THE CONFIDENCE GAME

President Carter's comments could have been used to describe the American condition in 2012. Neither President Barack Obama nor

Governor Mitt Romney uttered anything similar, however. In fact, they both expressed great confidence in America's future because of their confidence in the American people.

The American people, on the other hand, did not necessarily share the president's and the governor's confidence. Various polls taken in the last few months of the campaign cycle showed this to be the case. For example,

- A Pew Research Center report released in August 2012 indicated that "85% of self-described middle-class adults say that it is more difficult now than it was a decade ago . . . to maintain their standard of living." And, "43% of those in the middle class expect their children's standard of living will be better than their own." That compares to 51 percent of those surveyed in 2008.[2]

- Another Pew Center report released in September 2012 revealed that the number of people who classified themselves as "lower middle" or "lower class" had grown from "a quarter of the adult population to about a third in the past four years." Only 51 percent of those who saw themselves as lower class said that "hard work brings success." The report found 41 percent thought their children's standard of living would be "better" than their own and 35 percent predicted it would be "worse."[3]

- A Gallup poll released in late October showed that "For the first time in more than five years slightly more Americans are feeling financially better off than they were a year ago, rather than worse off, by 38% to 34%." That was good but not great news. One-third of the population that is "worse off" is still a lot of unhappy people.[4]

- Consumer confidence as measured and reported by the Conference Board also was up in October, to 72.2 percent. Again, that was good but not great news.[5] As *Bloomberg Businessweek* pointed out, "The consumer confidence index has fluctuated sharply this year. It's fallen five times in the past nine months . . ." And, "the index remains well below the reading of 90 that indicates a healthy economy."[6]

An October *Wall Street Journal/NBC News* political poll disclosed that these diminished circumstances and shrunken confidence caused registered voters to put an increasing importance of the outcome of the presidential election. Of those surveyed, 55 percent said "who wins the upcoming election" would "make a great deal of difference" in their lives.

Commenting on those results, Ezra Klein noted, "That's a 10 percentage point increase over the 2004 election, and more than double the percentage of voters who felt that way about the elections of 1996 and 1992. The stakes this year are higher—and most voters know it."[7]

While the voters knew it, many of those in the political class preferred pointing fingers and blaming one another. Those in the chattering class confined themselves to repeating the same tired old messages within their own echo chambers. When it came to depicting the full reality and the seriousness of our condition, the dominant sound was silence.

In spite of this lack of public acknowledgment by most in leadership positions, the nation and its citizens had moved beyond malaise. Our state at the end of 2012 remained one of misery, melancholy and mania. The country was at a major pivot point. We ignore it at our peril.

AMERICAN MISERY

In terms of misery, the numbers by themselves tell only part of the story. They take on meaning when they are put into context. Consider the following:[8]

- **7.7 percent**—the official unemployment rate in December 2012. The unemployment rates in December 2009, December 2010 and December 2011 were 9.9, 9.1 and 8.5 percent, respectively. So, there has been slow progress and positive movement. Unfortunately, the real unemployment rate is almost twice that reported when people who have fallen out of the workforce are considered. And, when workers who are in undernourished jobs have reduced wages or hours or are temporary in nature are considered, the job-constrained employment number grows to about 25 percent.

- **15.0 percent**—the official poverty rate for 2011. The poverty rate dropped slightly from 15.1 percent for 2010 when it was the highest that it had been in more than five decades. The 15.0 percent places 46.2 million in poverty and translates into 1 in 7 Americans living in poverty. And this number does not even include the millions of working poor who are above the poverty threshold.

- **51.0 percent**—the percentage of American adults who occupied the middle income tier in 2011. In 1971, this percentage was 61.0 percent. The middle income tier took in 46.0 percent of total U.S. income in 2011 compared to 62.0 percent of the total 40 years ago.

- **61.8 percent**—the percentage of job losses in the fourth quarter of 2010 that came from small businesses. In that same time period, small businesses only created 54.1 percent of all new jobs. That was the first time in recorded history that small business job losses were higher than jobs created.

- **39.0 percent**—the decline in the median net worth of American households between 2007 and 2010 from $126,400 to $77,300. According to the *Washington Post*, "That puts Americans roughly on a par with where they were in 1992."

- **2.2 percent**—GDP growth in the United States in 2012. That compares to 2.4 percent growth in 2010 and 1.8 percent in 2011. The numbers remain positive but anemic. While we had not technically fallen back into a recession, to many Americans it felt like it. We need to get GDP above 3.4 percent to start a job-creating recovery.

It's been said that misery loves company. That truism is borne out by the fact that most Americans are in this economically distressed state together.

Median household income, adjusted for inflation, declined for the fourth straight year in 2011 to $50,054. 2009 was the first time in recorded history that the annual median household income did not increase over the year before. The real median household income has fallen 8.1 percent since 2007.

It gets even worse. Here is a stunning statistic: *50 percent of U.S. workers earned less than $26,364 in 2010.*

A study released by The Rockefeller Foundation in 2010 substantiated that economic insecurity in the United States is not of recent origin and is intensifying. The study notes, "it appears that more than 60 percent of the American public experienced at least one drop of 25 percent or larger in their annual income over the decade ending in 2006. In short, economic insecurity appears more the rule than the exception in American life and more so over time."[9]

Misery is not just financial. It's psychological as well. The emotional impact of a job loss or significant reduction in earnings can have a significant impact on a person's attitudes and perspective on life. The Gallup Organization has been collecting daily data on self-reported well-being on 1,000 Americans each day since January of 2008.

Angus Deaton of Princeton University conducted a longitudinal review of that data in 2011. Not surprisingly, Deaton found that "In the fall of 2008, around the time of the collapse of Lehman Brothers, and lasting into the spring of 2009, at the bottom of the stock market, Americans reported sharp declines in their life evaluation, sharp increases in worry and stress, and declines in positive affect." Surprisingly, Deaton also found that in spite of continuing high unemployment, by the end of 2010 "these measures had largely recovered, though worry remained higher and life evaluation lower than in January of 2008." There was a startling caveat to Deaton's findings, however. He reported that asking political questions before the life evaluation question reduced the positive evaluation "by an amount that dwarfs the effects of even the worst of the (financial) crisis."[10]

In other words, what is going on in the political arena is definitely another pivot point. When bad things happen there—which is almost all that has been occurring politically for the past two years or even longer—it makes average Americans feel more miserable about their lives.

AMERICAN MELANCHOLY

Given these conditions, is it any wonder that so many Americans were wistfully looking backward and longing for the good old days? Two aptly named books that came out in 2011 captured the melancholy mood of the country: Thomas Friedman and Michael Mandelbaum's *That Used to Be Us*;[11] and William Harris and Steven Beschloss' *Adrift*.[12]

Friedman and Mandelbaum characterize themselves as "frustrated optimists." But the picture they paint in their book is not an entirely optimistic one. Early on they comment on the public's "sense of resignation . . . the sense that America's best days are behind it." They also observe, "We are dangerously complacent about this new world precisely because it is a world that we invented."

Friedman and Mandelbaum are not defeatists, though. They identify the five pillars (education, infrastructure, immigration, research and development, and regulation) that they think we need to build upon to define America's future. They close their book with a section titled "Rediscovering America," which calls upon us to "update" or "upgrade" those pillars that have been part of America's historic success formula.

Like Friedman and Mandelbaum, Harris and Beschloss caution us about complacency writing: ". . . we are forced to ask whether our national complacency has made it impossible to harness our intrinsic talent and reestablish our pre-eminence in the world." They also identify and recommend critical solutions in areas such as education, immigration, manufacturing and innovation that will help to restore American greatness.

Both of these books were insightful, thoughtful and well-reasoned. They challenged us to break out of the misery and the melancholy by coming together collectively in a shared enterprise between the government and the private sector. The threshold question, however, is the one that Harris and Beschloss ask in the title of the first chapter of their book: "Are Americans Still Capable of Bold Action and Common Purpose?"

Due to the political gridlock—verging on deadlock—that has come to symbolize Washington, DC, and the one-sided actions and viewpoints of the Tea Partiers on the right and the Occupiers on the left, the answer to that question may unfortunately be "No!"

AMERICAN MANIA

When the Tea Party first burst on the scene, it was mistakenly depicted by many in the press as a diverse group of non- or bipartisan citizens who were unhappy with the Great Recession, big government and so-called Obamacare. Based upon their groundbreaking research, professors David Campbell and Robert Putnam have put that myth to bed.

Here's what Campbell and Putnam found about the Tea Partiers.[13] They are:

- Highly partisan Republicans who are more likely than others to have contacted government officials on issues
- Overwhelmingly white
- Unified in holding immigrants and blacks in low regard
- Disproportionately socially conservative
- Desirous of seeing religion play a prominent role in government

Two chilling episodes in early Republican presidential debates provide insight into the Tea Party mentality. The first came when Rick Perry was asked to comment on the 234 convicts who had been executed on death row during his tenure as governor of Texas. As Perry responded that he had no qualms or concerns about his actions, the audience broke out in raucous applause.

The second came in a later debate when Ron Paul was asked by Wolf Blitzer if a man who is terminally ill without insurance should not be treated and allowed to die. Before Paul could get out his response, some in the audience cheered and yelled "Yeah!"

The Occupiers stood in stark contrast and as polar opposites to the Tea Partiers. Where big government was ostensibly the enemy of the Tea Party, the big financial institutions and fat cats were the enemy of the Occupiers.

Unlike the Tea Partiers who closely resemble and walk in lockstep with one another, the Occupiers, who burst onto the scene in September 2011 and then disappeared just about as quickly, were a highly disparate and motley crew. The ingredient that the mostly left-wing group shared in common with their right-wing counterparts was a strong ideology that caused them to take to the streets. The Occupiers were on Wall Street and other streets across the country, but they were neither Main Street nor mainstream.

One of the complaints against Occupiers for their short-lived existence was that, unlike the Tea Partiers, they didn't work inside the system to attempt to bring about change. The question is which is more problematic—a mania that is manifested by one minority group in large-scale group protests or a mania by another minority group to take over a political party?

The answer is neither and both. When and if mania wins, the middle loses. When the middle loses, America loses.

Experts have said that Americans tend to be center right or center left, depending on the issue. If mania prevails, there will be no center left. Without its center, the nation is hollow and democracy is sacrificed.

TIPPING POINTS, TURNING POINTS AND TALKING POINTS

The confluence of misery, melancholy and mania imperil the future of America and the American dream. They place the country at what we call a major pivot point.

Some might prefer to call this a tipping point, a turning point or a talking point. We strongly prefer the term "pivot point" because pivot point implies that we can "work" on that point and be proactive to bring about positive change to address it.

We define and explain the pivot point concept in the foreword to this book. Let us now talk about these other kinds of points and how they relate to each other and the pivot point.

In science, a tipping point is the "point in which a system is displaced from a state of stable equilibrium into a different state." A turning point can be defined as "an event marking a unique or important historical change of course on which historical developments depend." A talking point is a "succinct statement designed to support one side taken on an issue."

Tipping and turning points refer to a moment when something changes. Talking points, especially in the political sense, are used primarily for propaganda purposes and to make the same argument over and over again, to ensure that nothing changes.

The United States is definitely at a tipping point. We have moved from a state of relatively stable equilibrium to one of uncertainty and instability. We are also at a turning point, of somewhat indeterminate length, that has been marked by the "great recession" followed by a prolonged and painfully slow "recovery." What we have done and will do in response to that recession and the erstwhile recovery will dictate America and Americans' future.

WHY THIS BOOK? WHY NOW? WHY US?

This book extends and amplifies the message delivered in our book *Renewing the American Dream: A Citizen's Guide for Restoring our Competitive Advantage (Renewing)*, which we co-authored along with George Munoz in 2010.[14]

Renewing's premise was that the United States is a nation at risk and that we are at a critical crossroads. In that book, we observed that the actions that we take in this decisive decade (2010–2019) will determine the future of America and the American dream.

We decided to write this book because we are in a pivotal period in this decisive decade. In the first two years of the decade and as we moved into mid-2013, there was measurable and accelerating progress in the economy writ large. There was little, however, in the economy writ small. We witnessed the ongoing misery, melancholy and mania and felt compelled to speak out again.

We wrote our earlier book because we were disappointed and disturbed by the lack of unity of purpose from our leadership after the economic collapse of 2008. We had expected a coming together similar to what occurred after 9/11. That didn't happen. In fact, the exact opposite did. We became more fragmented than ever.

Unfortunately, in the following years, things have worsened. The environment in Washington, DC, became increasingly toxic. The vitriol and animus that flowed outward—across the banks of the Potomac—poisoned citizens' actions and attitudes nationwide.

For the most part, our business executives have been AWOL. Over the past few years, many large businesses have recorded record profits. For whatever reason, companies have not been investing in the United States and banks have been slow to lend. As a result, jobs are not being created and the economy continues to flounder.

And, our democracy is fast becoming a plutocracy. It's the 1 percent against the 99 percent, and the 1 percent are winning handily. Wealth is being redistributed, but it's from the middle class to the very richest in our society and not the other way around. Income inequality is on a dramatic rise.

In the time frame from 1980 to 2005, 80 percent of the total increase in American incomes went to the top 1 percent. Today, the richest 1 percent take home almost 24 percent of the annual income in the United States, compared to just about 9 percent in 1976. Jeffrey Sachs points out that the last time the distribution of income in the United States was this skewed was just before the Great Depression in 1929.[15]

Highly partisan and divisive politicians, unresponsive business executives and an extremely wealthy class claiming and demanding greater personal returns for themselves—these are the signs of a self-centered and stagnating society. We have written this book to shine a bright spotlight on those warning signs and to provide a framework for counteracting them.

We write this book, as we did our prior book, as concerned citizens who have lived the American dream and who want to make a contribution to seeing that dream sustained for all Americans and not just the privileged few.

As we noted in *Renewing,* "The real work starts when the words stop." Let us modify that a little bit here.

Only one letter separates word from work. Words, ideas and thoughts can become the basis for work. By concentrating on and working the pivot points, we can translate concepts into action and get America working again. Let's get to work!

1 | Pivot Points in American History: The Way We Weren't

As AMERICANS, WE TEND TO ROMANTICIZE THE PAST AND TO FORGET the enormous changes and progress that has been made at the major pivot points in American history. We also have a propensity to engage in selective interpretation of the facts and not to look at primary sources to secure a true understanding and appreciation of the context in which something took place.

REVISIONIST HISTORY

The decision to read the Constitution on the floor of the House at the beginning of the 112th Congress and the unquestioning infatuation with the Founding Fathers provide excellent examples of these tendencies.

On January 6, 2011, a number of House representatives participated in a "full" reading of the Constitution, including amendments. The text that was read, however, varied from the original document as it excluded passages that were superseded by amendments.[1]

This meant that there was no reference on the House floor to the "three-fifths" clause in the section of Article I, which made slaves three-fifths of a person for taxation and apportionment purposes. It also excluded entirely the reading of the Eighteenth Amendment to the Constitution, which imposed prohibition.

Our current Constitution contains nine parts that were later changed—including who had the right to vote (originally only white males over the age of 21), election of senators by state legislatures, and the original process set out for electing the vice president. While not reading these parts may seem insignificant, it is not. This is because it misrepresents history and understates the passage of time required and extreme difficulty in addressing those pivot points that changed the Constitution.

For example, the Constitution as approved by the delegates to the Constitutional Convention in September 1787 was the product of a compromise. It was not ratified by the states until 1790, after there had been substantial national debate and several close votes in state legislatures.

It took from 1790 and a civil war for former slaves to be made citizens and given the ostensible right to vote by the Fifteenth Amendment in 1870—80 years after the Constitution's ratification. But, African Americans didn't get unimpeded voting rights until the Twenty-Fourth Amendment, which eliminated the payment of a poll tax as a requirement to vote, was passed in 1964—174 years after ratification. Women did not get the right to vote until the Nineteenth Amendment was passed in 1920—130 years after ratification.

So, the Constitution was and is not perfect—nor were our Founding Fathers, in spite of the attempt from some to sanctify them. In fact, as students of history know, the Founding Fathers were also frequently not of one mind. Their genius was the ability to reach a compromise—Federalist and Anti-Federalist joining together in the best interests of the nation and its citizens to create the enduring framework for a "more perfect union."

That ability didn't make them superhuman, however. Each of the Founding Fathers (mothers were noticeably absent) had his own beliefs and peccadilloes. That might not square well with many in the American public today. For example, Thomas Jefferson did not believe that Jesus was the son of God nor did he accept the Trinity, the Virgin Birth or the Resurrection. And Alexander Hamilton was unapologetic about an affair that he had with a married woman, claiming it was nobody's business but his own.

THE PLATFORM FOR PIVOT POINTS

That's not to say that the Constitution and the Founding Fathers are not of substantial and significant historical importance and contemporary relevance. It is to argue that the brilliance of the document, as written by its drafters, is the fact that it was established as a firm but flexible platform upon which others could improve and the nation could be built.

This was accomplished by achieving a delicate balance among individuals, the states and the federal government. This balance, with the federal government as the linchpin, enabled the United States to grow and to prosper as a great nation—a nation that operates at the intersection of capitalism and community, individualism and the common good, and being and becoming.

The federal government has been, is and will be pivotal to America's success. Unfortunately, some (maybe many) do not see or realize this. They view the federal government at best as a necessary evil and at worst as a beast that should be starved or killed.

This perspective is a flummoxing one in that it denies the inextricable role that the federal government has played in making the American democracy the greatest and the country one of the most financially successful in the history of the world. Dennis Johnson provides a scholar's viewpoint on this in his masterful book *The Laws That Shaped America: 15 Acts of Congress and Their Lasting Impact.*

Johnson says, "What guided me in selecting these fifteen laws, was the answer to this simple question: 'Where would we be without this law?' How would America's elderly fare without the security of health care and social insurance? How congested and dangerous would our surface transportation system be without the backbone of the interstate highway system? . . . Each of these fifteen laws had a lasting impact on American society and history, and has had consequences far beyond its enactment."

Johnson observes that 15 laws was not a magic number. He said he could have picked 1 or even another 15—but the ones he chose to highlight appealed to him.[2]

Not all are blind to government's contributions. In his book *Bold Endeavors: How Our Government Built America and Why It Must Rebuild It Now,* written in 2009, financier Felix Rohatyn spotlights large and transformative events that contributed to America's growth, including the Louisiana Purchase, the Erie Canal and Lincoln's support of the transcontinental railroad.[3]

Thomas Friedman and Michael Mandelbaum quote Jeff Immelt, chairman and CEO of General Electric, as follows: "We worship false idols in terms of the power of a free market. The U.S. government has been the catalyst for change for generations."[4]

In spite of ringing endorsements such as these, there is a large and influential group of elected American officials and citizens who refuse to acknowledge or accept the fact that government has been a partner—and in many instances taken the lead—in creating the playing field for American businesses and citizens.

This may be because they do not understand history—which might be the case. The National Assessment of Educational Progress recently rated history as the subject at which students are least proficient, and a June 2010 *Times* magazine survey revealed that only 18 percent of Americans surveyed said that they knew a great deal about the Constitution. Or it may be because they have ulterior motives or an alternative agenda—they would prefer to bend the arc of history away from giving government credit for any of our accomplishments.

We prefer to believe that it is ignorance rather than intent. If it is a lack of knowledge that limits understanding, then fact-based evidence can provide the reason for changing one's mind and personal growth and development. It can also enable a shared construction of reality which—while it does not build consensus—can promote cooperation, collaboration and creative problem solving.

PIVOT POINTS ON PARADE

It is from that perspective that we come back to the concept of pivot points and the role that they have played over time in advancing America and the American dream for its citizens. As we noted in the preface, pivot points can be major, moderate or minor.

Over the short history of the United States, there have been scores of major pivot points that have determined the economic and social terrain for the nation and its citizens. These include but are not limited to:

- The Constitutional Convention
- The Bill of Rights
- The Civil War
- The Fourteenth Amendment
- The Morrill Act and the Homestead Act
- Teddy Roosevelt's trust busting
- The passage of Social Security
- The GI Bill
- Building the Interstate Highway System
- *Brown* v. *Board of Education*
- *Roe* v. *Wade*
- The Space Race
- The Civil Rights Act of 1964
- Medicare legislation

Entire books could and have been written on each of these pivot points. Our purpose here is not to provide an in-depth treatment or analysis of all of these points but rather to highlight a select few from different eras and to describe them briefly in terms of:

- The Context: What was the general situation at the time the pivot point occurred?
- The Response: What actions were taken/What was the outcome?
- Alternative Scenario: What might have happened if the course/ actions taken/or resolution of the point had been different from that taken?

These snapshots illustrate the manner and extent to which pivot points over time have, are and will shape the stream of American history and the nation's destiny.[5] Without further ado, let's proceed with the parade of pivot points and look at the following.

The Country's Founding

- The Constitutional Convention
- The Bill of Rights

Civil War Period

- The Morrill Act
- The Homestead Act

Beginning of the 20th Century

- The Sherman Antitrust Act and Trust Busting

The Great Depression

- The Social Security Act

Post World War II

- The GI Bill

The Constitutional Convention[6]

The Context

In 1786, the United States and many of the individual states were bankrupt. Congress had no money to pay the debts owed to foreign lenders who had supported the Revolutionary War or our soldiers who had fought it. Moreover, the states were involved in an endless war of economic discrimination against each other. This was attributable primarily to the fact that the Articles of Confederation that had been adopted in 1777 created a weak form of federal government and gave Congress virtually no power to regulate domestic affairs and absolutely no power to tax or regulate commerce. European nations were dismissing the United States as a "third rate republic." These and many other troubles with the existing Confederation of States convinced the Continental Congress in February 1787 to call for a Constitutional Convention "to devise such further provisions as shall appear to them necessary to render the constitution of the Federal Government adequate to the exigencies of the union."

The Response

On May 25, 1787, 55 delegates from 12 states (Rhode Island, which opposed the Constitution, sent no delegates) convened in Philadelphia. Four days after that, Governor Edmund Randolph of Virginia presented a plan (the Virginia Plan) chiefly drafted by James Madison that called for a strong national government with both branches of the legislature apportioned by population. The Virginia Plan included provisions for the national government to legislate when "separate States are incompetent" and for veto power over state legislatures.

In mid-June, delegate William Paterson of New Jersey put forward a competing plan (the New Jersey Plan). The New Jersey

Plan kept federal powers quite limited, did not call for a new Congress, and enlarged some of the powers held by the Continental Congress. Paterson made clear that the smaller states would not agree to any new plan that deprived them of equal voting power in the legislative body.

Over the course of the next three months, the delegates worked out a series of compromises between the competing plans. New powers were given to Congress to regulate commerce, currency and the national defense. At the insistence of the southern states, Congress was denied the power to limit the slave trade for 20 years and slaves were allowed to be counted as three-fifths of all other persons for apportionment and electoral votes. The Connecticut Compromise, advanced by delegate Roger Sherman of that state, called for representation in the House of Representatives to be based on population and for each state to be guaranteed an equal two senators in the new Senate.

On September 17, 1787, the final compromises were made and the vote was taken on the new Constitution. In the end, 39 of the 55 delegates from those attending supported adoption of the Constitution. That was barely enough to win majority support from each of the attending state delegations.

Alternative Scenario

Compromise and the reconciliation of competing plans were central to forging a Constitution that created a stronger national and federal government. If this had not been possible, the mostly likely alternative outcome would have been a "tweaking" of the "confederation model."

This would have strained an already financially strapped nation and most likely would have led to the end of the emerging Republic, survival of a few of the strongest states, and different results in the War of 1812.

The ability to expand across the nation and to grow new states and territories would have been greatly curtailed. The United States would never have become the superpower that it became in all areas—domestic, international and defense. Today, this country would most likely resemble the Eurozone with a few dominant economic players and a number of smaller, much poorer, and less influential ones.

The Bill of Rights[7]

The Context

Getting the Constitution adopted in Philadelphia was the easy part. Getting it ratified by the states required even further compromise. During the debates on adoption of the Constitution between 1787 and 1790, many citizens feared that that the Constitution gave far too much power to the central government and would result in tyrannical rule and a violation of civil rights similar to that experienced under the British. As a result, they demanded a "Bill of Rights" as part of the Constitution. Several states in their ratifications included and demanded such amendments. Others ratified the Constitution with the understanding that amendments would be offered and accepted.

The Response

Based upon this feedback, on September 25, 1789 (approximately two years after the Constitution had been adopted in Philadelphia), the First Congress of the United States proposed 12 amendments to the Constitution for consideration by the states. The first 2 proposed amendments, which related to the number of constituents for each representative and the compensation of Congressmen, were not ratified. Amendments 3 to 12 were ratified by three-fourths of the state legislatures.

These ten amendments, which became known as the Bill of Rights, were the first ten amendments to the Constitution. Four of the amendments deal with asserting or retaining affirmative rights (e.g., the right to freedom of speech) and six deal with protection against negative actions that the government might take (e.g., protection against excessive bail and cruel and unusual punishment).

One of the foremost advocates for the Bill of Rights was George Mason, a Virginia delegate to the Constitutional Convention. He had earlier written the Virginia Declaration of Rights, which influenced Thomas Jefferson in writing the first part of the Declaration of Independence for the United States. Mason left the Convention disappointed and became one of the Constitution's most vocal opponents because, as he said, "It has no declaration of rights." Mason's voice and words were heard. James Madison, who drafted the amendments to the Constitution, drew heavily upon Mason's ideas in the Virginia Declaration of Rights.

In spite of the addition of the Bill of Rights, passage of the Declaration was by no means a slam dunk. It just squeaked by in some states. The vote in Massachusetts was 187 for and 168 against. The vote in Virginia was 89 for and 79 against. Rhode Island was the last of the 13 states to ratify the Constitution on May 29, 1790, by the closest vote of 34 for and 32 against after the Constitution lost overwhelmingly in a popular referendum there in March 1788 by a vote of 237 for and 2,708 against.

Alternative Scenario

Compromise, again, is what ruled the day in shaping a constitution that was ratified and not one that was to be consigned to the boneyards of history. It is significant to note that, at over 200 years of age, the U.S. Constitution has stood the test of time. It has passed that test because it is a flexible framework and not a straightjacket.

What would have happened if the Bill of Rights had not been added as the first ten amendments to the Constitution? As noted earlier, most likely, given the strong opposition, it would not have passed and the United States would have been a loosely knit confederacy and ineffectual nation. Individual rights would have been state dependent and not "national" in their existence and enforcement.

Or, if the Constitution had passed without the Bill of Rights, the United States would have been a far different country—one that was truly controlled and dominated from the top and in which individual and states' rights did not matter. The Bill of Rights created the essential tension that made the United States the great representative democracy that it is and provided the basis for applying the rule of law in a manner that was even-handed and fair-minded rather than dictatorial.

The Morrill Act[8]

The Context

In the mid-19th century, higher education in the United States was provided by private colleges almost exclusively to the wealthy and elite. Several politicians and educators, however, wanted to make advanced education more easily available to the average American. The Morrill Act, which called for establishing "land grant" colleges, was drafted for this purpose. It was passed by Congress in a close vote (House: 105 to 100; Senate: 25 to 22) in 1859 but vetoed by President James Buchanan. Among the reasons Buchanan cited for his veto were that the bill was an unconstitutional infringement on states' rights and that it harmed existing private colleges and universities.

Opposition to the Morrill Act came primarily from the South and West and support came primarily from the North and East. In 1860, Abraham Lincoln was elected president and by 1862, 12 southern states had seceded from the union. The stage was set for passage and presidential approval of the bill.

The Response

The original Morrill bill, as proposed by Representative Justin Smith Morrill of Vermont, had been focused on agriculture. Morrill expanded the bill in 1861 to include the teaching of military tactics and mechanic arts (engineering). President Lincoln signed this bill into law on July 2, 1862.

The 1862 Morill Act granted 30,000 acres of public land to a state for each senator or representative in Congress. This meant that even the smallest state at the time got 90,000 acres of land. The state could sell this land and use the proceeds for the "endowment, support and maintenance of at least one college."

The Act specifically excluded benefits to those states that had seceded from the union. After the Civil War, however, the 1862 Act was extended to the former Confederate States and eventually to all states and territories, including those created after 1862.

In 1890, a second Morrill Act was passed that focused on the southern states to ensure that race was not a factor in a school's admissions criteria or else to designate a separate land grant institution for persons of color. This led to the creation of a number of today's historically black colleges and universities.

The Morrill Act drove the creation of the U.S. public higher education system. Today, the Association of Public and Land Grant Universities has 188 public and land grant universities as members. The total includes 74 land grant institutions, of which 18 are historically black institutions. The land grant institutions include many of the largest and most prestigious public universities such as the University of Illinois, Michigan State University and Ohio State University, and private institutions such as Auburn, Cornell and the Massachusetts Institute of Technology.

Alternative Scenario

The U.S. higher education system is the envy of the world. The Morrill Act ensured that there was an opportunity for advanced education for all. The importance of the land grant colleges to the growth of America and the American dream is incalculable and the nation's success without them is unfathomable.

If there had been no Morrill Act, the U.S. educational system would most likely have been a network of exclusive islands for the rich and privileged. Millions of American citizens would have been deprived of higher education and the costs to the American society in terms of the lost intellectual and economic capital are inestimable.

It should be noted that the 1862 Act was passed during a time of conflict—the Civil War—and not compromise. It is as important to note that the Act was extended to the former Confederate States and in the 1890 Act to those who might have been disenfranchised as an act of conciliation and compromise and not one of retribution and punishment.

The Homestead Act[9]

The Context

From the time of the Revolutionary War to the mid-1800s, public land use policy made land ownership financially unattainable for most would-be homesteaders. Then, as the nation and its citizens looked to and expanded westward, settlers began to claim "pre-emption"—the right to settle land first and then to pay later.

Homestead legislation to support this passed the House of Representatives in 1852, 1854 and 1859 but was defeated in the Senate.

In 1860, Congress passed a homestead bill that President Buchanan vetoed. In vetoing the bill, Buchanan appeared to be bending to the interests of northern factory owners who did not want to lose their cheap labor force and southerners who were afraid the western states would be populated by small farmers who would be opposed to slavery. As with the Morrill Act, the secession of the Southern states removed their opposition to the bill and the stage was set for its passage.

The Response

President Lincoln signed the Homestead Act on May 20, 1862. The Act provided that any adult citizen, or intended citizen, could claim 160 acres of surveyed government land and required them to "improve" their plot by building a dwelling and cultivating the land for five years. Then the homesteader was entitled to the property free and clear—except for a small registration fee.

The Homestead Act drove westward expansion of the United States. The evidence suggests, however, that expansion did not always take place according to the rules and was definitely not an unbridled success or panacea for the participants.

In the period between 1862 and 1904, only 80 million out of 500 million acres (16 percent) went to homesteaders (500,000 @ 160 acres/homesteader). Because of ambiguity in the law, the majority of the land went to speculators, cattlemen, miners, lumbermen and railroads. Before the law was finally repealed in 1986, it is reported that a total of 2 million homesteaders made claims on these parcels of 160 acres but only approximately 783,000 were successful (around 39 percent) in "proving up" and acquiring their deeds after five years.

Nonetheless, the Homestead Act stands as the benchmark for the beginning of an era that changed the geography, demographics and economics of the United States. It accelerated the westward movement substantially. And, even though originally focused on agriculture and free land ownership, in conjunction with the building of the transcontinental railroad, the Act sowed the seeds and supported the growth of industrial and commercial concerns in the West.

Alternative Scenario

As noted, the implementation of the Homestead Act was not without problems or faults. On the other hand, without the Act, with its flaws and failures, what would the United States look like today?

The West, most probably, would still be in a developing condition rather than a developed one. Some, such as environmentalists, might look at that as a good thing. Others, who realize that the Act contributed to an urban to rural shift and away from the highly industrialized cities of the East to the Midwest and areas such as Montana, Nebraska, Colorado, Kansas and the Dakotas, might look at that as a good thing as well. It's all a matter of perspective. No matter how one looks at it, however, this pivot point definitely changed the American landscape substantially and substantively.

The Sherman Antitrust Act and Trust Busting[10]

The Context

As the 19th century drew to an end, big business was growing bigger and bigger through consolidations and using its size and clout to dictate the terms of American economic exchange. The federal government, still recovering from the devastating effects of the Civil War, was doing little to nothing to regulate it. In an attempt to change that, in 1890 Congress overwhelmingly passed the Sherman Act, named after the bill's author Senator John Sherman (OH). The purpose of the bill was to prevent monopolistic practices and cartels and "to protect the consumers by preventing arrangements designed or which tend to advance the cost of the consumer."

In the decade following the passage of the Sherman Act it was rarely used. And when it was—such as in the case of the American Sugar Refining Company, which controlled 98 percent of the sugar industry—the Supreme Court ruled against the government's right to regulate "production of commodities within a state." Ironically, the only time an organization was deemed in restraint of trade was when the Court ruled against a labor union.

So, as the United States entered the 20th century, while the law of the land was antitrust, the reality was that trusts and big business were as strong as and possibly stronger than ever. Then, in September 1901, Vice President Theodore Roosevelt succeeded to the presidency after President William McKinley was assassinated. Things were about to change.

The Response

Even though President Roosevelt was wealthy and favorably disposed toward business in general, he felt strongly that businesses that controlled entire industries and increased prices to consumers should be constrained, or "busted." He decided to enforce the Sherman Act and to regulate those businesses that felt they could operate outside of or above the law.

In 1902, Roosevelt used the Act against the Northern Securities Company, a northwest railroad holding company organized by financier J. P. Morgan and empire builder James Hill. Roosevelt charged the company with attempting to monopolize the railroad industry. The company lost its appeal in the Supreme Court by a 5–4 margin and the Court ordered it to be dissolved.

The floodgates were opened. During his two terms as president, Roosevelt dissolved a total of 44 trusts, including monopolies in the beef, sugar, fertilizer and harvester industries. Roosevelt's successor as President, William Howard Taft, brought an end to 90 trusts in his one term.

Alternative Scenario

President Roosevelt's trust busting established the principle of government's right and ability to regulate businesses that were engaged in unreasonable practices and/or too powerful.

Many businesses in the early 1900s felt they were equal, or perhaps superior, to the government. For example, when Roosevelt brought the antitrust suit against J. P. Morgan's railroad combine, Morgan said, "Send your man to see my man and tell him to fix it up." Roosevelt responded, "That cannot be done . . . No private interest can presume to be equal to the government. The government must be superior to all of these."

If there had been no trust busting, the United States might have evolved into an autocracy or oligarchy. Virtually all wealth and power could have been concentrated in the hands of a few businesspeople. They would have been able to operate independently and with impunity and immunity. The American middle class might never have developed and the concept of the American dream might have died stillborn.

The flip side of this argument is made by conservatives and economists who are vehemently critical of antitrust law. For example, in his essay "Antitrust," Alan Greenspan condemns the Sherman Act as stifling innovation and harming society, stating, "No one can ever compute the price that all of us have paid for that Act which, by inducing less effective use of capital, has kept our standard of living lower than would otherwise have been possible."

The Social Security Act[11]

The Context

Before the Great Recession, there was the Great Depression. The Depression was worldwide and started in October 1929 with the crash of the stock market. It grew progressively in its intensity and impact, with national unemployment reaching 23.5 percent by 1932 and peaking in early 1933 at 25 percent. Between 1929 and 1933, more than 5,000 banks failed, businesses and families defaulted on loans in record numbers and hundreds of thousands of Americans became homeless.

Herbert Hoover, who was president during this time period, initiated a number of programs to reverse the economic collapse, including the Smoot-Hawley Tariff Act, which imposed a tax on imported goods to try to drive purchases of American-made products; establishment of the Federal Home Loan Bank Board to spur new home construction and reduce foreclosures; passage of the Emergency Relief and Construction Act to fund public works programs such as dams; and creation of the Reconstruction Finance Corporation to provide government-secured loans to financial institutions, railroads and farmers. In spite of these initiatives, the economic downturn continued to worsen.

The dreadful economy led to a landslide victory for Franklin Roosevelt as president in 1932. A New Deal was on the way. That Deal would include an array of programs directed, in Roosevelt's words, at "three great objectives—the security of the home, the security of livelihood, and the security of social insurance."

The Response

Roosevelt began his campaign for "social insurance" in June 1934 with a message to Congress, followed by a "fireside chat." He established a Committee on Economic Security and an Advisory

Council to study the problems and issues of social and economic security.

Based upon the committee's report, he presented a message to Congress in January 1935 calling for legislation to address four areas: unemployment compensation, old-age benefits, federal aid to dependent children through grants to states, and additional federal aid to state and local public health agencies. Congress acted immediately upon President Roosevelt's request with bills introduced in both the House and Senate, and on August 15, 1935, the president signed the Social Security Act into law.

There was some opposition to the Act from those who viewed it as "a governmental invasion of the private sphere," wanted exemption from payroll taxes for firms who adopted government-approved pension plans or questioned whether the Act went beyond the powers granted to the federal government in the Constitution.

The resistance to the Act before the bill was signed was relatively mild. The Conference Report on the Act passed by voice vote in both the House and Senate. There was some push back after the Act became law as opponents tried to get it overturned as illegal.

In two cases in 1937, however, the Supreme Court ruled the Social Security Act was constitutional. This stood in stark contrast to earlier Supreme Court rulings that found other pieces of New Deal legislation such as the National Industrial Recovery Act and the Agricultural Adjustment Act unconstitutional.

President Roosevelt signed amendments to the Social Security Act on August 11, 1939, approximately four years after the signing of the original Act. The primary amendment related to expanding the coverage from "old age" to "old age and survivors" insurance. The Social Security Act has been amended numerous times in the decades since then to change the scope and nature of the program and its financing.

Alternative Scenario

Social Security today is central to the economic health and well-being of America's elderly. Prior to Social Security, many elderly faced the prospect of abject poverty upon retirement.

Consider what would have happened to the elderly and other Social Security beneficiaries during the Great Recession of 2007–2009 and its aftermath if there had been no Social Security benefits. Imagine the impact and devastating effect the absence of these benefits and the cash flow they generated would have had on the entire economy. We do not think that is an exaggeration to say that without Social Security the Recession would have been a Depression.

There are certainly many issues related to Social Security's future direction and financing. The Bowles-Simpson Committee addressed these issues directly in its report and there have been numerous alternative proposals to change the "face" of Social Security.

The bottom line, however, is not whether there will be any Social Security at all. That is not a debating point or within the realm of consideration. America's Social Security system must be strong for America to be strong.

The GI Bill[12]

The Context

In 1944, as World War II began to wind down, American political leaders started to contemplate what should be done for our returning servicemen. Three primary factors drove this consideration:

- The desire to do what was right for those who had fought valiantly for the country
- Uncertainty regarding the potential economic and social consequences of dismantling the nation's war machinery
- The sad and vivid memory of the results of the veterans' Bonus March of 1932

The American economy had recovered somewhat in the period from 1932 to 1940 before the war. GDP grew 58 percent in those eight years and unemployment fell from a high of 25.2 to 13.9 percent when the draft started. GDP grew another 56 percent in the war years from 1940 to 1945.

Still, due to the extraordinary government expenditures to support the war, it was difficult to impossible to predict what would happen at the war's end. There was a concern that it might push the country back into a depression.

The greater concern, however, was to avoid a repeat of what had happened after World War I. The World War Adjusted Compensation Act (Bonus Act) did not become law until 1924—six years after the end of the war. President Warren Harding vetoed a version of the bill in 1922. President Calvin Coolidge vetoed the 1924 Bonus Act but Congress overrode his veto.

The Bonus Act basically provided 20-year insurance certificates to be paid on the veteran's birthday in 1945. With certain restrictions, the veteran could borrow against those certificates in advance of the payout.

Because of the effects of the Great Depression, a veterans' group marched on Washington in the summer of 1932 demanding immediate conversion and payment of the certificates in cash. They were rebuked—many veterans left but some stayed and encamped on the Capitol. After a conflict with police in which a few veterans were killed, President Herbert Hoover ordered the army to clear the veterans' site. Army Chief of Staff Douglas MacArthur carried out the president's orders commanding the infantry, cavalry and six tanks to evict the veterans and their families from their encampment.

There was a smaller veterans' Bonus March in 1933 at the beginning of President Roosevelt's administration. Finally, in 1936, Congress overrode President Roosevelt's veto to pay the WWI veterans' bonus years early.

Eight years later, near the end of WWII, the elected leaders in Washington were given a chance for redemption and to prove they had learned the lessons from the mishandling of the WWI veterans' "bonus."

The Response

They seized the moment. Congress passed and President Franklin Roosevelt signed the Servicemen's Readjustment Act (The GI Bill) of 1944 into law on June 22, 1944. Even given the background and compelling factors for passage of the GI Bill, there was some debate regarding the nature and substance of the bill.

The bill had three core provisions: support for college education or training, loans to buy homes and businesses, and unemployment compensation of $20/week up to a period of 52 weeks. The Senate and House easily agreed on the education and loans but there was a concern that the unemployment compensation would be extremely costly and might cause the veterans not to seek work.

The conference committee of the Senate and House was deadlocked 3–3 on this provision. Representative John Gibson

(GA), a member of the committee, had gone home to recover from an illness. Hearing of the impasse, he rushed back to the Capitol overnight and passed the deciding vote.

The rest is history. Few veterans availed themselves of the unemployment compensation—less than 20 percent of the funds set aside were used. In contrast, the educational and loan provisions were both outside of the ballpark, tape-measure grand slam home runs.

By the time, the original GI Bill ended on July 25, 1956, 7.8 million of 16 million WWII veterans had participated in an education or training program. From 1944 to 1952, nearly 2.4 million veterans got home loans backed by the Veterans' Administration. These are stunning statistics but the economic results are even more so.

Alternative Scenarios

The GI Bill fueled the growth and expansion of America during what in retrospect may be viewed as the country's economic golden era (1945 to approximately 1973). The U.S. highly educated class and its middle class expanded significantly, millions of new homes were built and hundreds of thousands of businesses were created. GDP, productivity and wages went up substantially.

Economic benefits were distributed relatively equally. The rising tide raised all boats. The American ship of state was one very good place to be for most citizens (except for those who were minorities).

Given the lessons learned from WWI and the Depression, some form of GI Bill was inevitable. There was some question at the time the bill was passed as to whether veterans would take advantage of the education and training provisions.

That question was answered with a resounding yes. As a result, this landmark piece of federal legislation became the springboard for launching and accelerating American creativity, capitalism and entrepreneurial behavior. It provides the perfect example of what can be done when the interests of the public and private sector align and citizens from all backgrounds can draw upon the benefits provided through governmental programs and apply typical American ingenuity to shape their future and that of the nation.

What would have happened if there had been no GI Bill or one of much lesser scope with only an economic payout, for example? Imagine the United States around 1945. Or, say 1940. Get the picture?

This is only a Whitman's sampler of the country's major pivot points. Think about the Context, Response and Alternative Scenarios for the points we mentioned earlier—such as the Civil War, the Fourteenth Amendment, the Interstate Highway System, *Brown* v. *Board of Education*, the Space Race and the Civil Rights Act of 1964—which we have not discussed here.

Think about the other pivot points that we have not mentioned— such as the Nineteenth Amendment, the Marshall Plan, Medicare, the internet (no, Al Gore was not its father but he did play a role and the federal government was instrumental in its establishment), the Environmental Protection Act—and the full implications become apparent. What is done at the pivot point has incredible potential and power to make America stronger and better or weaker and poorer.

PIVOT POINT TAKEAWAYS

The role the federal government plays and how pivot points are handled matter enormously. That's the basic takeaway from this brief historical review. There are additional takeaways that an analysis of this data suggests:

- **Memory Matters:** Or, our American memory should. George Santayana famously said, "Those who do not remember the past are condemned to repeat it." An understanding of the contexts and back stories at pivot points facilitates the development of knowledge and insights for forward progress. A partial or inaccurate recollection retards momentum and leads to inertia—intercranial and otherwise. Based upon this, we offer the following adaptation to Santayana's saying: "Those who remember, or want to go back to, a past the way that it wasn't are condemned to no future." *Back to the Future* made good movie theater but it cannot be the basis for a successful country.

- **Mindsets Matter:** Even when citizens do recognize government's role, there is no agreement on the level or importance of its contribution. If one reviews the accomplishments that government has spurred in American history, it would seem there might be some agreement on that. But quite the contrary is true. If you review the pivot points in this chapter, you'll see the same arguments being played out continuously and over and over again in eras from the time of the Constitution. Howard Fineman describes this phenomenon in depth in his book *The Thirteen American Arguments: Enduring Debates That Define and Inspire Our Country*.

- **Momentum Matters:** The accomplishments at these pivot points were not achieved instantaneously. In many cases, it took years and repeated efforts to achieve the final results. That demonstrates the need for persistence and movement forward. Compromise was also an essential ingredient.

While the evidence of government's contributions may be incontrovertible, the importance one assigns to them is not inarguable. That's the American way and the way it should be. The perception of the conservative will differ from that of the liberal or progressive, but the definition of the facts should not.

If that can be the starting point, and we acknowledge that our differences are matters of opinion or on alternative approaches to solve a mutually agreed upon problem, then there is the chance for persons of goodwill to negotiate in good faith to work the pivot points.

Without that starting point, there can be no finish line. There can be no ways and means. There can only be wills and wails. This is the case where conflict and confusion prevail over courage and compromise. This is where we stood in the United States at the end of 2012 and moved midway into 2013.

2 | The Deficit and Debt Crisis: Poised on a Pivot Point

In 2011, RESPONSIBLE AND LEGITIMATE CONCERNS ABOUT AMERICA'S debt and deficit crisis turned into a forum for political posturing, finger pointing and gamesmanship.

This was too bad because a substantial amount of good work had been done before 2011 by a variety of individuals and bi- and nonpartisan groups to develop comprehensive recommendations to address the crisis. Then, in came the politicians, and not only was the baby thrown out with the bathwater but there went the bathtub, too.

Thus in 2013, the nation still confronted the deficit and debt crisis pivot point with few meaningful answers in place. The question of whether we are poised, paralyzed or impaled by this crisis will be determined and answered over time.

The story on how we got to this state, however, provides a case study on how the manner in which pivot points are handled produces sub-optimal or no results. Let's start that story not at the beginning but in the spring of 2011.

THE DEBT CEILING DEBACLE

Addressing the debt ceiling is one of those prototypical Washington exercises engaged in relatively regularly and routinely. Since 1941, Congress had approved 91 "ceiling" bills—73 of which raised the ceiling. The ceiling was raised seven times under George W. Bush and three times under President Obama with virtually no consternation or commotion.[1]

Then in the spring of 2011, the debt ceiling became the vehicle for discussing the nation's deficit and debt situation (the debt ceiling stood at 14.3 trillion) when the Republican leadership (spurred on primarily by new freshman "Tea Party" legislators) refused to raise the ceiling unless substantial spending cuts were made in association with it. Once the issue was framed that way a debate began that seemed like it would be never ending.

In reality, it lasted for only approximately four months, from late April to early August. But the debate's contentious nature, the blame-placing and the apparent unwillingness of either side to be reasonable and to listen to the other put the Washington political process under a magnifying glass. The image was not a pretty one for either the process or politicians involved.

The Republicans argued that not raising the debt ceiling wouldn't matter and that the United States would continue to pay its bills. The Treasury and the Democrats asserted that failing to raise the ceiling would cause the government to default on its legal obligations, thus causing a severe financial crisis. In fact, both sides were exaggerating to make their case and score their points.

After all of the haggling, the debate ended in a truly anticlimactic manner. An agreement of sorts was reached, which called for raising the ceiling until 2013 and spending cuts of $2.4 trillion over ten years. The agreement included the establishment of a Joint Select Committee on Deficit Reduction (known as the Super Committee) to make those cuts and for an automatic reduction of over $1 trillion if the Committee did not accomplish its task.

President Obama signed the legislation into law on Tuesday, August 2—the day on which at midnight the United States would have gone into default on its debt. The bill had passed the House 269 to 161 and the Senate by 74 to 26. The leaders in both bodies tried to characterize the bill as bipartisan and some felt satisfied that the doomsday scenario had been avoided.[2]

But the fact is that while the financial crisis had been averted, the public perception and confidence crisis had not. The debt ceiling debate had done its damage to the psyche of the American public and the already tarnished reputation of our elected officials.

The Pew Research Center conducted a national survey in late July right before the debt ceiling legislation was signed. The survey found that, in general, the nation's citizens were distraught and distressed by the spectacle that had been the debt ceiling debate. The respondents characterized the debate with highly negative words such as "ridiculous, disgusting, stupid and childish." These responses cut across party lines, with over 70 percent of Democrats, Republicans and Independents offering negative assessments.[3]

So, the debt ceiling debate did accomplish one thing. It united the American people in their perception that the Congress was inept and irrelevant. It didn't have to be that way. Let's look at why and how things unraveled.

THE "DEBATE" IN CONTEXT AND PERSPECTIVE

There had been considerable concern about the debt and deficit well before the 2011 debt ceiling debate.

David Walker, while comptroller general of the United States, launched a "Fiscal Wake-Up Tour" in conjunction with The Concord Coalition, The Brookings Institution and The Heritage Foundation to educate the American public about the country's financial condition and debt level and the fact that it was unsustainable. In his 2009 book *Comeback America: Turning the Country Around and Restoring Fiscal Responsibility*, Walker proposed a number of measures to address the fiscal problems, such as wage indexing of Social Security and establishing some type of consumption tax.[4]

In September 2009, the bipartisan Committee for a Responsible Federal Budget (The Committee or CRPB), a group comprised of some of the nation's leading budget experts, issued a paper titled *Deficit Reduction: Lessons from Around the World.*[5] The Committee described six lessons learned from studying deficit reduction strategies that countries worldwide have employed over the past 30 years. They boiled down to two key factors:

1. Put a deficit reduction (fiscal consolidation) plan in place as soon as possible.
2. Phase that plan in gradually.

In December 2009, The bipartisan Peterson-Pew Commission on Budget Reform (The Commission)—a group of experts formed by Pete Peterson, businessman and former U.S. Secretary of Commerce—the Pew Charitable Trusts and the CRFB in its paper, *Red Ink Rising: A Call to Action to Stem the Mounting Federal Debt,* outlined a six-step approach to stabilize the debt by 2018. The Commission noted that its approach would "require significant policy changes and raising taxes and cutting spending."[6] This Commission concluded its work in December 2011.

In his fiscal year (FY) 2011 budget introduced in February 2010, President Obama put forward his recommendations. They included balancing the primary (noninterest) budget by 2015 and stabilizing the debt-to-GDP ratio by the end of the decade.

On January 27, 2010, Conservative Congressman Paul Ryan (R-WI) presented a radical alternative to the Peterson-Pew Commission and the president's approaches in his Roadmap for the American Future. The center lane for Ryan's "roads" included capping government spending and major changes to Social Security, Medicare and Medicaid policy, including actively promoting the privatization of Social Security for future generations.[7]

Ryan's roadmap received only modest recognition, responses and support from his Republican peers at the time of its introduction. Things changed dramatically when the conservative Republicans elected in November of 2010 took office in January 2011.

SIMPSON-BOWLES MOVES CENTER STAGE

At this juncture, the plot thickens. On February 18, 2010, President Obama appointed a bipartisan commission (the National Commission on Fiscal Responsibility and Reform) to take an in-depth look at the country's deficit and debt problems and to develop a report on how to resolve them.[8] The President named ex-Senator Alan Simpson (R-WY) and Erskine Bowles, investment banker and former White House Chief of Staff for Bill Clinton, to head the Commission.

The Commission had 18 members: 12 from Congress—6 each from the House and Senate, and 6 private-sector members. The division of the members by party affiliation was 8 Republicans and 10 Democrats.[9]

The Commission deliberated for approximately eight months from the time it was established until co-chairs Simpson and Bowles put forward their draft proposal on November 10, 2010.[10] The proposal, which formed the basis for the Commission's full report, had five parts:

- Tough discretionary spending caps
- Comprehensive tax reform
- Health care cost containment
- Mandatory savings
- Social Security solvency

A super majority of 14 of the 18 members had to vote for the report for it to be approved. On December 3, 2010, only 11 of the 18 members did so.[11]

Five of the seven opposing votes came from the six representatives from the House (all three Republicans and two Democrats) on the Commission. The other two opposing votes came from two Democrats, Senator Max Baucus (D-MT) and Andy Stern, former President of the Service Employees International Union. All three Republican House opponents indicated they could not vote for the report because of "tax increases" and inadequate "health care spending reforms."

One of those was Congressman Paul Ryan, who in his statement for the Record on his vote stated "the Commission relies too heavily on revenue increases, $2 trillion over a decade, with the tax collections reaching 21 percent of gross domestic product." Another was Jeb Hensarling (R-TX), who stated, "I am unable to support it because at its core it calls for massive tax increase without fundamentally addressing the largest, long-term driver of our nation's debt crisis—rising health care costs."[12]

Co-chairs Simpson and Bowles had had their day. Congressman Ryan was about to have his. Congressman Hensarling was waiting in the wings.

PAUL RYAN'S PRIVATE WAR GOES PUBLIC

The congressional elections held in November 2010 dramatically changed the dynamics of the debt and deficit discussion in the nation's capital. The Republicans achieved a landslide victory in House races nationwide, picking up 63 seats and becoming the majority party with 242 Republicans in the House versus 193 Democrats.[13]

This made John Boehner the speaker and nominal leader of the Party. The new center of power and influence, however, was Paul Ryan, who had been named Chairman of the House Budget Committee.

In that position, Congressman Ryan developed a budget plan called the "Path to Prosperity." Ryan announced the plan on April 5, 2011, proclaiming "Our budget cuts $6.2 trillion in spending from the President's budget over the next 10 years and puts the nation on track to pay off our national debt."[14]

While the Republican budget was a "Path" and not a "Roadmap," it bore strong resemblance to Congressman Ryan's earlier work. Key plan ingredients included major cuts in domestic discretionary spending, repealing Obama's health care act, making dramatic cuts to Medicaid and transforming Medicare into a voucher-like program for those under 55.

The new "Tea Party" Republican House members—who had asserted themselves early on by saying that it wasn't going to be business as usual in the halls of Congress—embraced Congressman Ryan's approach to budget cutting and deficit reduction. So too did their other Republican colleagues.

As a result, on April 15, 2011, the House passed the Ryan-promoted budget plan for 2012 by a vote of 235–193, largely along party lines. Four Republicans opposed it and no Democrat voted for it.[15]

A week after the House GOP budget was announced President Barack Obama squared off with Congressman Ryan by introducing a deficit reduction plan of his own. The President's plan called for achieving a $4 trillion reduction in 12 years and included spending cuts, changes in government health care programs and tax increases.

In announcing his plan, the President drew a stark contrast between his proposed approach and Ryan's. He immediately went on the offensive by declaring, "It's a vision (the House Republican budget) that says that in order to reduce the deficit, we have to end Medicare as we know it and make cuts to Medicaid that would leave millions of seniors, poor children and Americans with disabilities without the care they need."[16]

In response, the President was accused by Senator Tom Coburn (R-OK), a member of the Simpson-Bowles Commission who had voted for the Commission's deficit reduction report, of engaging in "campaign style political attacks" against those "who have a different vision of government."

From that point forward, the deficit reduction battle became a series of punches and counterpunches between Congressman Ryan and President Obama. In late April, a Gallup poll showed the match being pretty well even with 44 percent of Americans favoring the Democratic plan proposed by Obama and 43 percent preferring the Republican plan proposed by Ryan.[17]

THE STUPOR COMMITTEE

Chronologically, that brings us back to the debt ceiling debate that started in April and ended on August 2, 2011. As noted earlier, the act extending the ceiling to 2013 called for spending cuts of $2.4 trillion over ten years. It also established a Super Committee (the Committee) to make those cuts.

The Committee had twelve members: Six appointed by the Speaker and Minority Leader of the House and six by the Majority and Minority Leaders of the Senate. The Speaker of the House and the Senate Majority leader each appointed a member as co-chair.

Four of the twelve appointees, Senator Max Baucus (D-MT) and Representatives Jeb Hensarling (R-TX), Dave Camp (R-MI), and Xavier Becerra (D-CA) had been on the Simpson-Bowles Commission. All four had voted against the Fiscal Commission's plan. Congressman Hensarling was Speaker Boehner's choice as co-chair.

As the old saying goes, "Well begun is half done." Given this composition, the Super Committee was not well begun. That's not to say that the Committee might not have been able to succeed. But it would have had to overcome significant ideological barriers and intransigence in order to do so.

One way of accomplishing that could have been by forming bipartisan teams to develop mutually agreeable solutions. That's not what was done, however.

Before the Committee started its formal work, each side met separately to develop its "respective strategies." Many of the subsequent meetings were also held along party lines. The Democrats met alone with the President at the White House. The Republicans met alone with their congressional leaders.

This was a perfect way to build barriers and not bridges and to foster conflict rather than compromise. It violated the basic principles of negotiation espoused by Roger Fisher and his Harvard colleagues in the classic work *Getting to Yes*. (See our detailed discussion on *Getting to Yes* in chapter 4.)

So, the Super Committee had two strikes against it: flawed team membership and a flawed process. The third strike was a flawed and completely unrealistic timeline. In approximately 90 days (between mid-August to November 23), the Committee was supposed to achieve a mutually agreed upon solution, which the Simpson-Bowles Commission couldn't achieve in an eight-month time frame.

The logic was that by holding a gun (the approximately $1.2 trillion in automatic cuts) to the Committee's head it would be forced to cooperate and collaborate in a compressed time frame. That logic was disproved on November 21, when Congressman Hensarling and his co-chair, Senator Patty Murray (D-WA), released a statement saying, "We have come to the conclusion today that it will not be possible to make any bipartisan agreement available to the public before the committee's deadline."[18] There might have been a gun but it was loaded with blanks.

The Committee ended its work with a whimper. As a result, the sequestration process that put across-the-board cuts in both the defense and domestic budgets was triggered. These cuts were to total $1.2 trillion over a ten-year period and would have taken $109 billion out of the budget in January 2013.

FREE FOR ALL

With the failure of the Super Committee, the ball officially was in no one's court. Individuals and groups both inside and outside of the government continued to try to seize the initiative and to work toward a positive resolution of the debt and deficit discussion. Among the most prominent were the Gang of Six and the Moment of Truth Project.

The Gang of Six was a group of six senators led by Democrat Mark Warner (VA) and Republican Saxby Chambliss (GA) that convened independently after the report of the Fiscal Responsibility and Reform Commission was not approved. The other four senators in the Gang had been members of the Commission who voted for approval: Tom Coburn (R-OK), Mike Crapo (R-ID), Dick Durbin (D-IL) and Kent Conrad (D-ND).

Working together outside the normal processes of the Senate, the Gang developed a deficit reduction plan that drew heavily upon the work of the Commission. It presented its plan in a briefing to about half of the U.S. senators on July 19, 2011.[19]

The Gang's plan received initial support from a number of senators on both sides of the aisle and President Obama who called the plan "a very significant step" that is "broadly consistent with the approach that I've urged." The House Republicans and conservative groups such as the Heritage Foundation, on the other hand, were highly critical of the plan because of its "tax hikes" and "lack of details."[20]

The Gang's plan was set aside when the debt ceiling legislation was signed on August 2. When the Super Committee failed to accomplish its mission successfully, the Gang resurrected its efforts but little progress was made before the end of 2011 and virtually nothing was done during the presidential year of 2012.

The Moment of Truth Project bore a strong resemblance to the efforts of the Gang of Six. That's because it was initiated by the bipartisan Committee for a Responsible Federal Budget when the Fiscal Commission's report was not approved.

The Project took its name from the title of the Fiscal Commission's report, which declared that the country's "era of deficit denial is over." The Project's purpose was "to use the Fiscal Commission's findings to spark a national discussion . . . and to help further develop the policy reform ideas to improve the nation's fiscal outlook."[21]

As with the Gang of Six, the Project was less relevant while the Super Committee was at work. After the Committee's failure, the Project declared on its website "the momentum behind enacting a bipartisan, comprehensive fiscal plan based on the framework put forward by the Fiscal Commission has continued to grow." There may have been momentum but there was little tangible progress.

STUCK IN A TIME WARP

If all of this seems like we've seen this movie before, it's because we had. This was Bill Murray's *Groundhog Day* at its worst—waking up every day expecting things to be better or different but they weren't. Why not?

There are undoubtedly a variety of reasons. But at the heart of the matter was the absolute refusal to consider any form of "tax increase" as part of a comprehensive solution to addressing the problem of deficit and debt reduction.

Given this refusal, the question must be what is more important—solving a concrete problem facing the county or adhering to an abstract political principle? For one group—namely conservative House Republicans, as the evidence shows unequivocally, the political principle came first and the problem solving came second.

This is not to say that those House Republicans did not have a right to take this position. It is to say that when they did they not only cut off debate and negotiations, they also used their power as the majority in the House to try to dictate and control the congressional and national agenda.

The House's proposed Cut, Cap and Balance Act of 2011 provides an excellent example of this. The bill passed the House on July 19 by a vote of 234–190 largely along party lines.

The Cut, Cap and Balance bill called for cuts in FY 2012 "non-security discretionary spending; capping future spending to a declining % of GDP over the next 10 years; and, a constitutional amendment to balance the budget. The balanced budget amendment would have required that any future tax increase be supported by a supermajority of two-thirds in both the House and the Senate."[22]

The issue of "no tax increases" is a transcendent one and to this point was the primary stumbling block to solving the deficit and debt crisis. The focus on tax increases was a peculiar and particularly misguided one in light of the fact that a large part of the current deficit was due to tax cuts and not increases.

When Bill Clinton left office, the nation had a budget surplus of almost $1 trillion. The tax rates at that time were 39.6 percent on individuals and 35 percent on corporations. Since the imposition of the Bush tax cuts, the government's revenue collected as a percentage of GDP declined from close to 21 percent in 2000 to 15 percent in 2010.[23]

Ezra Klein did an excellent job of summarizing what he considered to be "three of the best analyses of what's happened to the federal budget since 2001." According to Klein, the Pew Fiscal Analysis Initiative attributed about two-thirds of the growth in the federal debt to new legislation—40 percent of that amount was due to tax cuts and 60 percent was due to spending increases. E21, on the other hand, asserted that about 50 percent was due to spending increases and that less than "one quarter was due to tax relief of any kind." The Center on Budget and Policy Priorities analysis shows that "By themselves, in fact, the Bush tax cuts and the wars in Iraq and Afghanistan will account for almost half of the $20 trillion in debt that, under current policies, the nation will owe by 2019."[24]

Based upon this data, it is obvious that the United States has had both an expense and revenue problem. It would seem that thoughtful approaches would have taken this into account. Unfortunately, thoughtfulness did not appear to matter much to some elected officials and others in the country in these tumultuous times. When it came to taxes and the debt ceiling debate neither did public or expert opinion.

In July 2011, poll after poll showed that the majority of the American public was clearly in favor of a balanced approach of spending cuts and tax increases. A Pew Research center study showed that the proportion favoring a "mixed approach" was 65 percent—about the same as it was in December 2010.[25] A Quinnipiac poll revealed that 67 percent of respondents supported increasing taxes on the wealthy and corporations. An MSNBC-*Wall Street Journal* poll disclosed that 81 percent of Americans favored a surtax on millionaires and 68 percent favored phasing out the Bush tax cuts. A *New York Times*-CBS News poll showed that 56 percent of Americans did not believe that corporations pay their fair share of taxes.[26]

It wasn't just Joe Six Pack who wasn't being heard. Those with independent and/or objective expertise were ignored as well. A Media Matters report released on September 21, 2011, reported that based upon an analysis of three major cable news programs (CNN, Fox News and MSNBC) only 4.1 percent (52 out of 1,258) of guests were "actual economists." According to Media Matters, "This lack of credible economic experts helped create a media environment in which political and media figures could spread misinformation."[27]

NONCOMPROMISING POSITIONS

As 2011 drew to a close, the deficit and debt discussion had come full circle—if not to a full stop. The combatants had dug in their heels and there seemed to be little room for maneuvering or forward progress. Pure partisanship and politics were prevailing over policy making and problem solving.

There was a need to address the deficit and debt pivot point in a "fair and balanced" manner. Sound bipartisan solutions abounded. What was lacking at that time was not a lack of answers but a lack of will.

Will demands political and personal courage. It requires being able to see things from the other side of the aisle and putting country first. It requires both standing up for what you believe in and standing down those who will not compromise.

We should point out that compromise and broad bipartisan support is not always the right or good thing. The war in Iraq was concluded on December 15, 2011, after ten years with much uncertainty regarding the final results and outcomes.

There was no doubt, however, about the investment of American blood and treasure in the war: 4,487 U.S. dead; 32,226 U.S. wounded; 170,000 peak troop level; 1 million Americans who served; and a total cost of almost $1 trillion. The $1 trillion was a substantial contributor to the nation's deficit.

There was far too little debate in the run-up to the Iraq war. There had been far too much about the deficit and debt. As 2011 ended, it was time, well past time, for Congress to act and to get off of this pivot point. As we shall see in the next chapter, they did not.

3 | Attention Deficit Disorder: Show Me the Money

THE OBSESSIVE FOCUS ON THE DEBT AND DEFICIT FOR MORE THAN two years, the failure to resolve these issues in 2011 and the hollow rhetoric of the political campaigns of 2012 regarding them did the nation and its citizens a tremendous disservice.

Admittedly, it drew attention to a very real problem: excessive government spending. However, it constrained us from focusing in depth on an even more serious problem, our ongoing human tragedy: the disappearance of the middle class; rising economic inequality; and the debilitating conditions of the jobless, underemployed and those with diminished and wasting assets.

During this time frame, we suffered from a serious case of attention deficit disorder regarding those "human" issues. These were the pivot points that should have been central to the debate and dialogue as the 112th Congress wrapped up its business and the 113th began its work.

Instead, the sad fact was that the Congress remained focused primarily on "financial" issues. Enter the fiscal cliff, sequestration, the new budget and, believe it or not, the debt ceiling again. This may not have been déjà vu all over again, but the view definitely looked familiar.

The sadder fact is that while we were consumed with talking about going over the fiscal cliff, we should have been consumed by determining how to climb the economic summit. The real need long term is to grow revenue. That can only be done through economic development, creating good-paying jobs, and promoting the individual economic well-being of our citizens.

We begin this chapter by chronicling Congress' financially related activities at the end of 2012 and in the first quarter of 2013. We then examine why human concerns are much more critical to the future of the American economy and provide our pivot point recommendations for addressing them. We conclude the chapter by reflecting on why this not-so-magnificent obsession took place and debt and deficit issues were so difficult to resolve

FISCAL CLIFF OR BUNNY SLOPE?

In October 2012, Superstorm Sandy was a disaster brought to us by mother nature. The fiscal cliff that the United States approached at the end of the year was brought to us by human nature. Which was worse? Time will tell.

What we can tell right now is that Sandy was unavoidable. The cliff, on the other hand, was completely avoidable. We should not have gone over it, fallen off of it, or even slipped at all while working our way down it.

The so-called "fiscal cliff" was created due to the expiration of all of the Bush-era tax cuts and across-the-board spending cuts to be triggered by the sequestration process.

Federal Reserve Chair Ben Bernanke is widely credited with coining the term "fiscal cliff." He "implored Congress" in his testimony before the Senate Banking Committee on July 17, 2012, to avoid it.[1] The cliff was indeed real—even if it was man-made—but there are a number of reasons that we shouldn't have approached it and resolving this apparent crisis should have been a no-brainer.

First, we have had a basis for a solution to the cliff since December 3, 2010. That's the date that the members of the National Commission on Fiscal Responsibility and Reform (better known as the Simpson-Bowles Commission named after its co-chairs Alan Simpson and

Erskine Bowles) failed to pass the Commission's Report by a super majority. As noted earlier it needed 14 out of 18 votes. It received 11 and some bipartisan support.

It's not just the work of the Commission that could have been employed in the cliff problem solving. As Erskine Bowles pointed out in an article for the *Washington Post* the day after the 2012 national elections, "We already have the blueprints. It's the type of bipartisan package toward which the commission I co-chaired . . . , the Domenici-Rivlin group, the Senate's 'Gang of Six', and the Obama-Boehner negotiations all worked."[2]

Second, the Congressional Budget Office (CBO) released a report during the negotiations highlighting the negative impact of "fiscal tightening in 2013." The CBO projected that GDP would drop by 0.5 in 2013 and that the unemployment rate would rise to 9.1 percent.

It went on to state, "Output would be greater and unemployment lower in the next few years if some or all of the fiscal tightening scheduled under current law—sometimes called the fiscal cliff—was removed. The CBO predicted, however, that even if all of the fiscal tightening was eliminated the economy would remain below its potential and the unemployment rate would remain higher than usual for some time."[3]

Third, before the election, a group of CEOs from approximately 80 large companies such as Allstate, Deere, Walgreen, Caterpillar and Boeing signed a "manifesto" calling on Congress to reduce the federal deficit with tax increases as well as budget cuts. In their statement, they endorsed the Simpson-Bowles approach—about $3 in spending cuts for every $1 of tax increases—as an "effective framework."[4]

This group was organized by the Campaign to Fix the Debt (The Campaign). On November 14, Jeff Immelt of General Electric, David Cote of Honeywell, and other backers of The Campaign met with President Obama at the White House to discuss the need to address the fiscal cliff. The Campaign had a $40 million budget and ran advertisements with slogans such as "Just Fix It" to heighten public awareness of the need to solve this problem now.[5]

Fourth, while the average citizen may have just begun to focus on this issue, informed citizens had already proven that the people know best. In May 2010, the Committee for a Responsible Federal Budget

(CRFRB) put up an online "Stabilize the Debt" simulator. The simulator allowed individuals to make choices regarding what they would do to drive down the debt.[6]

In April 2012, the CFRB reported that over 250,000 people had used the simulator. 94 percent of the respondents reduced the deficit through a combination of spending and revenue changes. The CFRB noted that "71 percent of Democrats supported raising the retirement age and 82 percent of Republicans supported letting at least some of the 2001/2003 and 2010 tax cuts expire."

Fifth, on the spending cuts or sequestration side, this was not an October surprise or an unexpected storm for the Congress. This was a men- and women-made catastrophe created by our legislators who kicked the can down the road on August 2, 2011, when they approved the continuing resolution and established a Super Committee to make cuts of approximately $1 trillion and called for automatic reductions if the Committee did not accomplish its task.

On November 21, 2011, the Super Committee announced that "We have come to the conclusion today that it will not be possible to make any bipartisan agreement before the committee's deadline." From that point forward until the run-up to the presidential election in September 2012, Congress paid virtually no attention and made no legitimate attempt to address the debt problem. It became a campaign talking point but not a policy pivot point.

So there we have it. After much wasted time, the country and Congress was staring reality in the face and it was not pretty. It was now time, as Erskine Bowles put it in his *Washington Post* op ed, "for both sides to move beyond contentious electoral politics and come together in the spirit of good governance to replace the abrupt and mindless spending cuts and tax increases set to take effect Jan. 1 with a gradual and intelligent deficit reduction plan."

America's debt and deficit problem had been studied to death. Almost all of the information and plans introduced in 2011 and what little was done in 2012 were slight variations on old themes. There was no new knowledge being created or insights being gained.

There were a variety of viable options that could have been used to construct a "gradual and intelligent deficit reduction plan" comprised of spending cuts and tax increases. The 112th Congress was at the juncture where it had to do the right thing and that was not necessarily the right wing thing.

FROM CLIFF DWELLING TO MOUNTAIN CLIMBING

We're not certain if Congress did the right thing. But at least they did something. They passed a "fiscal cliff" bill on January 2, 2013.[7] Our thumbnail assessment of that bill follows: Much sound. Some fury. Simplifying nothing.

Nonetheless, those members of Congress who worked together in a bipartisan fashion to construct and pass the "cliff deal" are to be commended. The major presenting short-term problem of the expiration of "middle class" tax cuts was addressed. Significantly and appropriately, tax rates for the "wealthy" were increased. In addition, the alternative minimum tax was corrected, expiring jobless benefits were extended and cuts to Medicare reimbursements were prevented.

This congressional compromise pulled us back after we went over the cliff for a very short period of time. The unavoidable truth, however, is that we were still cliff dwellers. Much more remained to be done than got done with this bill.

Consider the following: The sequestration process for automatic budget cuts to defense and domestic programs was extended by only two months. Operating on a continuing resolution instead of having an agreed-upon budget became a cause célèbre. The debt ceiling reared its ugly head again. Social Security, Medicaid and Medicare solvency and management remained wide open issues. And, most importantly, job creation and economic growth were not central to the ongoing deficit and debt discussions.

Erskine Bowles and Alan Simpson, co-chairs of the Deficit Reduction commission, stated that the fiscal cliff bill was "truly a missed opportunity to do something big to reduce our fiscal problems."[8] We agree with Bowles and Simpson that the bill was not "something big."

In no way could this be considered a grand bargain. On the other hand, given the composition of the 112th Congress and its track record over the past two years, a grand bargain in this constrained a time period was probably impossible because of the grand canyon—i.e., the ideological chasm—that separated the extreme Tea Party conservatives in the House from the Democrats and even their more moderate Republican brethren.

Looking at it objectively, the fiscal cliff bill contains elements and produces consequences that offend partisans on both sides of the aisle. While the middle-class tax breaks were protected, the payroll tax break was eliminated. It is estimated that this will cost "an average of $1,000 for a household at the national median income."[9] While "new taxes" were on the table, spending cuts were off. The bill generates $620 billion in new tax revenue, which seems like a lot but pales in comparison to what is required.[10] Moreover, the Congressional Budget Office estimates that the bill will reduce revenues over ten years by $3.64 trillion and increase spending by $332 billion.[11]

So the bad news was that we were still cliff dwellers. The good news was that the cliff was no longer the exclusive province of those within the Beltway. It was now occupied by the American public and voters as well.

The results of the national elections sent a loud and clear message that the public was expecting and demanding compromise. They also sent a message that it would be unacceptable to extend the Bush-era tax cuts uniformly. Finally, they sent the message that the voters were paying close attention to the negotiation processes surrounding the cliff and the behavior of our elected officials in resolving the debt and deficit crisis.

The passage of the fiscal cliff bill with an overwhelming bipartisan majority in the Senate and a sound bipartisan majority in the House was a clear sign that some in Congress had gotten the message. Let us hope that this collaborative action by the departing 112th Congress was a harbinger for the 113th. (See the epilogue for our analysis and observations on the activities of and prognosis for the 113th.)

Right after the elections, the Pew Research Center conducted a survey that revealed that in general voters were "pessimistic about partisan cooperation" in politics going forward. As we started the New Year, Congress gave the citizenry a reason to replace this healthy skepticism with guarded optimism.

A year-end *Washington Post*–ABC poll showed that 75 percent of the registered voters responding felt that the "economy is still in a recession."[12] If that is the perspective from those at the bottom and the middle of the cliff one to two years from now, all of the pick and shovel work done to try to address the debt and deficit crisis by only focusing on cost cutting and shrinking government will have been in vain.

Congress needs to be about more than green eyeshades and expense reduction. It also needs to be about investing and revenue generation.

It needs to start working the pivot points that matter to the populous and not just those that matter to the proletariat. We need much less Wall Street and much more Main Street, side streets, blue highways and back roads.

The American people deserve this. They should be given the opportunity to be mountain climbers rather than cliff dwellers. They should not have been sequestered. But they were.

SEQUESTRATION NATION

For most of 2012, there was little serious and substantive attention paid to the deficit and debt and the impending sequestration on Capitol Hill. Then, as Congress began to wrap up its work in August and September before heading home to campaign for re-election, there were hearings about the impact of a potential sequester and the need to avoid it but no affirmative action was taken before adjournment.

The lobbyists got out their long knives and began fighting for the segment of turf they were there to protect during the lame duck session of Congress that would be held after election day and the sequester that was initially scheduled to take effect at the beginning of January. In the final presidential debate, President Obama declared that the sequester "will not happen."[13]

From there on the sequestration dance unraveled as follows:

- Congress moved the date of the sequester back two months to the beginning of March 2013.

- The President, his cabinet members and other representatives went around the country in campaign-style mode describing the serious and eminent danger that was coming with the sequester.

- Various factions of Congress tried to negotiate different cuts other than the across-the-board ones stipulated in the sequester bill.

Then, on March 1, 2013, what the President said would not happen—happened. The sequester went into effect as passed and the jousting match was over—at least for the time being. It appeared that the real negotiations over what and where to cut would take place as part of the budget process or debt ceiling negotiations later in the year.

Some conservative pundits reacted with glee a day or two after we were sequestered pointing out the world had not ended, the economy had not collapsed and things were going on pretty much as usual. They were correct. But, as more neutral analysts noted, the full effect of the sequester would not begin to be felt until the second half of the year and it would be felt disproportionately across the country.

In the three months after the sequester went into effect, the news media ran a wide variety of stories regarding its impact. For example: In May, *Forbes* ran a piece headlined "Federal Budget Sequester Not Having Effect on the Economy Thus Far." In that same month, NBC News had a piece titled "Businesses Slash Jobs as Sequester Impact Hits." In June, Inc.com wrote "Four Months After the Sequester the Economy Continues to Improve." In contrast, in June, finance.yahoo.com wrote, "Remember the Sequester? It's Finally Dinging the Economy."[14]

The difference in these differing "angles" or perspectives can be easily explained. What you see and what you report depends on where you look and what you measure. As the experts had predicted, the impact of the sequestration on the economy was variable and disparate.

This was borne out by a study released by the Economic Policy Institute (EPI) in June 2013 that looked at the effect of the sequester on state budgets. According to EPI, the sequester would result in a cut of $5.1 billion from the previous year's funding level to states. The five states with the biggest percentage losses due to the combined effect of the continuing resolution that was approved on March 26 were Louisiana, Indiana, Maine, Connecticut and Massachusetts.[15]

In summary, the bottom line for the sequester is unequivocal. It will not be beneficial for the economy in general or specific terms.

Rest assured, it has already caused and will cause pain. It will yield little to no gain. And there will definitely be more than a few migraines because of the sequester and its aftermath negotiations before this is all over.

FUSS BUDGETS

The same can be said about the tussle over the budget that took place in 2013. On March 21, 2013, the House approved Budget Committee Chairman Paul Ryan's budget by a vote of 221–207. Ten Republicans voted against the budget as did all Democrats.[16]

On the same day that the House passed its budget, the Senate rejected it by a vote of 40–59. Five Republicans—Susan Collins (ME), Dean Heller (NV), Mike Lee (UT), Rand Paul (KY) and Marco Rubio (FL)—joined all of the senate Democrats to vote against the bill.[17]

The Senate passed its first budget in four years on March 23 by the slim margin of 50–49. No Republican voted for the budget and four Democrats—Max Baucus (MT), Mark Begich (AS), Kay Hagan (NC) and Mark Pryor (AK), all facing tough re-election races in 2014—voted against it.[18]

As might have been expected, there were monumental differences between the two budgets in terms of structure and substance. The Senate budget developed by Budget Chair Patty Murray (D-WA) included $1.2 trillion in additional taxes and included increased spending of $100 billion to boost economic growth and workforce development. The House budget called for cutting taxes, repealing the 2010 health care law and slowing the rate of government spending.[19]

The House budget was designed to cut $5.7 trillion in spending and achieve a balanced budget within ten years. The Senate budget was designed to cut the deficit by $1.85 trillion in ten years through a blend of spending cuts and new revenue but not to achieve a balanced budget within that time frame.

The President delivered his own budget on April 10—two months late according to the White House because of the uncertainty of the fiscal cliff debate. It was much was more conservative than the Senate budget with less tax revenue and more entitlement cuts.

The President's 2014 budget included a chained CPI proposal for Social Security designed to reduce future benefits by adapting a new way of calculating benefits and significant reductions in Medicare benefits and higher premiums for those couples making over $170,000 a year. The budget also called for major decreases (over 30 percent) from his 2013 budget for agencies such as Housing and Urban Development, Labor and Homeland Security and major increases (over 30 percent) for agencies such as Commerce and Transportation.

In introducing his budget and talking about the entitlement cuts the President acknowledged, "I don't believe that all of these ideas are optimal, but I'm willing to accept them as a compromise." Those in the President's own party agreed they weren't "optimal" either and shouldn't be part of a compromise. Immediately after the President's announcement, Democratic House leaders like Nancy Pelosi (CA), Steny Hoyer (MD) and James Clyburn (SC) said Social Security should be taken off the table and not dealt with as part of the budget and deficit debate. From the Republican side, House Ways and Means Chair Dave Camp (R-MI) complimented the President for taking a "step forward on entitlement reform" but said they would not sign on for any increases in tax revenue as part of a budget package.[20]

Then, the fussing and tussling began for real as the parties began working to try to reconcile the budgets and to reach an agreement. We do not know what the final resolution will be as we go to press with our book. We do know that it will be a budget that the country will have to live with and that none of the combatants will be completely happy about.

ONE MAN'S DEBT CEILING/ANOTHER MAN'S FLOOR

The budget fight was an opening bid in the negotiations on the deficit and debt ceiling. If the fiscal cliff bill was act one, the budget was act two and the debt ceiling was to be act three of this financial three-act play.

In January the House GOP voted to suspend enforcement of the federal debt limit through May 18 to avoid a nasty early confrontation and spectacle with a promise to their conservative members to try to get a balanced budget agreement when the debt ceiling negotiations were held.[21]

The President agreed to the "suspension" gambit but made no commitment other than to abide by the extension. White House Press Secretary Jay Carney said, "clearly, we support extension of the debt ceiling without drama or delay."[22]

While there was no drama then, there was a little drama in the days leading up to the debt ceiling negotiations. President Obama invited a dozen senators to the White House for dinner on April 10. During the dinner the President and the senators agreed to exchange papers on the deficit even though, as one lawmaker said, the chances of reaching a grand bargain on the deficit were less than 50/50.[23]

At about the same time, the White House endorsed a conference committee as the best path forward for a deficit deal. The committee was proposed by Senate leader Patty Murray (D-WA) and house budget chair Paul Ryan (R-WI) to try to reconcile the "vastly different budget resolutions that had been passed by the House and Senate."

In announcing the support for the conference committee, Acting White House budget director Jeff Zients proclaimed that "Regular order is the way to proceed." Zients made it clear, however, that the President would not negotiate behind closed doors over an increase in the debt ceiling and the $16 trillion limit will have to be raised again this summer.[24]

In spite of the attempt to achieve "regular order" and the expressed need to raise the debt ceiling, nothing happened. May 18 came and went. No agreement was reached and the ceiling was not raised.

Therefore, on May 19 the debt limit was reset to $16.699 trillion and the CBO reported that the Department of Treasury would be "employing its well-established toolbox of extraordinary measures (e.g., suspending the issuance of new securities to the Civil Service Retirement and Disability Fund and the issuance of new state and local government securities) to allow continued borrowing for a limited time." The CBO projected "those measures will be exhausted in either October or November of this year."[25]

The debt ceiling bullet was dodged due to these "extraordinary measures" and the fiscal legerdemain of the Treasury. That was a good thing. As Manu Raju and John Bresnahan noted in *Politico* on June 11, "Three months after President Barack Obama began his charm offensive with Senate Republicans, the two sides have yet to even agree on the scope of the spending or deficit problems—let alone what's needed to solve it."[26]

So in 2013 things picked up and played out in essentially the same manner as they had two years or so ago. And it looked as if the summer and fall of 2013 would look like the summer of 2011.

We hope we are proved wrong and that this time the results are different. They need to be. That's not only our opinion, it's also that of Simon Johnson, chief economist of the International Monetary Fund in 2007 and 2008 and currently a professor at the Massachusetts Institute of Technology and Senior Fellow at the Petersen Institute for International Economics.

On June 4, 2013, Johnson testified before the Senate Budget Committee hearing on "The Fiscal and Economic Effects of Austerity." Main points in his testimony included the following:

- There is no meaningful evidence that we "need" to cut federal deficits in this year or next year, or even over the next five years.
- It is far more important to get the economy back on a sustainable growth path . . .
- The ongoing sequester is a perfect example of how not to manage fiscal policy . . .
- Significantly cutting federal discretionary domestic spending below current projected levels will . . . actually reduce attainable growth rates in the United States.

In a posting for Bloomberg News shortly after his testimony, Johnson cautioned, "The real danger is that the political process will produce another scary, needless confrontation over the debt ceiling that will significantly slow the recovery. The debt ceiling should be completely taken off the table."[27]

We hope that Congress heeds Johnson's warnings. We know that we could have and should have known and done better in the past. That was true not only in the nation's capital but outside it and around the country as well.

A TALE OF TWO COUNTRIES

On March 5, 2013, the Dow Jones index hit a record high and kept on climbing for some time. On March 28, the Dow Jones and Standard and Poor 500 indexes both hit record highs. On May 3, the indexes did it again.

In the first quarter of 2013, corporation after corporation announced record or near-record profits. The wealthy who were invested in the markets and other exotic vehicles continued to rake it in. They gained the money back that they had lost at the beginning of the Great Recession and then some. Large business organizations such as the Conference Board and Business Roundtable were bullish on the country's economic prospects.

In June 2013, the Conference Board reported that its consumer confidence index "jumped to 81.4, the highest reading since January 2008."[28] And in June as well, writing in a front page article for the *New York Times*, Nelson D. Schwartz revealed that a "number of economists . . . are now predicting something the United States has not experienced in years: healthier, more lasting growth."[29]

God was in her heaven and all was well with the United States economy. Or was it?

In a devastating opinion piece published in *The New York Times Sunday Review* on March 31, 2013, David Stockman, former budget director for President Ronald Reagan, called the question not only on the apparent economic and financial successes but on the manner in which they were being achieved. Stockman observed, "Over the last 13 years, the stock market has crashed and touched off a recession . . . I predict this latest Wall Street bubble, inflated by an egregious flood of phony money from the Federal Reserve, rather than real economic gains, will explode, too."

Stockman pointed out that Main Street was failing and Wall Street was succeeding now because of exceedingly favorable treatment from and an invidious relationship with Washington, D.C. He proposed a number of radical reforms to both the political and financial systems to correct that.

Stockman recommended, on the banking side of the ledger, "purging the corrosive financialization that has turned the economy into a giant casino since the 1970s. This would mean putting the great Wall Street banks out in the cold to compete as at-risk free enterprise, without access to cheap Fed loans or deposit insurance. Banks would be able to take deposits and make commercial loans, but be banned from trading, underwriting and money management in all its forms."[30]

Stockman was not alone in his call to reform financial services institutions. In an opinion piece for the *Washington Post* on March 29,

Thomas M. Hoenig said, "The fuel of the largest firms is subsidized, and the public bears the cost." Hoenig called these subsidies "corporate welfare" and proclaimed, "The way to return the financial services industry to the free market is by separating trading from commercial banks and by reforming the so-called shadow banking sector. Government guarantees should be limited primarily to those commercial banking activities that need it to function: the payments system and the intermediation process between short-term lenders and long-term borrowers."[31]

Although there was a small and elite group of organizations and individuals apparently doing well, they were unwittingly putting us and the economy at risk. There was a much larger group in the economy that was and continued to be at risk. They were the jobless and underemployed. They were the middle class.

According to *The Economist* in a March 23, 2013, article, "Since the end of 2007 the population over 16 has grown by 11.6m people and the labor force (those either working or looking for work) has grown by just 1.6m." *The Economist* went on to observe, "Even after accounting for demographic shifts, participation among men aged 25 to 54 has still fallen much more sharply in America in the past decade than in other rich countries. That suggests America does a poor job of keeping the unemployed, particularly the unskilled, in the workforce."[32]

In June 2013, at the same time there were buoyant reports in the media regarding the economy, Paul Wiseman, AP economics reporter, wrote an article pointing out that the recovery was not being felt by the middle class. In it he noted that because of factors such as lagging home values and losses in "real income," "Americans are still not shopping with enough gusto to add much momentum to the economy."[33]

Near the end of June 2013, the Commerce Department validated Mr. Wiseman's reporting on a flagging economy when it released a report that lowered the gross domestic product (GDP) for the first quarter to 1.8 from 2.4 percent. According to Reuters, "The biggest surprise was the pace of consumer spending, which grew at 2.6 percent, not the 3.4 percent rate previously estimated."[34]

The sad truth is that in mid-2013 too many Americans were still falling through the economic cracks. They were not invisible. But, they were not being helped by the invisible hand. Both presidential candidates recognized and discussed this during their campaigns in 2012.

IT'S THE ECONOMETRICS STUPID

Although they disagreed on much during their election campaigns, there was one thing on which President Barack Obama and Mitt Romney, the Republican candidate for President, seemed to agree: That it was time to renew America and the American dream.

President Obama made his view explicit during a 2012 Afghanistan visit when he stated, "Let us . . . reclaim the American dream that is at the heart of our story".[35] The President called for unleashing innovation and creating new jobs as part of his formula for reclaiming the dream. Later, after the Bureau of Labor Statistics announced that 115,000 jobs were added to the workforce in April, candidate Romney called for the economy to create 500,000 jobs a month and achieving an unemployment rate of 4 percent.[36]

The bottom line for both men was that, in spite of the fact that the economy as measured by GDP had been in recovery mode since mid-2009 and had created 4½ million jobs in that time period, the results to date had been insufficient. That's because what is needed to complete the turnaround of the American economy and the American dream is renewal rather than recovery. Let's look at why.

The paradoxical nature of our current situation is best portrayed by the perspectives of journalist Daniel Gross and economist Paul Krugman. In the cover article for the May 7, 2012, issue of *Newsweek*, Gross commented that the United States had made significant economic progress since the collapse of 2007 and was well-positioned against the rest of the world.[37] Krugman, in contrast, in his 2012 book titled *End This Depression Now,* asserted that, while we are not technically in a recession or depression, the economic conditions for many Americans are similar to those experienced in the 1930s.[38]

Who is right? Both—it all depends where you want to put your focus. Do you want to look at things through a macroeconomic or a microeconomic lens?

We made this point in our book, *Renewing,* when we observed, "GDP was never intended to function as an indicator of well-being and

GDP is insensitive to the distribution of income within a country." We went on to quote Nobel Prize–winning economist Joseph Stiglitz, who said, "No single measure can capture what is going on in a modern society, but the GDP measure fails in critical ways. We need measures that focus on how the typical individual is doing."[39]

That analysis was relevant almost two years ago. It remains so today. Consider the following.

Throughout 2012, many corporations across the industry spectrum reported record profits and the United States as a nation is as productive as it has ever been. Still, there were 5 million fewer workers employed than prior to the recession. Hours worked remained flat, wages were stagnant and income inequality was increasing. There was a significant disjuncture between recovery at the macro level and renewal at the individual or micro level.

Laura D'Andrea Tyson, professor and former chairwoman of the Council of Economic Advisors under President Clinton, explained the source of this disjuncture in a 2012 *Economix* posting for the *New York Times* titled "Structural Unemployment and Good Jobs" in which she wrote, "Despite several quarters of growth in private sector employment, the American economy is still far from full employment. The primary reason is weak aggregate demand, the painful and predictable consequence of a deep balance-sheet recession."

Professor Tyson went on to note that there is no evidence of a "larger-than-usual mismatch between employer needs and worker skills," but that there has been a significant decline in middle-skill jobs that has been especially harmful "to the earnings and labor force participation of workers without a college degree, especially men."

In an earlier *New York Times* column, on July 29, 2011, Professor Tyson noted "Like many economists, I believe that the immediate crisis facing the United States is the jobs deficit, not the budget deficit."[40] Although we are not economists, we agree unreservedly with that assessment.

That's because when it comes to renewing America as opposed to continuing a slow-motion recovery, it's about the econometrics, stupid. It is a matter of straightforward economics and the fundamental laws of supply and demand.

Supply-side economics is fine as an abstract concept. Demand-side economics, however, drives real-world economic growth and positive results for individuals. In America, historically there have been three critical levers that have stimulated demand: a plentiful supply of jobs, decent wages and a national psychology of upward mobility and opportunity. Those levers are not present today.

More importantly, we are engaged in two national debates that divert our attention from addressing these root causes of our economic problems on the demand side. One is about our budget deficit. The other is about income inequality.

Some, who have made the budget deficit discussion central to our national dialogue for well over two years now, would have us believe that all we have to do to improve the economy is to curb rampant governmental spending by embracing an austerity agenda. There is no question that we need to bring government spending under control.

There is considerable question as to whether this would do anything to make the average citizen's economic circumstances better. It might make the rating agencies and the financial industry happier. It might make the expense side of the nation's balance sheet look better.

We are not aware of any economic model, however, that predicts improvement in individual economic well-being caused by reducing the nation's deficit and debt problem. Without improvement there and on the revenue side of the balance sheet, it will be impossible to restore economic stability for the country and prosperity for its citizens.

We would also argue that the current focus of the discussion on income inequality is misplaced. Many are contending that addressing income equality is a matter of fairness. In our opinion, this frames the issue incorrectly.

There is certainly a fairness concern to income inequality. But that concern tends to be philosophical and revolves around the type of society and nation we want to be. The pragmatic concern with income inequality is that malapportionment of wealth and resources diminish demand and reduce the tax base.

THE ECONOMIC ABYSS

At the beginning of 2013, it looked as if there might be an emerging recognition that it was the human issues and the econometrics as we call them that were retarding the financial recovery of the country and its citizens.

In a major speech at the American Enterprise Institute (AEI) in early January, House Majority Leader Eric Cantor (R-VA) called for Republicans to "focus our attention really on what lies beyond the fiscal debates" and to create "conditions for health, happiness and prosperity."[41]

It seemed the national conversation was about to pivot from an almost obsessive concentration on big government and expense reduction to a concern for the well-being of the individual citizen and revenue generation. That was good news because while the majority of the politicians and pundits were talking about the fiscal cliff the American public was staring at an economic abyss.

What was the nature of the abyss? Here are a few facts and figures:

- *Gross Domestic Product*: The GDP in Q4 of 2012 was 0.1 percent, the first quarter of negative GDP since the second quarter of 2009. Some freakish factors such as a 22 percent reduction in defense spending accounted for this and economists didn't feel that the performance was signaling a recession. On the other hand, Bank of America was only forecasting GDP growth of 1.0 for Q1 of 2013— hardly the sign of a robust recovery.[42]

- *Unemployment/Joblessness*: The Bureau of Labor Statistics' official unemployment rate stood at 7.9 percent. When workers who have fallen out of the workforce are taken into account that rate is 9.3 percent. The Federal Reserve projects that the unemployment rate will not fall to 6 percent or below until 2015 or later.[43]

- *Wage Stagnation*: From 2000 to 2011, the median income for working-age households shrank 12.1 percent to $55,640. According to the Economic Policy Institute, since 2000, productivity has increased by 23 percent but wages have stayed essentially the same.[44]

- *Income Inequality:* The share of wages going to the top 1 percent went from 7.3 percent in 1979 to 12.3 percent in 2010. Emanuel

Saez, an economist at the University of California at Berkeley, found that 65 percent of the nation's income growth from 2002–2007 went to the top 1 percent of households.[45]

What is the future nature of the abyss? Here is what some experts and indicators are suggesting:

- *Sequestration:* The Congressional Budget Office projected the across-the-board sequester process could eliminate 1.4 million jobs. The Bipartisan Policy Center says the process would eliminate at least 1 million jobs in this year and the next.[46] The Pew Research Center noted that "Overall, about one-fifth of federal grant funding to states will be cut . . . But, the percentage of funding in each program area that would be vulnerable to any cuts varies greatly."[47]

- *Small Businesses: Start-Ups and Job Creation:* According to the Bureau of Labor Statistics, the number of "new establishments" rose until 2006, then from 2007 through 2010 they declined by an average of 40,053 per year with a slight increase in 2011 of 29,316.[48] A Gallup poll released in December 2012 reported that small business owners expect to add fewer new jobs in 2013 than at any point since the depths of the recession in 2008.[49]

- *Construction Industry Performance:* The McGraw Hill Construction Industry Forecast for 2013 projected a total U.S. construction increase of 6 percent to $483.7 billion. This compared to $641 billion in 2007. As Juan Rodriguez noted in writing for aboutconstruction.com, however, these projections are "completely unpredictable as funding for construction projects will become the most important factor."[50] Anirban Basu chief economist of Associated Builders and Contractors made a similar observation, noting, "the fiscal cliff represents a nonresidential construction industry cliff as well."[51]

- *Innovation Stagnation:* Economists Tyler Cowen of George Mason University and Robert Gordon of Northwestern argued that U.S. economic growth has been and will be retarded into the future because of the lack of transformative technological breakthroughs comparable to other industrial eras. Cowen labeled this the "Great

Stagnation." In his paper titled *Is U.S. Economic Growth Over? Faltering Innovation Confronts Six Headwinds*, Gordon asserted that "continuous economic growth is not inevitable" and speculated that "future growth in consumption per capita for the bottom 99 percent of the income distribution could fall below 0.5 percent per year for an extended period of decades."[52]

- *Economic Rewards System*: A recent study revealed that one-third of the overall increase in income going to the richest 1 percent has resulted from increased corporate profits. In contrast, wages, which have typically been around 50 percent as a percent of GDP, have been on a steep decline since 2001 and hit a record low of 43.5 percent in 2011. There is nothing we have seen to indicate a reversal of these trends going forward.[53]

Sum them all up and the bottom line from these prognostications is that—unless some positive intervention is made—the abyss deepens and the future for the average American will look more abysmal rather than less.

This should be unacceptable. We need a national jobs agenda and we need it now. That agenda should build upon traditional American strengths such as manufacturing, innovation, quality, productivity and entrepreneurship. We present our pivot point recommendation for that jobs agenda in this chapter. We present our recommendations on how to address the individual economic well-being needs of our citizens in chapter 6.

THE SKILLED WORKER SHORTAGE FALLACY

Some would have us believe that America has a serious shortage of skilled workers and that is a primary cause of our lack of job creation. Right? Wrong!

We were bemused for the past few years as an ecumenical group of business leaders, academics and experts put forward the argument that training and developing a more skilled workforce would help drive job creation. It seems to us that this is a basic misunderstanding of cause and effect.

We can have a philosophical debate about which came first, the chicken or the egg. But when it comes to job creation there should be no such argument. Organizations and individuals who create new organizations are the chicken—they are the job creators. Employees and skilled workers are the eggs—they are the job holders.

That's not to say that we don't need skilled workers in the United States. But as a wide variety of studies have demonstrated, the extent to which the skills of the workforce influences business decisions is a modest one and the actual "skill deficiencies" of the current American workforce may be significantly overstated.

For example, in a March 2012 *Harvard Business Review* article, Michael Porter and Jan Rivkin reported that a survey that they had done revealed that by far the leading reason that a company would move out of the United States was "Lower wage rates in the destination country—70 percent." 31 percent of the survey respondents cited "Better access to skilled labor" as a "reason for leaving." But, 29 percent cited "better access" as a "reason for not leaving."[54] So that makes "skilled labor" a "push" rather than a clear and compelling driver of job creation for the United States.

After examining labor demand data from the Chicago Federal Reserve, Matthew O'Brien, associate editor of *The Atlantic,* in June 2012 wrote, "We should expect wages to be rising much faster in sectors where employers can't find enough qualified workers. But that hasn't been the case." Instead, in the period from May 2006 through May 2011 there was a "general shortfall of demand" for the "low, medium and high skill workers" that has moved "more or less in tandem."[55]

Professor Peter Cappelli of The Wharton School supported O'Brien's position in a June 12, 2012, article for *Time Business* titled "The Skills Gap Myth: Why Companies Can't Find Good People." After analyzing a Manpower survey which showed that "roughly half of the employers were reporting having trouble filling their vacancies," Professor Cappelli astutely noted, "roughly 10% of the employers admit that the problem is that the candidates they want won't accept the position at the wage level being offered." He continued to observe for those who indicate there is a skill shortage, "by far the most important shortfall they see in candidates is a lack of experience doing similar jobs."[56]

In June 2012, the Bureau of Labor Statistics reported that there were approximately 3.4 million job openings in the United States. *Our careful review of the top 50 occupations, with the most projected openings for 2010–2020, posted by CareerOneStop of the Department of Labor current job openings on its careerinfonet shows that the majority of these current and future openings will be "low skill," requiring less than high school or high school degrees.*

So if skill shortage was not central to the country's job creation dilemma, what was? In our opinion, America has had significant problems since the beginning of the great recession on the following five key factors that drive significant job creation:

- *Small businesses and entrepreneurial start-ups*: Although Congress has passed some legislation aimed at assisting small businesses, they still indicate difficulties in getting loans and financial assistance. The Bureau of Labor Statistics reports that there was a steady decline in new business start-ups from a high of 670,000 in 2006 to a low of about 500,000 in 2010 with a slight increase to about 530,000 in 2011.[57]

- *Large corporate growth and development:* In general, American businesses and the multinationals have continued to expand and create more jobs outside the country while learning to do much more with less and replacing people with technology here. Many are also sitting on record profits rather than expanding. Our byzantine tax system creates incentives for doing business abroad and provides loopholes that can bring a company's effective tax rate down to zero.

- *Government investment*: State and local governments across the nation continue to be cash strapped and to cut government jobs (teachers, police, fire, agency employees) and eliminate public works and other types of projects that create private-sector jobs. The stimulus bill provided a little short-term relief from 2009 until 2011. But its transitional benefits are long gone now.

- *Clustering and construction*: After prior recessions, new construction—both commercial and residential—has been at the heart of economic recoveries. In the early 2000s, America was significantly overbuilt, so that cannot be the case in the near term.

Our infrastructure is crumbling, but we lack the political where-withal to deal with that condition.

- *Consumer demand:* According to a June 18, 2012, U.S. Census Bureau press release, "U.S. median household net worth declined by 35 percent between 2005 and 2010."[58] As reported in *Business Insider* on June 12, 2012, almost 24 percent of mortgages nationwide were still "under water."[59] People are struggling to make ends meet and do not have discretionary income. In its cover article for its July 14–20, 2012, issue, *The Economist* observed that in the period from 1982 to 2007, consumer spending "on goods, services and houses rose from 67% of GDP (growth) to 74%." It goes on to note that "in the three years since the recession ended. . . . Consumer spending and housing contributed just 65% of growth."[60]

Small businesses and entrepreneurial start-ups, large corporate growth and development, government investment, clustering and construction, consumer demand: those are key factors in the job creation algorithm. Appropriately weighted and aligned they produce the output, which is jobs. They are out of synch now. We need to correct this.

The citizens and the country have begun to mobilize and there is an emerging consensus that this is a complex demand side issue that must be addressed in an integrated and coordinated manner. It can and will not be corrected simply through training and development or increasing the supply of skilled workers. It's time to set the concept of a skilled workforce shortage aside—unless, of course, it's applied to the current status of Congress.

PIVOT POINT RECOMMENDATION: CREATE A NATIONAL JOBS AGENDA

Thomas Kochan of MIT wrote a *Huffington Post* blog in 2012 titled "The Jobs Crisis: Time to Treat It as a National Emergency." In his post, Professor Kochan recommended developing a "Jobs Compact" and major investments in job creation.[61] We called for a similar comprehensive and sweeping approach in *Renewing* and call for it again.

We need to implement a national agenda that will manufacture American jobs in large numbers. There is nothing more important than a plentiful supply of good-paying jobs to create the conditions for individual and national prosperity.

We recognize that recommending a program of the size and scope we are proposing is not politically correct and given the current configuration of Congress is not politically palatable either. That does not mean it is not necessary or the proper intervention, however. As we have said, and will say throughout this book, not addressing a pivot point correctly can only result in failure.

Failure here should not be an option. There is no piece of legislation that is more important to America's future than a national jobs agenda. There is no better investment of taxpayer's dollars. There is no better way to "make life work"—as Majority Leader Cantor titled his AEI speech—than to put Americans to work in jobs that promote their self-worth and economic well-being.

A jobs agenda does that. Therefore, we strongly recommend that Congress implement a robust jobs bill. To have maximum impact, the bill must be structured and designed correctly. Much like a strong strategic plan, the bill must be targeted and designed for speed of implementation and impact.

The bill should be structured to:

- Generate the largest number of "high-quality" jobs in the shortest period of time
- Focus on jobs that will have the greatest multiplier effects on local economies as well as consumer spending and confidence
- Ensure the federal government disperses funds according to an established timeline
- Ensure that state governments and other recipients use the funds to create new or replacement jobs instead of protecting existing jobs or to cover operating costs

The primary focus of the jobs bill should be to put *job-ready and skilled workers back to work* and *new, well-educated entry-level workers to work in as short a time frame as possible.* At a minimum, the bill should include the following components:

1. *Small Business Component:* Major appropriation for direct and guaranteed loans to small businesses; targeted jobs tax credits; tax incentives, such as payroll tax credit with Social Security match; reduced and accelerated depreciation for capital investments for creating jobs that meet established criteria

2. *Public Service Employment Component:* Major appropriation for job creation at state and local levels to restore government services and for the establishment of the Works Progress Administration and Civilian Conservation Corps-type programs focused on "shovel-ready projects" addressing the needs of America's crumbling infrastructure

3. *Community Service Component:* Major appropriation for employees to work in nonprofit, community-based, and other service organizations to restore and increase social safety net services

4. *Manufacturing for Export Component:* Major appropriation that uses the Golden Rule to our advantage—whoever has the gold sets the rules. Increase funding for manufacturers and suppliers of products for exports, and increase funding of the U.S. Export-Import Bank so that it can finance American exports.

The bill should be targeted in terms of the priority groups to be reached and the priority industries/sectors in which jobs should be created. At a minimum, the priority groups should include 45- to 65-year-old age groups, millennial age groups, highly skilled and educated professionals and white-collar workers; entry-level workers with college degrees and high school diplomas, and disadvantaged minorities. At a minimum, priority industries should include manufacturing, construction, infrastructure development and modernization, information technology, and education.

We won't put a dollar amount on the bill we recommend, but it should be designed to help create 300,000 or more jobs per month if it is going to be sufficient to convert an extremely fragile macroeconomic recovery into one that has the capacity to make a difference at the microeconomic level in consumers' pocketbooks and spending patterns. We need to create around 150,000 jobs a month just to keep up with new workers entering the workplace. We need the additional jobs created and not just saved to start reducing the unemployment rate.

The jobs bill should have a time limitation and not be considered permanent. It should be in place long enough to jump-start the economy and to move it back to "normal," but no longer. Given the current continuing estimates for a jobless recovery, we anticipate this to be three years.

The bill should have a strong performance management framework to ensure its proper rollout through appropriate planning, involvement and execution.

In conclusion, jobs should be job one for Congress. The real question is why haven't they been? To answer that we need to look at the philosophical, political and psychological divides that separate our elected officials. We address those in the next chapter and in the epilogue to the book and contemplate the impact they will have on working the pivot points going forward.

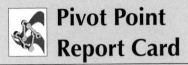

Pivot Point
Report Card

Instructions

This report card is provided to allow you to reflect upon and assess the progress in this pivot point area. To use the report card:

1. Review the recommendation for the area.

2. Evaluate the progress made in the area to date and assign a letter grade using the system that follows: A–excellent progress. B–substantial progress. C–some progress. D–little progress. F–no progress.

3. Describe the nature of the progress and the rationale for your rating.

We will be posting our assessment for this area on an occasional basis. To see that assessment and to provide your input and feedback on the area, visit *http://www.workingthepivotpoints.com.*

Recommendation

- Create a National Jobs Agenda

Grade

Reason

4 | Congressional Dysfunction: Beltway Blues

THE 112TH CONGRESS, WHICH WAS IN OFFICE FROM JANUARY 3, 2011, to January 3, 2013, may have been the worst Congress in history.

That's hard to determine objectively. It is easy to determine, however, that the 112th was the least productive Congress ever.

The 112th was also held in exceptionally low regard by the American citizens. Let's look at the facts and the implications they have both for Congress as a pivot point and Congress' working on pivot points in the future.

THE 112TH'S REPORT CARD

If we were to assign a letter grade to the 112th's performance it would have to be an "F" for "farcical." The overall explanation for that grade would be "Present but not accounted for." Come to think of it, they weren't present as much as they were in the past either. Let's look at the 112th's output and effort.

During its two years, the Congress passed 220 laws—18 percent of them related to things like renaming post offices or federal buildings. That was by far the lowest of any Congress in more than half a century. The next lowest was 333 public laws passed by the 104th Congress—almost 50 percent more than the 112th. Excluding these low points, in the period from 1948 to 2010, in general, Congress tended to pass somewhere between 500 and 600 public laws.[1]

The *Washington Times* labeled this past Congress the "least productive ever" based upon the 112th's performance on its Legislative Futility Index, which tracks floor activity in both chambers. The Index looks at six measures: time spent in session, number of pages added to the Congressional Record, conference reports between the House and Senate, floor votes, the total number of bills that cleared each chamber and the number of laws enacted that began in each chamber.

The Times has been maintaining its Index for 33 Congresses. According to the *Times*, in this Congress:

- The House and Senate produced only 10 conference reports—the worst ever.

- The Senate cleared a total of only 350 bills and had 66 of its own bills signed into law—both the worst ever.

- The House had only 567 bills clear the chamber—the fewest ever— and 162 bills enacted into law—a record low.[2]

These final results and futility throughout the course of its two-year tenure led many knowledgeable observers to evaluate the 112th Congress harshly. While Congress was stuck in the morass of the debt ceiling debacle (which we describe in detail in chapter 2) during the summer of 2011, Norm Ornstein of the American Enterprise Institute wrote an article for *Foreign Policy* titled "Worst. Congress. Ever."[3] In the next issue of *Foreign Policy*, Sarah Binder of the Brookings Institution agreed with Ornstein in an article titled "Yes, It's Really That Bad." As did Beverly Gage, who teaches history at Yale, in her article titled "Trust Me, This Congress Is Historically Inept."[4]

The comments were not any kinder as the 112th wrapped up its desultory performance in 2013. Walter Hickey of *Business Insider* wrote, "[It was] the least effective and most disliked legislative body in years." Jonathan Allen of *Politico* wrote, "The 112th Congress came in with a bang, but it is crawling out with the soft whimper of failure." David Horsey of the *Los Angeles Times* was even more damning. He wrote, "The 112th Congress worked hard on just one thing: competing to be known as the most worthless, incompetent, do-nothing gathering of lawmakers in the nation's history."[5]

YOU CAN'T GET THERE FROM HERE

So what is it that the 112th Congress did not get done that caused this flood of opprobrium? Ezra Klein described this perfectly in a *Washington Post* blog,

> What's the record of the 112th Congress? Well, it almost shut down the government and almost breached the debt ceiling. It almost went over the fiscal cliff . . . It achieved nothing of note on housing, energy, stimulus, immigration, guns, tax reform, infrastructure, climate change, or really anything.[6]

Reading Klein's assessment, it struck us that over the past several years—most especially in the past two—our nation's capital has become a very misdirected place. That's true not only on a political but on an experiential level as well. Trying to drive anywhere in or around the city proves that the transportation grid is a reflection of the gridlock that has dominated the debates or lack thereof in political circles.

You can't turn left on a light—or an issue. You can turn right—from either side of the aisle, at any time. You can make a U-turn anywhere you want—that's what's called Washington logic and consistency.

Washington, D.C., may have more roundabouts than any other city in the United States. And, if you miss your cross street off the roundabout, you just keep going around and around and around and getting nowhere—this is similar to the holding of endless congressional hearings and the drafting of meaningless legislation doomed to failure.

This all reminds us of an old joke that goes something like this: A traveler on a country road comes to a creek where the bridge has been swept away by a recent flood. The traveler sees an old farmer standing next to where the bridge used to be and asks, "Is there a way to backtrack and find somewhere else to get across the creek?"

The farmer responds, "Yep. Just, go back two miles, turn right and . . . No, go back one mile and turn left . . ." The farmer stops for a minute, shrugs his shoulders, scratches his head and then says to the traveler, "Come to think of it, you can't get there from here."

Welcome to Washington, D.C.! A city where for two years there were no bridges being built (not even to nowhere) and few bridge builders.

In 2011, the Senate did pass a veteran's "jobs" bill with unanimous bipartisan support in both the Senate and House. This might have been viewed as a sign that repair work had begun. In fact, just the opposite was true. The "carve out" for veterans from the President's substantial jobs proposal was a no-brainer.

Voting against this bill would have been like voting against motherhood and apple pie. Voting for it was not a profile in courage but of political expediency. It gave the appearance of doing something when in fact it did very little to address the underlying problems of the American economy. The truth was that this vote was one of avoidance rather than commitment.

The President's American Jobs Act of 2011 was a comprehensive package that included a number of provisions that had previously been endorsed and supported by Republicans. Rejecting it too was a no-brainer. All it required was for partisan politics to prevail rather than reasoned discussion leading to joint problem solving and compromise.

Unfortunately, compromise has become a dirty word in Washington. Compromise was on the wane in our nation's capital before the elections of 2010. It became virtually nonexistent after that.

This is sad, even tragic, given that this nation's constitution was a product of compromise. Those newly elected officials who came to Washington, D.C., in 2011 after the elections of 2010 with a professed admiration and belief in the Constitution and what it represents did not seem to comprehend or chose to ignore this fact.

As we note in chapter 1, the Constitution was not handed down from on high. It was hammered out in the halls and backrooms in Philadelphia by Founding Fathers who frequently didn't agree with one another but saw the necessity for coming together.

This willingness to compromise in order "to form a more perfect union" is best illustrated by Benjamin Franklin.

On September 17, 1787, when the Constitution was read aloud for the first time, Franklin wrote these words, "I confess there are several parts of this constitution which I do not at present approve, but I am not sure I shall ever approve them." Franklin continued to request "that every member of the Convention, who may still have objections to it, would with me on this occasion doubt a little his own Infallibility, and make manifest our Unanimity, put his name to this instrument."[7]

The 112th Congress was a place of no compromise and a setting in which domination or subjugation of a political opponent triumphed over the interests of "We The People." There were few elected officials with Franklin's stature, intellect and insights in this most recent Congress.

Infallibility ruled and "my way or no highway" was the mantra. This was the case during the entire 112th Congress for a variety of reasons—most of them political and personal. It was also the case because most of what didn't get done or what got done was posturing rather than policy making. Here's a case in point.

IN GOD WE TRUST

In God we trust. So proclaimed the U.S. House in November 2011 when it overwhelmingly passed a resolution to reaffirm that statement as the official motto of the United States.

Congressman J. Randy Forbes (R-VA), the resolution's sponsor, said the measure was needed because of a "disturbing trend" of ignorance regarding the motto and to "firmly declare our trust in God" as the nation faces "challenging times."[8] This was another example of misplaced congressional priorities and focus.

Our country was indeed experiencing a "disturbing trend." And many of our citizens were confronting incredibly "challenging times." The trend and times, however, were characterized by a dramatic rise in social and economic inequality **and not** by a lack of belief or commitment to the Almighty.

That is why instead of talking about God our legislators should have been consumed with doing all that was required to address these conditions and their root causes. Specifically, they should have been engaged in a thoughtful dialogue about the common good, what should be a public good, and then compromising and collaborating to solve our problems. They should have been working on reaffirming our trust in good as well as God.

The concept of "goodness" has been at the center of philosophical and political discussions dating back to the times of Plato and Aristotle. This was not the case in the United States during most of the 112th Congress—reason and rational discourse were replaced by rancorous rhetoric.

At the end of the constitutional convention, a woman asked Ben Franklin what type of government the constitution was bringing into existence. Franklin responded, "A republic—if you can keep it." Given the country's downward spiral, we are in danger of losing that republic and becoming a virtual theocracy controlled by an activist minority group of the rich, powerful and special interests who will dictate the agenda for the majority and the nation.

In his book *The Price of Civilization: Reawakening American Virtue and Prosperity*, economist Jeffrey Sachs described our national condition as follows: "Our society has turned harsh, with the elites on Wall Street, in Big Oil, and in Washington among the most irresponsible and selfish of all."[9] George Packer, staff writer for the *New Yorker*, in his essay "The Broken Contract: Inequality and American Decline" in the November/December 2011 issue of *Foreign Affairs* magazine, concurred with Sachs and declared, "The more wealth accumulates in a few hands at the top, the more influence and favor the well-connected rich acquire, which makes it easier for them and their political allies to cast off restraint without paying a social price."[10]

These are not descriptions of a vibrant and vital representative democracy. They are depictions of an eroding value system and a country that favors the rich over the poor, the few over the many, and the business contract over the social contract. They are warning signs that it will not matter how much trust you put in God if you lose the trust of the people.

TRUST-BUSTING

In the early 20th century, Teddy Roosevelt engaged in "trust-busting"—eliminating the powerful control of a few robber barons over the country, its citizens and our democracy. That was a good thing.

In the early part of the 21st century, we had a different form of trust-busting going on—inept, illegal and amoral acts engaged in by some businesses, politicians and individuals that were destroying the bonds of confidence and faith in each other that bind the citizens and the nation together. That is a bad thing.

On April 18, 2010, the Pew Research Center released a report titled *The People and Their Government: Distrust, Discontent, Anger and Partisan Rancor*. The Pew study, which was conducted in March 2010, asked people to give their opinions on the effect (positive or negative) that various institutions/groups were having "on the way things are going in the country today." The *highest positive effect ratings* were given to small businesses (71 percent), technology companies (68 percent), churches and religious organizations (63 percent) and colleges and universities (61 percent). The *lowest positive effect ratings* were given to banks and other financial institutions (22 percent), Congress (24 percent), large corporations (25 percent) and the federal government (25 percent).

The same Pew study asked who "gets more attention from the federal government than they should." The groups who received the *highest more attention than they should ratings* were Wall Street (50 percent), business leaders (45 percent) and labor unions (34 percent). The groups who received the *lowest more attention than they should ratings* were small businesses (8 percent), the middle class (9 percent) and poor people (17 percent).[11]

In a poll issued on June 4, 2011, Gallup found similarly to the 2010 Pew study that the public's institutional confidence was waning. The poll's lead sentence read, "Americans' confidence in U.S. banks has dipped to a record low 21%." Only two institutions got lower marks than banks: health maintenance organizations (19 percent) and Congress (13 percent).[12]

These polls showed that we were definitely at a pivot point in terms of the country's social contract. America and the American dream are held together by faith in our dominant institutions, a belief that the voice of the individual citizen matters and an undeniable hope for upward mobility and personal success. These factors have all been compromised. Public trust is on a teeter-totter.

This trust trauma has captured the attention of commentators ranging from economists to columnists and ethicists. In a June 17,

2011, Sunday *New York Times* article titled "Broken Trust Takes Time to Mend," Tyler Cowen, a George Mason economics professor, wrote, "America is witnessing a collapse of trust in politics, including the shaping of its broad economic policy."[13] In the same issue of the *Times*, columnist Maureen Dowd in her article "Moral Dystopia" broadened the trust-busting perspective far beyond politics by asking, "Have our materialism, narcissism, and cynicism about the institutions knitting society—schools, sports, religion, politics, banking—dulled our sense of right or wrong?"

Ms. Dowd turned to James Davison Hunter, a professor of religion, culture and social theory at the University of Virginia, for the answer to that question. She quotes Professor Hunter, "We know more, and as a consequence, we no longer trust the authority of traditional institutions who used to be carriers of moral ideals." Hunter goes on to assert, "Now we experience morality more as a choice that we can always change as circumstances call for it . . . And what you end up with is a nation of ethical free agents."[14]

We don't necessarily agree with Professor Hunter's conclusions regarding the American culture and individual behavior. We do know, however, that numerous studies have indicated a serious breakdown of trust in our dominant institutions and the potential for an individual to achieve the American dream through education, hard work and determination.

As we pointed out in chapter 1, at the beginning of the 20th century, many businesses felt they were equal, or perhaps superior, to the government. For example, when Teddy Roosevelt brought an antitrust suit against J. P. Morgan's railroad combine, Morgan said, "Send your man to see my man and tell him to fix it up." Roosevelt responded, "That cannot be done . . . No private interest can presume to be equal to the government." And, with that said, President Roosevelt went into the trust-busting business.

Today, near the beginning of the 21st century, we are confronted by a different form of trust-busting. For the United States as we have known it to survive and to avoid moving backward to where we were at the beginning of the 20th century, we must bust the trust busters. We must engage in trust-building.

Trust-building can only be done by government, business and societal leaders coming together and setting their personal and political interests aside and working cooperatively in the interests of the public and the American citizen. Trust-building requires concentrating on and emphasizing what unites us rather than what divides us.

Congress must be central to the trust-building. To be worthy of its trust, Congress must regain the respect of the citizenry.

CONGRESS AT THE CROSSROADS

Unfortunately, as 2013 began, Congress was being held in contempt. That contempt came from the American people.

A poll released in early January by Public Policy Polling (PPP) revealed that contempt is deep and broad. Congress got only a 9 percent favorability rating in the PPP study. That's actually the good news for the institution. The bad news is that the survey respondents rated Congress considerably less popular than a number of other "distressing" things such as colonoscopies, root canals and being stuck in traffic.[15]

These ratings would be funny if they weren't—and they aren't. They were clear indicators of a public that is fed up and turned off by the manner in which Congress is conducting or not conducting its business.

This poll was taken shortly after the vote on the "so-called" fiscal cliff deal and reflected the public's dissatisfaction with the three ring circus leading up to, during and after the vote. Even though a bill was passed, the spectacle surrounding it was ugly and unnecessary.

Columnist Eugene Robinson expressed his disenchantment in a column that he began, "To say that Congress looked like a clown show this week is an insult to self-respecting clowns."[16] Political analyst Bob Schieffer was not quite as condescending in his comments during an interview on *Face the Nation* but he was extremely critical nonetheless.

Schieffer began by stating, "Watching the blundering ineptitude and the vulgar partisanship of last week made me think of other days our modern politicians may have forgotten—an era when Washington actually worked." He proceeded to cite examples such as the collaboration between Senators John McCain (R- AZ) and Russ Feingold (D-WI) on campaign reform and Senators Sam Nunn (D-GA) and

Richard Lugar (R-IN) on arms control. Schieffer concluded by observing, "The rearview mirror has a way of making things look better, but those things really happened, and we used to say Washington was a place of giants. You don't hear that much anymore."[17]

But we should! The sorry performance of the 112th Congress has brought the perception of this once-esteemed body to an all-time low. Our representatives in the 113th Congress are at a crossroads. How they comport themselves will determine how the public sees them. (See the epilogue of this book for our assessment and predictions regarding the performance of the 113th Congress based upon its performance to mid-2013.)

We write this as citizens who know and have much respect for many current elected officials but with extreme concern for the quicksand in which they are now stuck. We write this as citizens who see politics as Robert Kennedy did, as "an honorable profession." Kennedy said, "An honorable profession calls forth the chance for responsibility and the opportunity for achievement; against these measures politics is a truly exciting adventure."[18]

Over the past decade and then some, that "adventure" has become much less worthwhile for many involved or those who would consider engaging in it. That's because the political environment has become extremely toxic for a variety of reasons, including a broken political process, more bellicose politicians, 24-hour press coverage, extremely partisan pundits, and incessant and inflammatory internet postings.

It didn't use to be that way. Politics wasn't bean bag in the past. But, it and the contestants and citizens were somewhat kinder and gentler.

We were reminded of this with the recent passing of Richard Ben Cramer who wrote a great book, *What It Takes*, about the 1988 presidential campaign. The candidates in that campaign were Democrats Joe Biden, Michael Dukakis, Richard Gephardt and Gary Hart and Republicans George Bush and Bob Dole. Cramer treated them all with respect and his in-depth profiles provided insights that caused us to understand and like each one of them.

Margalit Fox's obituary of Cramer for the *New York Times* explains the reason for this perfectly: "Mr. Cramer's book is at bottom a psychological study of towering ambition and the toll of public life.

Where it succeeded most notably, in the view of many critics, was in its depiction of the candidates not as mere archetypes but as flesh-and-blood human beings."[19]

The politician's life was never an easy one. It is much less so today. The continuous climate of confrontation and combat has squeezed much of the humanity and dignity out of the process. As the PPP poll results attest, it has also substantially shrunk the public's view of those in office. We are in dire need of a transformation and turnaround.

Americans believe in the God of second chances. The 113th Congress has been given that chance. If it conducts the public's business with a sense of civility, equanimity and propriety, it will recapture public confidence. If this becomes déjà vu all over again, and the 113th replicates the behavior of the 112th, Congress' prestige will be driven so far underground that it may never again be resurrected.

Just a little more than a century ago, Teddy Roosevelt said, "It is not the critic who counts; not the man who points out how the strong man stumbles, or where the doer of deeds could have done them better. The credit belongs to the man who is actually in the arena."[20]

Like Roosevelt, we believe the credit still belongs to the "man and woman" in the arena. That arena, however, should not be one for extreme boxing or cage wrestling. It should be an honorable place, where honorable people come to practice an honorable profession, thus earning the citizens' respect and proving they should be considered "giants" and not "participants in a clown show."

GETTING TO MAYBE

"Saying No" was the modus operandi of the 112th Congress. For far too many of our elected representatives were in that body; as former Senator Tom Daschle (D-SD) said, there were too many individuals focused on "standing their ground" rather than finding "common ground." Progress for the American economy and Americans was compromised because there were few attempts at compromise.

Now that there is a new Congress, our fondest hope is that the legislators realize that they are in Washington, D.C., to do the people's business. They are there to solve problems and craft pragmatic legislation rather than to impose their own personal and partisan agendas and ideologies. They are there to negotiate, not to negate.

We don't expect the members of the 113th Congress to be able to move directly from Saying No to *Getting to Yes* (the title of Roger Fisher and William Ury's classic book on negotiations).[21] But perhaps they can start by Getting to Maybe.

Getting to Maybe establishes a framework for meaningful discourse and dialogue and the consideration of a range of acceptable alternatives, options and trade-offs. From there it should eventually be possible to Get to Yes and by doing so to restore citizen respect for this badly tarnished and increasingly reviled institution.

We are not delusional or naive enough to expect that Getting to Maybe will be an easy task. We recognize that over the past few years, compromise in Congress has become an oxymoron and bipartisanship a dirty word.

On the other hand, we are not skeptical or jaded enough to think that Getting to Maybe is impossible. That's because getting there is a necessity for continuing our democratic system of governance and our country. Put us in the camp of former Defense Secretary Robert M. Gates who, speaking at an event in September sponsored by the Center for Strategic and International Studies and other organizations, said, "My hope is following the presidential elections whatever adults remain in the two political parties will make the compromises necessary to put this country back in order."[22]

It takes courage to compromise—especially when you are reaching across party lines and defying conventional party wisdom. We saw that courage demonstrated by the five senators—Tom Coburn, (R-OK), Mike Crapo (R-ID), Judd Gregg (R-NH), Dick Durbin (D-IL) and Kent Conrad (D-ND)—on the National Commission on Fiscal Responsibility and Reform who voted for approval of the Commission's full report. We have seen it early in the 113th Congress as a bipartisan group of senators worked together on the immigration bill. (See chapter 10 of this book for our discussion on this.)

Unfortunately, this type of compromise has become more and more unusual. That's because, as E. J. Dionne pointed out in a post-presidential election column, "Democrats, a more moderate and diverse party, believe in compromise far more than Republicans do." Dionne explains this is true for both the Democratic Party faithful and their candidates for office and indicates that the Tea Party influence has changed the composition of the Republican Party and their candidates to make them extremely more conservative and unwilling to compromise.[23]

Thomas Mann and Norm Ornstein, two of the foremost scholars on the operations of Congress, made a similar but much more strongly expressed point in their book *It's Even Worse Than It Looks: How the American Constitutional System Collided with the New Politics of Extremism,* published in early 2012. In it, they write, "Today's Republican Party . . . is an insurgent outlier. It has become ideologically extreme; contemptuous of the inherited social and economic policy regime; scornful of compromise; unpersuaded by conventional understanding of facts, evidence and science; and dismissive of the legitimacy of its political opposition, all but declaring war on the government."[24]

This is a harsh assessment and possibly overstates the case. We do know unequivocally, however, that the Republicans and Democrats are at very different points on the compromise continuum. The majority of Democrats tend to be in the middle, malleable and movable, while the majority of the Republicans are far right, intractable and intransigent.

If that's the situation, how do we begin Getting to Maybe? We recommend the following as starting points:

1. Change the mindset
2. Change the rules
3. Change the methods

Change the Mindset: Today many legislators believe aligning themselves with those from the other party on an issue is an act of cowardice and surrender. As long as this attitude prevails and leaders punish those who cross over, the journey to Maybe cannot start. We need to replace it with the understanding that compromise is an act of courage and success. It is a necessary pre-condition for achieving shared solutions, not a capitulation or sacrificing of principles. The subtitle of Fisher and Ury's book *Getting to Yes* is "Negotiating Agreement Without Giving

In." That says it perfectly. Negotiating to reach a common ground is getting things done, not giving in.

Change the Rules: Steve Kroft did a *60 Minutes* segment titled "The Broken Senate" on the Sunday before Election Day, 2012. During that segment, Majority Leader Harry Reid (D-NV) pointed out that when Lyndon Johnson was leader of the Senate he had to try to override one filibuster compared to 248 for Reid. The filibuster allows the minority to thwart the will of the majority because it requires 60 votes to get a piece of legislation passed. Scholars Mann and Ornstein place it at the top of the list for reform in a chapter they devote to "Reforming U.S. Political Institutions" in their book. The nonpartisan group No Labels also has the filibuster near the top of its 12 proposals to Make Congress Work. We are not in complete agreement with all of the No Label proposals nor with all of the Mann/Ornstein recommendations.[25]

We are in absolute agreement, however, with the need to change the rules and to make Congress work. We should note that the Senate did make a modest change to its filibuster rules early in 2013. But in our opinion, those changes are insufficient to deal with the institutional ossification that almost paralyzes the Senate.

Change the Methods. One of the main reasons that Congress doesn't work is that is has become so balkanized. There is virtually no effort at coming together to work together. It didn't used to be that way. As Senator Olympia Snowe (R-ME) said in the *60 Minutes* segment when Bob Dole was majority leader, "He would say go to my office at 8:30 in the morning and work it out. He was so intent on making sure that we came up with a solution to the issue that was before the Senate."[26]

In contrast, today the Senate and House members often convene in private and purely intraparty meetings and sessions where the emphasis is on competition, not collaboration. One such gathering is Democratic caucus lunches, a lot of which, according to former Senator Evan Bayh (D-IN), are about, "OK, we're a team. We gotta stick together. We got to beat the daylights out of the other side. We can't afford straying from the team. If you do, that doesn't help us."

These one-sided meetings in which a group develops and hardens its own positions without input or participation from the other are counterproductive and conflict producing. They lead to what Fisher and Ury call "positional bargaining" in which each side opens with a position and then the two positional combatants struggle mightily and frequently futilely trying to reach a common agreement.

To correct this, Fisher and Ury recommend "principled negotiation" as opposed to positional bargaining. The four principles of this approach are (1) separate the people from the problem; (2) focus on interests, not positions; (3) generate a variety of options before settling on an agreement; and (4) insist that the agreement be based on objective criteria.

As we stated, changing the mindset, changing the rules and changing the methods are starting points for Getting to Maybe. There are other areas that need to be addressed in order to Get to Yes. We address them in our congressional pivot point recommendations, which follow.

Our focus here, however, is on getting started on Getting to Maybe. The good news is that what is required is not costly in financial terms. It is elected men and women of good will with the courage to compromise. The bad news is that getting started requires true leadership (both official and unofficial).

When Senator Coburn was asked during the *60 Minutes* interview why it has been so difficult to compromise, he responded, "It's leadership. It's pure leadership. When the goal is always to win the next election, rather than to put the country on the right course, whether it's a Republican leading it or the—a Democrat leading it, the Senate is not going to work."

If the Senate doesn't work and the Congress doesn't work, the country doesn't work. With this new Congress, we will see if we now have courageous leaders who realize this and are prepared to begin the journey to Maybe and to compromise by putting country first rather than party first.

PIVOT POINT RECOMMENDATIONS: WORKING ON "YES"

Subject matter experts have provided numerous excellent recommendations for reforming Congress, political institutions and our governance process. In our opinion, the three most important areas to be addressed relate to creating a framework that will make Congress more functional, representative and collaborative and thus move it closer to "Yes". They are:

- Structure: Break Up the Island States of America
- Knowledge: Make Congress Smarter
- Finance: Control the Big Money Interests

Structure: Break Up the Island States of America

- *Implement a national fair districting initiative.*
- *Revamp the primary voting rules and processes.*

Right after the national election, the secessionists received a lot of attention with their petitions to leave the union because Barack Obama won re-election as president. While their appeals were headline grabbing and fabulous fodder for talk radio and cable TV for a short period of time, this group was and is substantively and politically unimportant and impotent.

The issues of true significance for the future of our representative democracy are (1) the structure of the federal congressional districts and the senate and house districts within the states; and (2) the rules for voting in primaries within each state. We examine why and what needs to be done to address these problems with this recommendation

First, however, let's dispense with the secessionists. These folks are what we refer to as the looney tunes fringe of the electorate. They have a right to their own opinion and we would like to see them have rights as individuals clustered together to secede from the United States.

John Donne said "No man is an island, entire of itself." Nonetheless, we say grant the men, and the few women (Neil Caren's research shows that these petition signers, which numbered approximately 300,000 as of November 16, 2012, were disproportionately male) that were part of this nascent secessionist movement, individual island state status.[27]

Then, take away, all of their privileges and benefits that derive from being part of the United States of America. These would include the use of highways subsidized by federal funds, assistance from the National Guard, defense by our nation's military, access to national parks, emergency management and medical services, educational assistance, Social Security and Medicare.

We could call these new free-floating entities "barrier island states" or the independent island states. Based upon the initial surge of petitioners, the largest of these new states would be located in Texas with 100,000 signers and the following five states that had 25,000 signers or more: Alabama, Florida, Georgia, Louisiana and North Carolina.[28]

It's not these artificial island states that we have just invented that threaten our representative democracy, however. It is those individual island states that have been legitimately constructed that put it at risk. Those island states are the federal congressional districts and the senate and house districts in the majority of our states.

Because of gerrymandering, these districts are insular and polarizing by design. The districts are also designed to protect those in office. As Paul Kane noted in his *Washington Post* column on the day after the national elections, "Many incumbents survived because of a redistricting process that left a record low number of competitive seats, cloistering Republicans and Democrats together into geographically odd—but politically homogenous—districts."[29] If you can't change the butts in seats, it becomes very difficult to change behavior.

Both parties are very good at gerrymandering, but the Republicans excel at it. Here's some evidence:[30]

- At the national level, there are 435 congressional districts. In this most recent election, 241 leaned toward Republicans. 194 leaned Democratic.

- The Democrats won the presidency and U.S. Senate seats in Pennsylvania, Ohio, Wisconsin, Virginia and Florida. The breakout of the House winners in those same states follows. Pennsylvania: Republicans 13 seats. Democrats 5 seats. Ohio: Republicans 12 seats. Democrats 4 seats. Wisconsin: Republicans 5 seats. Democrats 3 seats. Virginia: Republicans 8 seats. Democrats 3 seats. Florida: Republicans 17 seats. Democrats 10 seats.

- At the state level, in January 2013, over two-thirds of the states will be under single party control of both the executive and legislative branches: 24 states will be Republican and 14 will be Democratic.

No matter which party or candidate wins as a result of the gerry-mandering process, the losers are the potential for bipartisanship and compromise. This problem is compounded by the primary systems in many states that preclude participation by independents and nonpartisans unless they declare as a Republican or Democrat.

According to a 2012 Pew Research Center study, in this national election year 38 percent of voters indicated they were independents compared to 32 percent who declared as Democrats and 24 percent as Republicans.[31] Excluding this large and growing group of voters—who tend to be more centrist and moderate in their positions—from the candidate selection processes means that they tend to be controlled by the fringes (think "Tea Party or conservative" on the right and "liberal or progressive" on the left).[32]

Many of the district island states are controlled by a small group of islanders. They are like-minded folks who choose representatives who resemble them to do their bidding.

We need to break up the island states and their stranglehold on our political process. There are a number of actions that can be taken to accomplish this. The two key ones are:

- Implement a fair districting approach within each state controlled by a nonpartisan independent commission as opposed to politicians.

- Reform primaries to ensure processes and systems that are fully inclusive of the registered voter population rather than those that are restrictive and exclusive.

In the most recent election cycle, California and Florida provided positive examples of how changing the districting and primary approaches can produce different outcomes.

California went from a party primary system to one in which the two candidates with the most votes in an "open congressional primary" moved on to the general election. This resulted, as Juan William reported, in seven incumbents losing their seats "as they ran in more diverse districts—in which candidates had to appeal to more diverse neighborhoods and political groups." Williams continued to comment, "The bottom line is that voters have more choice among candidates competing for the middle ground, not to be a champion of one political extreme."[33]

Florida was redistricted by the state legislature according to guidelines set out in a constitutional amendment that banned "gerrymandering" that was passed by the state's citizens with over 62 percent of the votes casts. The redistricting helped the Democrats pick up four congressional seats and seven seats in the state legislature.[34]

In conclusion, if we want our democracy to work and to represent the interests of all the people and not those at either extreme, we need to succeed and not to secede. To succeed, we need to renew and reform our electoral processes to put the emphasis on the United States of America instead of the Island States of America.

Knowledge: Make Congress Smarter

Upgrade the quantity and quality of expert knowledge utilized in congressional decision making.

No, we aren't advocating brain transplants or remedial education courses. What we do need to do, however, is to ensure that Congress gets access to more comprehensive and objective expert input and insights for consideration in the policy-making process.

In December 2012, the New America Foundation published a paper authored by Lorelei Kelly titled *Congress' Wicked Problem: Seeking Knowledge Inside the Information Tsunami.*[35] To our knowledge, to this point, that paper has received scant attention from either the politicians or the pundits. The findings in the paper and its recommendations deserve and demand a full review and thoughtful corrective actions.

The opening sentence in Ms. Kelly's paper reads, "The lack of shared expert knowledge capacity in the U.S. Congress has created a critical weakness in our democratic process." She continues to note that Congress lacks "basic knowledge management" and it is "not so much venal and corrupt as it is incapacitated and obsolete."

In our opinion, Kelly's paper hits the bull's-eye. It calls the question on the manner in which Congress organizes and operates itself as a "learning organization." Key points she makes include the following:

- Less than 20 years ago Congress operated one of the world's premier scientific advisory bodies. It had an extensive network of shared expert staff and before 1995, committee staffs were also large and more often shared.

- There is a difference between information and knowledge. Members of Congress and staff do not lack for access to information. But information backed by financial interests and "high decibel" advocacy is disproportionately represented, and because of changes there is a "lack of institutional wisdom."

- There is a "knowledge asymmetry" of "trusted quality expertise" inside the institution. An example is that the committees on Capitol Hill have the "lion's share of expertise" compared to D.C. personal staff and those back home in the state or district.

- There is an asymmetry in two areas: knowledge provision (who is the source) and knowledge sharing (who gets easy access to it).

- Congressional focus on information that addresses the "here and now" of the electoral and budget cycle timelines is typically provided to the members' offices by the "most influential providers" such as lobbyists and the politically oriented.

Key recommendations in Kelly's paper to address these deficiencies include restoring congressional budgets for legislative branch staff on the Hill and in support agencies, improving the capabilities and capacity of the Congressional Research Service, establishing better relations and linkages with universities for knowledge sharing, and strengthening the connections to local experts and media.

This paper resonated and struck a responsive chord with us. One of our key recommendations in the Government chapter of *Renewing* was "Build Congress' capacity and capabilities for performance management."[36] We made that recommendation because we felt then and still feel now that Congress lacked the breadth and depth of experience and expertise required for knowledge and performance management.

If we want high-quality policy and decision making, we need to make the investments in congressional staff and systems that facilitate and enable that. If we don't, then we will get the performance or lack thereof that we deserve.

Finance: Control the Big Money Interests

Conduct a study, develop and implement recommendations to control big money interests in the political and legislative process.

We had originally planned on titling this section "Break the Big Money Stranglehold." Then we reflected that the goal should be realistic and attainable: Breaking the stranglehold—probably not. Controlling it—maybe so.

In any case, Congress should convene an independent, bipartisan commission to conduct a comprehensive review of political recruitment, candidacy, selection and legislative participation. The Commission's inquiry should include campaign fundraising, legislator financial capacity and the connections between legislation and financing.

The amount of money raised and spent in this past election was absolutely obscene—especially obscene was the involvement of the Super PACs and wealthy individuals who tried to tilt the electoral races in their favor with major contributions. Fortunately, during this past election cycle, that form of "big money" obscenity did not do too well at the polling place. As we point out in the epilogue to the book, in the game of campaign moneyball in 2012, time and again small money and smart money trumped big money.

Regardless of these victories, we need campaign finance reform. As long as the lobbyists, special interests, and those with the biggest checkbooks have the most control over not only who gets nominated, what gets proposed and how business is done, the system cannot and will not heal itself. Those with the money will rule and those with the most money will rule the most.

The Supreme Court's egregious Citizens United decision, with the subsequent influx of "anonymous grassroots" campaign groups, made this situation even worse. It elevated "free speech" of the corporation above that of the citizen. When the corporation's voice can speak louder than the citizen's, democracy is at risk.

Personally, we would like to see a complete reform of financing and walking back of the Citizens United decision and support the positions of the groups who are advocating large-scale changes. At a minimum, there should be transparency and full disclosure from all individuals and organizations supporting candidates, office holders and/or their positions.

One of the more interesting changes over the past several years and even before is the increasing economic distance and differences between the elected officials in Washington, D.C., and the people they represent. The Center for Responsive Politics released a report in December 2012 that revealed that the median net worth of the members of Congress went up 15 percent from 2004 to 2010. During that same time frame, the net worth of the top 10 percent remained essentially flat and the median net worth of all Americans dropped 8 percent.[37]

Looking back further, in 1984 the median net worth of a House member, adjusted for inflation, was $280,000. By 2009, the adjusted median net worth of a House member was $725,000; adding in the Senate members raises the median net worth to $913,000. This compares to the adjusted median net worth of the average American in 1984 of $20,600 and $20,500 in 2009.[38]

It is obvious that the people sitting on the seats in Capitol Hill are doing much better than the people sitting in the seats around the dining room tables in most of the homes in America. And the economic circumstances of those holding the seats in Congress are continuing to improve as well.

This is attested to by the fact that the 112th House freshmen class of 106 members elected in 2012 had an inflation-adjusted median net worth of $864,000—26 percent higher than the median net worth of the freshmen elected in 2004. One of the likely causes of this is the increasing cost of political campaigns. According to Eric Lichtblau of the *New York Times*, in 2010 a successful Senate run cost around $10 million and a successful House race cost $1.4 million. Since 1976, according to the Federal Election Commission, the inflation-adjusted average cost of a successful House race has quadrupled.[39]

It is apparent that national politics is becoming a rich person's game. Lichtblau notes that "Congress has never been a place for paupers."

He goes on to observe, however, "But, rarely has the divide appeared so wide."

The size of that divide matters because, as Peter Whoriskey points out in an article for the *Washington Post,* academics have found that "The growth of income inequality has tracked very closely with measures of political polarization, which has been gauged using the average difference between the liberal/conservative scores for the Republican and Democrat members of the House. Whoriskey cites studies that show that a person's financial circumstances, life experience and occupations all play a role in how they legislate.[40]

The bottom line from all of this is we are increasingly getting those with better bottom lines in Congress. As part of this Commission study, we need to investigate alternatives such as public financing and campaign spending limits to give those of more modest financial means a fighting chance in electoral contests. We know there are no easy answers here but we need to ask the tough questions. It may be that the media bringing these economic differences to the public's attention will help to level the economic playing field somewhat and brings things more into balance.

Balance is also what Lorelei Kelly calls for in the development of our public policy. Right now that policy debate process is controlled by lobbyists. Kelly says that retired representative Lee Hamilton (D-IN) sees lobbyists as part of the normal deliberative process but quotes him as follows: "Our challenge is not to shut it down but to make sure it's a balanced dialogue."[41] Kelly's recommendations could help to establish that balance.

One other area that should be addressed in terms of balance is the relationship between the financial interests of elected officials in Congress and their investments and contract awards. In late 2011, Peter Schweizer created a brouhaha with his book *Throw Them All Out,* which showed among other things a connection between high-level briefings of members of Congress and the sale and purchase of stock.[42]

Two 2011 studies of the investment portfolios of congressional members showed different results. One indicated the portfolios outperforming the market. The other found the portfolios performed somewhat worse.[43] We do not have enough information to determine which study is valid nor do we want to. What we want to do, however, is to invoke the full transparency and disclosure principle.

It is common knowledge that those who support winning politicians do have a relative advantage in terms of support for contracts/investments, appointments to positions and even invitations to dinners and special events. It would seem to us that an easy way to deal with this issue is just to append a page to each piece of legislation, appointment, or any other form of transaction that notes the contributions or input of those who are the beneficiaries of the congressional action. That would bring things more into the sunlight and make the work of good government and investigative reporters easier if not quite as revelatory.

In conclusion, we need to address and solve those problems that are the root causes of our electoral dysfunction. If we do not, our country and its citizens will be stuck in a perpetual cycle of electoral rigor mortis.

The American voting public will replace one set of "rascals" with another set of "rascals" and expect better results. It won't happen! The reason for this is that the overriding issue is just not who sits in the seats in Congress but the fact that we have a broken political governance system. Until we fix that system, the most that can be expected are marginal or incremental changes around the edges.

Congressional dysfunction will continue. And we as citizens will continue to suffer the Beltway blues.

Pivot Point Report Card

Instructions

This report card is provided to allow you to reflect upon and assess the progress in this pivot point area. To use the report card:

1. Review the recommendations for the area.
2. Evaluate the progress made in the area to date and assign a letter grade using the system that follows: A–excellent progress. B–substantial progress. C–some progress. D–little progress. F–no progress.
3. Describe the nature of the progress and the rationale for your rating.

We will be posting our assessment for this area on an occasional basis. To see that assessment and to provide your input and feedback on the area, visit *http://www.workingthepivotpoints.com*.

Recommendations

- Working on "Yes"
  - Structure: Break Up the Island States of America
  - Knowledge: Make Congress Smarter
  - Finance: Control the Big Money Interests

Grade

Reason

5 | Citizenship Dysfunction: Coming Together or Coming Apart?

Many think that the official motto of the United States is "e pluribus unum"—from many one. It is not. In fact, given the national drift toward divisiveness over the past few years, that saying should probably be reversed to "e unum pluribus"—from one many.

It appears that citizenship is not what it once was. And it may never have been what folklore and conventional wisdom would have us believe it was.

In this chapter, we examine the current nature and state of citizenship as it has played out recently and then take a quick look at the history of American citizenship. We conclude with our recommendations for enhancing civic engagement and citizen civility going forward.

THE GREAT DIVIDE

In the middle of 2012, before the national presidential campaigns kicked into high gear, the Pew Research Center released a report titled *Partisan Polarization Surges in Bush, Obama Years*, which looked at trends in American values from 1987 to 2012.[1]

The report noted that overall there had been "much more stability than change across the 48 political value measures." But it went on to state, "the average partisan gap has nearly doubled over this 25-year period"—from 10 to 18 percentage points."

The issues on which the partisan divisions were the largest in the 2012 survey in terms of the differences between Democrats' and Republicans' attitudes, along with the differences for 1987, are displayed in the following table.

Largest Partisan Divisions Comparison			
Value	1987 Gap	2012 Gap	Difference
Social Safety Net	23	41	+18
Environment*	5	39	+34
Labor Unions	20	37	+17
Equal Opportunity	17	33	+16
Gov't Scope and Performance	6	33	+27
Immigration**	4	24	+20
Business	16	24	+8

* Value first included in 1992 survey.
**Value first included in 2002 survey.

The average gap on these seven areas in the 1987 survey was 13 compared to 33 in the 2012 survey. That's a difference of +20 or more than 2.5 times greater. That's not a gap. It's a chasm.

As Pew notes, both the Democrats' and Republicans' attitudes have shifted considerably. The Republicans have become much less concerned about protecting the social safety net and the environment. The Democrats, in contrast, according to Pew, "have become more secular, more positive in their views of immigrants and more supportive of policies aimed at achieving equal opportunity."

Interestingly, the differences in values or opinions by social class did not change much between 1987 and 2012. So the explanatory factor in terms of the shift in the respondents' responses was party affiliation. These wide differences are some of what helped to account for the confrontational and disputative nature of the 2012 election contest.

THE POLITICS OF DIVISION AND SUBTRACTION

Pew and others referred to this phenomenon as the "partisan polarization" of the parties. We think, however, that an equally appropriate description of what was going on then and now is "the politics of division and subtraction."

That's because as the parties polarized they grew the divide between them and subtracted a large number of registered voters from their rolls. This increased the ranks of reported independents substantially.

In the study cited above, Pew reported that 38 percent of voters indicated that they were independent as opposed to 32 percent who declared as Democrats and 24 percent who declared as Republicans. Pew observed that "independents are more numerous than at any point in the last 70 years."[2]

Many of the independents leaned toward one party or the other. Pew reported that for the 2012 presidential election, only 23 percent of the independents were swing voters based upon those who were "undecided or not certain" who they would support at the time of the survey. That meant that 15 percent were "leaners" toward one party or the other.

Some might view the increase in independents and swing voters as a good thing. We do not. That's because given the way that our political system works, these voters have little input and influence in selecting candidates for office and even less in the policy-making process. They are basically disenfranchised.

It is frequently said that the citizens of the United States tend to be either center-right or center-left depending on the issue. Historically, our parties have reflected that centrism in their membership. Today, however, in both parties there is virtually no center left.

The centrists have been forced into the independent ranks. The politics of division and subtraction has altered the fundamental balance that has made our democracy work for almost the past century. It has eliminated the middle. When there is no middle, there can be no middle ground. There can be no basis for compromise and closure. There can only be conflict and chaos.

While many of our elected officials have been criticized because of their confrontational and contentious nature, they are not independent agents. To a greater or lesser extent, they are mirrors reflecting the highly partisan values and perspectives of the voters who select and then elect them. As the voting base of each major party has shrunk and become more extreme (i.e., much, much more conservative in the Republican Party and slightly more liberal in the Democratic Party), the impetus to work cooperatively across the aisle has practically disappeared.

The independent and swing voters can have some modest impact on this gridlock. As Linda Killian pointed out in her book *The Swing Vote: The Untapped Power of Independents*, the independents have played a role in who has won national elections in the past.[3] They did again in the 2012 election as well—especially in the swing states. In addition, "bipartisan" groups such as Americans Elect and No Labels have focused attention on the need to reform our governance system.

These organizations and individuals who are involved in trying to change the toxic political climate are to be commended. There is one overriding limitation with these "outsider" approaches, however, and that is they are playing at the margins rather than affecting the political mainstream.

For better or worse, America is, and for the foreseeable future will remain, a two-party system. Therefore, to make America work for all Americans we need to make the two-party system work—for the better and not for the worse. The only way to do that is to restore the middle and give the center more of a voice in the political process.

We presented our pivot point recommendations on how to accomplish this through open primaries, fair districts and campaign finance reform in chapter 4. Now, let's peel back the layers of the onion a little bit further and go beyond party labels to see what more we can learn about citizens as members of the electorate and the impact it has on the manner in which campaigns are run and the results achieved.

HIGH ANXIETY, LOW INFORMATION, MODERATE EXPECTATIONS

Frequently, citizens' votes have more to do with who they are rather than who the candidates are or what their ads say. That's why when it comes to winning elections in close races understanding psychographics trumps demographics.

Voters can be classified into three broad psychographic categories: High Anxiety, Low Information and Moderate Expectations. Political campaigns typically do a good job of connecting with the first two categories and a relatively poor job with the "moderates." Let's examine the reasons for this.

High anxiety voters are the "true believers" in either party or for either candidate. They bleed true blue or true red. They live or die by their candidate's defeat or victory. It is virtually impossible for them to understand how someone could support the other side. They are easy to reach and mobilize.

Low information voters are of two types. On the one hand, they are many of the high anxiety voters who only consume intake—i.e., drink the Kool-Aid—from the right or left. Their information comes from one channel—Fox or MSNBC, depending on their political predisposition. On the other hand, they are almost completely disinterested voters who either use a party label; the candidate's race, religion or some other characteristic; a single "wedge" issue; or some idiosyncratic or personal preference to make their voting decision. They are "narrow band" and easy to reach as well.

Voters of moderate expectations, in contrast, cover a wide spectrum. They don't see government as the root of all evil or the solution to all problems. They are frequently maligned as being disinterested or as low information voters. The truth is that unlike the high anxiety voters they are not consumed by politics and unlike many of the low information voters they are not indifferent to varied input. They weigh and balance the alternatives. They do their homework, put things to the reasonableness test and decide who will get their votes.

Columnists David Brooks and Ross Douthat of the *New York Times* wrote articles during the 2012 political campaign season focused on the moderate and undecided voters. Brooks devoted an entire column to providing his description and delineation of the "moderate." One of the points he made is that "Just as the moderate suspects imbalance in the country, so she suspects it in herself. She distrusts passionate intensity and bold simplicity and admires self-restraint, intellectual openness, and equipoise."[4]

Douthat admitted that "many undecided voters do tend to be ill-informed bandwagon jumpers with little coherence or consistency to their world view." But he argued that there are also high information voters "with views somewhere near the American median (who) might still regard this November's decision as a harder-than-average call."[5] Those are the voters that we and Brooks refer to as moderates.

In 2011, based upon its research, the Pew Research Center developed a new political typology of registered voters that was a blend of demographics and psychographics.[6] That typology is presented in the following table.

Party Affiliation/Categories	Registered Voters
Mostly Republican	
– Staunch Conservatives (highly engaged Tea Party supporters)	11 percent
– Main Street Republicans (conservative on most issues)	14 percent
Mostly Independent	
– Libertarians (free market, small government seculars)	10 percent
– Disaffected (downscale and cynical)	11 percent
– Post-Moderns (moderates, but liberal on social issues)	14 percent
Mostly Democratic	
– New Coalition (upbeat—equal number majority-minority)	9 percent
– Hard Pressed (religious, conservative, financially struggling)	15 percent
– Solid Liberals (across-the-board liberal positions)	16 percent

When we looked at the distribution of registered voters in this table, two things jumped out: (1) Even though they were classified as "mostly independent," the Libertarians and Disaffected registered voters tended to lean Republican. If they were combined with the 25 percent mostly Republican voters, the Republican total became 46 percent versus the Mostly Democratic total of 40 percent. (2) So the battle in a national election, and most importantly in the swing states, was for what Pew calls the Post-Moderns. Pew noted that this voting group was "largely white, well-educated and affluent."

The good news for the Democrats was that, according to Pew, most of these voters "lean Democratic." The bad news was that they were "moderate." That meant that they were persuadable in either direction.

We should note that many of these moderates had probably already made their decisions and were reflected in the polling numbers. The presenting question or problem for the Obama and Romney campaigns moving toward Election Day in 2012 was how to convince those moderates still withholding judgment.

The answer, based upon our analysis of the moderates' thinking and decision-making style, is that they should have been allowed to convince themselves. They shouldn't have been communicated with in the same manner as the high anxiety or low information voters. They couldn't be hectored, tricked or scared. They were looking for information and data and the chance to exercise their free wills.

The best way to reach out to them would be by applying a variant of the golden rule. The golden rule says "treat someone as you would like to be treated." Our version is "treat someone as she or he would like to be treated." That's the critical thing the campaigns needed to remember as they put together their final messages and appeals to try to gain the favor of those remaining undecided moderate voters. They needed to understand that it was not about who you are but who they are that mattered.

The Obama campaign figured that out and reached beyond its own base to become inclusive. The Romney campaign remained stuck in the same old ruts. The rest is Election Day history. One of the Republican ruts related to one of the "G" words—God.

THE DIVINE RIGHT: CONSERVATIVES, GOD, POLITICS AND POLICY

Whose side was God on in the 2012 presidential election?

The Republicans—both at and subsequent to their convention—actively laid claim to God's mantle and gave the Almighty credit for most things American. The Democrats only begrudgingly acknowledged God in the platform at their convention—after a contested three-vote fight of the delegates.

Still, we're of the opinion that God—being omniscient, omnipotent and all caring—was on neither side and was upstairs rooting for the party that would do the right thing—not the "right wing" or "left wing" thing—for humankind generally and America specifically. We're fairly certain that the frequency of mention of God's name does not enter into the Creator's calculus and decision-making equation when it comes to passing along blessings.

That's not to say that invoking God's name does not have an impact with someone more earthbound than heavenly. That someone is the "God voter." That's who Jonathan Haidt described in detail in his book *The Righteous Mind: Why Good People Are Divided by Politics and Religion.*[7]

During the 2012 election campaign, the Republicans had a substantial edge in making their appeal to this constituency. Let's look at the evidence.

At the Republican convention, both vice-presidential candidate Paul Ryan and presidential candidate Mitt Romney near the end of their speeches gave God credit for our Constitution and the rights it contains. Candidate Romney put it this way, "That America, that united America, will uphold *the constellation of rights that were endowed by our Creator and codified in our constitution.*"[8] Candidate Ryan went even further to state, "They are self-evident and unchanging, and sometimes, even presidents need reminding, that *our rights come from nature and God, not from government.*"[9]

We must have missed that lesson in our history book. But, as far as we know, our rights and our Constitution were not passed down from on high on a set of tablets. They were painstakingly crafted by our Founding Fathers after much debate and discussion. The good and enduring work of the Founding Fathers shows that they definitely had divine inspiration during their deliberations but provides no testimony to divine intervention.

In fact, the word "God" does not appear in the Constitution. That's not because the Founding Fathers were "godless" but because they were not of one mind on the subject of religion and wanted the Constitution to be seen as a secular rather than a religious document. They also saw a need for the separation of church and state.

The most outspoken "founder" with regard to God was Thomas Jefferson, a Deist, as quoted in the religious beliefs section of *http://www.monticello.org*, who wrote to his nephew, Peter Carr, in 1787, "Question with boldness even the existence of a god; because if there is one, he must more approve the homage of reason, than that of blindfolded fear." Jefferson also declared, "But it does me no injury for my neighbor to say there are twenty gods, or no god. It neither picks my pocket nor breaks my leg. . . ."[10] We may be wrong but we don't think that this Founding Father would have been very welcome at the 2012 Republican Convention.

That's especially true because at the convention God was exalted from the podium and in the platform. According to Dorian de Wind in his September 12 *Huffington Post* blog, the Republican platform included 12 references to God.[11] Based upon its analysis of transcripts from the Federal News Service, on September 6 the *New York Times* posted an interactive that showed that Republican speakers used the word "God" 35 times during their presentations.[12]

The verbal commitments did not end in Tampa. Shortly after the convention, Mitt Romney went to Virginia Beach on September 9, and after reciting the Pledge of Allegiance, proclaimed, "That pledge says 'under God.' I will not take 'God' out of the name of our platform. I will not take 'God' off of our coins, and I will not take 'God' out of my heart. We're a nation bestowed by God."[13]

Candidate Romney's ringing endorsement of God was in perfect alignment with a Republican-sponsored resolution passed boldly and overwhelmingly by the House in November 2011 to reaffirm "In God We Trust" as the official motto of the United States. As we said in chapter 4, this is another example of misplaced congressional priorities. We are at a pivot point. To save the United States as we have known it, we need to put things into proper balance and perspective. We need to reaffirm our trust in good as well as God.

We don't know where George McGovern would stand on our statement. We do know he did not square with the political mainstream of either party in his forthright opinions regarding God.

Here's what he said in an April 3, 2003, article for *The Nation*: "As a World War II bomber pilot, I was always troubled by the title of a then-popular book, *God Is My Co-pilot*. My co-pilot was Bill Rounds of Wichita, Kansas, who was anything but godly, but he was a skillful pilot, and he helped me bring our B-24 Liberator though thirty-five combat missions . . . I give thanks to God for our survival, but somehow I never quite picture God at the controls of a bomber or squinting through a bombsight deciding which of his creatures should survive and which should die."[14]

We should point out that when Senator McGovern ran for president against Richard Nixon in 1972, he received only 37.5 percent of the popular vote and a grand total of 17 electoral votes out of 537 cast. His comments on the previous page were made almost 30 years after his candidacy. We don't know what impact they might have had back then or if they would have possibly made his defeat any worse. We do know that they would not ingratiate him at all today with the God-Voters.

We wonder, on the other hand, if they might get him God's vote. As religious people, we believe that God judges us by our actions and not by our words. We further believe that God and goodness is in the details and how we care for the least among us and not by public pronouncements or pious platitudes.

While In God We Trust may be our motto, In Good We Trust must be our motive. As long as "we the people" make choices based upon a motive and not just a motto this democracy will endure.

That's our story and we're sticking to it. So help us God!

A CASE STUDY: GUN CONTROL VS. MIND CONTROL

While God was frequently mentioned during the 2012 presidential election, guns were hardly ever talked about. Gun control was not at the forefront of anyone's agenda. Then the tragic shootings at the Sandy Hook Elementary School unleashed a torrent of public discussion and legislative proposals on gun control.

Nationally, however, we expect this will result in only small changes to our existing gun laws. In part, that will be due to political calculations. More importantly, however, that's because, given the state of our American psyche today, mind control trumps gun control.

That's not true just for gun lovers. It's also true for the general public as well. A poll conducted by Time/CNN/ORC International on January 14–15, 2013, revealed fairly strong support for a variety of gun control measures including:

- 92 percent background checks for gun purchases at a gun store
- 69 percent required gun registration
- 58 percent ban on high-capacity clips

- 56 percent ban on assault weapons
- 54 percent putting armed guards in every school

In contrast, more survey respondents (48 percent) agreed with the positions of the NRA than disagreed (42 percent).[15] The only measure that the NRA agreed with completely and advocated for is "putting armed guards in every school." Thus, this survey discloses the cognitive dissonance of the public on the gun control issue. While it leans toward more control, especially after violent incidents, in general it is more laissez-faire.

That's because gun control is not a compelling "wedge" issue for the vast majority of the public. Of the survey respondents, 18 percent said it was not a "major issue" and 62 percent said it was "just one of many factors" in their voting decisions.

It is important to note that the attitudes of the public regarding gun control have changed dramatically over the past two decades. The Pew Research Center has been tracking opinions on gun control since 1993. In that year, 57 percent of the public felt it was "more important to control gun ownership" and 34 percent felt it was "more important to protect the rights of Americans to own guns." In subsequent polls until 2008, those seeing "controlling gun ownership" as more important ranged from a high of 66 percent to a low of 54 percent.

Since April 2009, however, there has been almost an equal divide among those prioritizing gun control and those prioritizing protecting gun rights. In April 2012, before the mass shootings in Aurora, Colorado, the opinions were 45 percent for gun control and 49 percent for gun rights. After the shooting, in a July survey, it was 47 percent for gun control and 46 percent for gun rights.

In a December 2012 survey, almost immediately after the Sandy Hook incident, the opinion divide was 49 percent for gun control and 42 percent for gun rights. In a survey conducted in January of this year, the divide was approximately the same: 51 percent for gun control and 45 percent for gun rights.[16]

While those percentages seem close and tilting toward more control, a Pew Research Center study in early 2013 revealed a huge "activism" gap. The Center report on its findings notes "Nearly a quarter

(23%) of those who say gun rights should be the priority have contributed money to an organization that takes a position on gun policy, compared with just 5% of those who prioritize gun control." People who favor gun rights are also about twice as likely as gun control supporters to have contacted a public official about gun policy (15 vs. 8 percent).[17]

Here is the bottom line: Gun rights is top of mind for a much larger percentage of the American public than gun control. And those folks put their money and mouths where their minds are—in a big way.

As Geoffrey Stone observed in a *Huffington Post* blog, "The nation's largest and most potent anti-gun control organization, the National Rifle Association, increased its annual revenue to the present by approximately 400%. It now has an annual operating budget of approximately $300 million and 4.3 million dues-paying members." This compares to the Brady Center to Prevent Gun Violence's annual budget of $6 million and 30,000 dues-paying members.[18]

Given these enormous differences in financing and in "share of mind," the playing field is definitely uneven. Mayor Michael Bloomberg of New York City has weighed in, and given his wealth and commitment to the issue, which can provide a bit of a counterbalance on the dollars side. What Mayor Bloomberg cannot do, however, is to control citizens' minds and to place this issue more prominently on their personal radar screens.

A CITIZEN'S MIND

As we have shown, we as citizens are definitely not of one mind. And sometimes some of us change our minds based upon the types of information and input that we receive.

What we have in common as citizens, however, is the fact that we all share certain common characteristics. These include hardened beliefs, personal style preferences, selective reception of data, decision-making and thinking flaws, and a tendency toward irrationality.

Hardened beliefs are a person's core values, attitudes and opinions. They are usually developed early in life and relate to areas such as abortion, same-sex marriage, religion and race relations.

Social psychologist Milton Rokeach from Michigan State University was one of the foremost experts on belief systems. His research disclosed that Americans basically share the same values, but we each have a value hierarchy and the ranking of the values in that hierarchy varies considerably from individual to individual.

Rokeach also developed a psychology of dogmatism. He found that dogmatism was a measurable personality trait created by the convergence of a closed cognitive system, authoritarianism and intolerance. The dogmatic, or closed-minded person, has immutable values and opinions that can't be changed no matter what. As voting citizens, the dogmatists live at the extremes and can neither be influenced nor persuaded.[19]

Personal style determines who we are and how we act as individuals. One of the most common ways of looking at style is in four major areas: (1) introvert/extrovert, (2) feeler/thinker, (3) big-picture focused/detail focused and (4) present oriented/future oriented. Peoples' styles affect their approaches to communications and problem solving. People tend to associate with others who have styles similar to theirs and to avoid those who don't.

As humans, most of us tend to be imperfect collectors and analysts of data. A study led by researchers from the University of Illinois and Florida found that many people do not even attempt to secure data if it does not agree with their viewpoints. Another study found that if some people were provided with accurate information on something and then read a blog that provided incorrect information, they tended to believe the blog even if they were informed it was not true.[20]

Even if one is systematic in data gathering and rigorous in decision making it is still frequently difficult to avoid ideological biases. Political scientist Philip Tetlock found this when he evaluated predictions from "experts" in different fields regarding specific events and compared them to the predictions of well-informed laypeople. The laypeople did just as well as the experts in most instances and outperformed them in many.

Tetlock labeled the laypeople "foxes" because they had an open mind and no preconceived positions. In contrast, he labeled the experts "hedgehogs" because they had strong filters through which they interpreted things.[21]

There are a number of other traps that can impede the objective decision-making process in addition to the "hedgehog" trap. Some of the most common include "the assumption that everyone thinks like I do," "too much has been invested to pull the plug," and "it's obvious, we don't need any more data to support our decision."

Finally, after the economic collapse of 2008, behavioral economists such as George Akerlof, Robert Shiller, Cass Sunstein and Richard Thaler did an excellent job of disabusing us of the "rational man theory" of economics. Akerlof and Shiller, based upon their analysis, discovered that as investors, we substantially overestimate upside potential and significantly underestimate risk and the consequences on the downside.[22]

To sum up, we as citizens are not robots and are imperfect vessels. That's the bad news. That's also the good news. That's what the founders knew when they constructed the Constitution—knowing full well that they were not perfect themselves.

CITIZENSHIP IN THE UNITED STATES

If the founders had thought they were infallible either collectively or individually, they would never have achieved the Great Compromise that resulted in the Constitution and would have cast the document in stone, making no provision for amendments. They would also have frozen citizenship in time as it was when the drafters approved the Constitution in Philadelphia in September 1787 with a 3/5 compromise that counted slaves as 3/5 persons for apportionment and electoral purposes.

Fortunately, the Founding Fathers implicitly understood the concept of pivot points and the need for this brilliant document to be a flexible framework and not a straitjacket. And the first thing added to the document in order to ensure its passage and ratification by the states were the first ten amendments, known as the Bill of Rights. (See our discussion of the Constitutional Convention and Bill of Rights as Pivot Points in chapter 1.)

As noted in chapter 1, four of the Bill of Rights amendments deal with asserting or retaining our affirmative rights (e.g., the right to freedom of speech), while six protect us from negative actions (e.g., protection against excessive bail and cruel and unusual punishment that the government might take to deprive us of our individual rights).

In reviewing these rights, it becomes obvious that the Founding Fathers sought to achieve a delicate balance between individuals, states and the federal government—a goal they achieved. Federalist and Anti-Federalist came together and compromised to add these basic "citizenship" rights to the Constitution.

There have been 17 additional amendments to the Constitution since the original 10. As presented in the following table, six of these amendments directly expanded the American dream for citizens or extended it to previously disenfranchised classes.[23]

Amendment	Key Content	Year Ratified
XII	Abolished slavery.	1865
XIV	Clarified citizenship status of persons born or naturalized in the United States.	1868
XV	Gave the right to vote regardless of race or color or previous condition of servitude.	1870
XIX	Gave women the right to vote.	1920
XXIV	Eliminated the payment of poll tax as a requirement to vote.	1964
XXVI	Gave 18-year-olds the right to vote.	1971

EDUCATION, CIVIC EDUCATION AND THE CIVIC LITERACY GAP[24]

Just as the concept of citizenship evolved over time so too did the American approach to education and civic education. The evolution of universal American public education with a strong focus on citizenship is a testimony to the genius and commitment of passionate and principled citizens and leaders from the public, private and academic sectors. Unfortunately, as we shall see later, we are living today in devolutionary rather than evolutionary times.

There was no mention of education itself in the Constitution. Therefore, what carried the day in terms of the establishment of the U.S. educational system was the Tenth Amendment, which was part of the Bill of Rights and reserved all powers not granted to the federal government to the states. This made education the primary but exclusive province of each state.

The common school reform movement started in Massachusetts, and that state was the first to require compulsory schooling in 1852. By 1918, all states then in existence had adapted some form of required education. The Morrill Act, which was passed by the federal government in 1862, spawned the development of "public" land grant colleges in all states and became the backbone of the still unrivaled American higher education system. (See the discussion on this as a pivot point in chapter 1.)

Later pieces of federal legislation that shaped the educational system and our citizens included the GI Bill (1944), which increased access to higher education significantly (see the discussion on this as a pivot point in chapter 1); *Brown* v. *Board of Education* (1954), which made education an equal and civil rights issue; and Title IX (1972), which placed education at the center of the drive toward gender equality.

There have been many towering figures in the development of the American education system and making the connection to citizenship. Three of the most important have been Noah Webster, Horace Mann and John Dewey.

Webster was a newspaper publisher and a dictionary developer (Merriam-Webster). He was a firm advocate and influential proponent for educating all of the youth in America. In 1788, he wrote, "In our American republics, where [government] is in the hands of the people, knowledge should be universally diffused by means of public schools." He emphasized, "every child in America should be acquainted with his own country. He should read books that furnish him with ideas that will be useful to him in life and practice."[25]

Mann was a former Massachusetts legislator and businessperson who almost single-handedly created the common school movement in the United States. After a visit to Prussia in 1837 and studying its approach, which included normal schools for developing teachers, he came back home and worked tirelessly to ensure that the state of Massachusetts developed its educational system patterned after the Prussian model.

Dewey was a philosopher, psychologist and educator who lived from 1859 to 1952. His reform ideas drove the development of the progressive and populist approaches to schooling implemented in the

United States during the first half of the 20th century. Dewey believed that proper schooling was essential to establishing a civil society and democracy and that one of the key responsibilities of education was to develop informed and knowledgeable citizens.

It wasn't just the members of the boys' club who made citizenship central to education. In April 1930, Eleanor Roosevelt wrote a seminal piece for *Pictorial Review* titled "Good Citizenship: The Purpose of Education."

In her article, Ms. Roosevelt asserted, "In our schools are now given courses in civics, government, economics, current events. Very few children are as ignorant as I once was. But there still remains a vast amount to be done before we accomplish our first objective—informed and intelligent citizens, and secondly, bring about the realization that we are all responsible for the trend of thought and the action of our times."[26]

Fast forward more than 80 years—from the 20th to the 21st century. It appears that students are much more ignorant about citizenship and democracy than Ms. Roosevelt was in those halcyon days of civic education. At least, that's what those who research civic learning and engagement are finding. A series of studies done over the past decade revealed that[27]

- Less than 30 percent of 4th, 8th and 12th graders were proficient in civics
- Less than 50 percent of 8th graders knew the purpose of the Bill of Rights
- The majority of students were not able to explain the purpose of the Declaration of Independence
- Only 1 in 10 demonstrated an acceptable knowledge of checks and balances among the legislative, executive and judicial branches

In large part, this is attributable to the fact that civics is no longer taught in many schools and that few states have standards specifically related to civic education. Today most states have adapted the common core standards for education and most schools teach to the test. Much of that test, though, relates to proficiency in Science, Technology, Engineering and Math (STEM). There is no test on civics.

In STEM and other education areas, the United States has embarked on a race to the top. For most of the past decade, the contest in the civic education and engagement arena has been primarily a race to the bottom.

TIME FOR 21ST CENTURY CITIZENSHIP

So, as we reflect on it, we as citizens of the United States have come a long way on the citizenship journey. But given the present conditions and circumstances, we still have a very long way to go.

As we ponder what paths to take, we need to begin by asking, "Who is the good citizen and what does the good citizen do?" That question is as old as and has been debated since Aristotle's *Politics*.

President Barack Obama brought the issue of *citizenship* front and center in his acceptance speech at the Democratic convention when he declared, "But we also believe in citizenship—citizenship, a word at the very heart of our founding, a word at the essence of our democracy, the idea that this country only works when we accept certain obligations to one another and to future generations."

President Obama went on to emphasize that "We the people— recognize that we have rights as well as responsibilities." The emphasis throughout the President's speech was on shared obligations and responsibilities.[28]

Presidential candidate Mitt Romney also addressed the concept of citizenry indirectly in his acceptance speech at the Republican convention when he stated that immigrants came here to become citizens "not just in pursuit of riches but for the richness of this life. Freedom. Freedom of religion. Freedom to speak their mind. Freedom to build a business. With their own hands. This is the essence of the American experience." The emphasis throughout candidate Romney's speech was on individual advancement and economic opportunities.[29]

Which vision and version of citizenship is correct? The answer should be both. Early in this 21st century, however, where partisanship has been elevated to the new art of war it appears that neither may be. As we have stated, polls show that the divide between the parties and the perspectives of their loyalists was widening. The extent of that divide was reflected in the substance and tenor of the two conventions.

David Brooks did a good job of capturing this difference in separate columns after each convention. In his August 30 *New York Times* column following the Republican convention, Brooks observed, "But there is a flaw in the vision the Republicans offered in Tampa. It is contained in its rampant hyper-individualism . . . There was almost no talk of community and compassionate conservatism. There was certainly no conservatism as Edmund Burke understood it, in which individuals are embedded in webs of customs, traditions, habits and governing institutions."[30]

Following the Democratic convention, in his September 7 *New York Times* column, Brooks wrote "during the hours between 7 and 10 o'clock when the party was appealing to its own activists, the social issues overshadowed the economic ones. Any time a speaker mentioned the tools of social empowerment—reproductive rights, same-sex marriage, contraceptive freedom—the crowd rose to its feet." He continued to note that "Democrats have an indifference to business and an attachment to lifestyle libertarianism that is off-putting to American majorities." In spite of this, Brooks concluded that because Clinton and Obama are "able to project balance" while the Republicans have not, the Democrats have an advantage in this year's presidential race.[31]

E. J. Dionne also emphasizes the need for balance in his masterful new book *Our Divided Political Heart: The Battle for the American Idea in an Age of Discontent,* in which he provides an in-depth and historical examination of the current state of our political condition and how we got to where we are. In the final chapter Dionne argues for a more "consensual balance" from both parties—especially from the Republican Party, which he argues has lost its commitment to classic conservatism and communal values due to the stranglehold of the Tea Party.[32]

We agree with Dionne and Brooks about the importance and necessity for rebalancing. But we think that our balance will be restored by citizens rather than though the political parties and their leadership.

That's because many of the avid advocates (elected officials and party members) in each party have only fear and loathing for those on the other side. They will tolerate no room for common ground or compromise. Civil discourse and dialogue are alien terms to them.

Today, with the movement to the extremes and the hardening of positions, the center is weak in both major parties—virtually non-existent in one. There is a centrism vacuum.

Nature and politics abhor a vacuum. That vacuum must be filled—and it will be by what we refer to as a 21st century citizen. That citizen is:

- *Interested*: concerned about the common good and the American community as opposed to purely pecuniary or personal concerns

- *Issues-oriented*: focused on areas of civic and social concern as opposed to rigid ideologies

- *Informed*: dedicated to gathering and analyzing objective data as the basis for civic and social engagement

- *Independent*: committed to exercising personal judgment as opposed to taking totally partisan positions

- *Involved*: engaged actively in addressing those issues that are of paramount concern to our citizens, communities and the nation[33]

The 21st century citizen is a good citizen. In his *Politics*, Aristotle stated, "The conclusion to which we are thus led is that excellence of the citizen must be excellence relative to the constitution."[34]

Twenty-first century citizens understand that the Constitution is the starting line and not the finish line. They are problem solvers, not blame placers. They are future-focused and not fault-focused. They are proactive rather than reactive.

Citizenship, like patriotism, is not a partisan concept. The U.S. Constitution and our democracy belong to the people and not a party. The nation's greatness and genius come from the many and not the few.

Senator Bill Bradley recognized and celebrated this at the end of his new book *We Can All Do Better* when he wrote, "Wisdom is where you find it. . . . Wisdom acts for the long term. . . . It tells us that our great country needs to be revived and that its citizenry deep down wants to reclaim American democracy from the stranglehold of money and ideology. And it has faith in those citizens to succeed in that task."[35]

We have faith in those citizens too. And that is why we say, now more than ever, *it is time for 21st century citizenship* that promotes both individual striving and shared responsibility. With that in mind, we present our pivot point recommendations on citizenship.

PIVOT POINT RECOMMENDATIONS: ALL FOR ONE AND ONE FOR ALL

American citizenship has rights and responsibilities. For the past decade or more the emphasis has been much more on the rights than the responsibilities. The emphasis has been more on the "me" rather than the "we." Our pivot point recommendations are targeted at reversing this orientation through a process of:

- Education: From STEM To STERN
- Collaboration: National Service Not Military Service
- Participation: Voter Expression Not Suppression
- Celebration: Interdependence Day—Celebrating the "Us" in USA

Education: From STEM to STERN

Prepare future generations of citizens by teaching civics and civic engagement in middle school.

Our educational system places tremendous emphasis on Science, Technology, Engineering and Math (STEM). We need to place a comparable emphasis on Students Together Engaging to Renew the Nation (STERN).

Former Supreme Court Justice Sandra Day O'Connor identified the lack of sufficient and appropriate civic education as one of the most significant problems in America today. She has put addressing that problem at the top of her personal agenda now that she is a private citizen again.

Justice O'Connor worked with the Georgetown University Law Center and Arizona State University to develop a website and an interactive civics curriculum for seventh- through ninth-grade students called Our Courts. According to Justice O'Connor, "At least half of our states no longer make the teaching of civics and government a requirement for high school graduation."[36]

This leaves a huge gap, and we should not forget that a primary purpose of public schools in America has always been to help produce citizens who have both the knowledge and skills and the values to sustain our republic as a nation, our democratic form of government.

The federal government should make civics a requirement and provide adequate funding to support implementation of scalable and replicable civic education and civic engagement programs on a national basis. State legislatures should provide support for and make civics a requirement as well. Foundation support should be solicited to magnify the efforts.

These civic education and engagement programs should be designed to build knowledge, attitudes and skills. They should be targeted to middle school, in-school, and after-school classes because educational research indicates that formation of a positive orientation toward an area earlier in a student's career increases the potential for sustained interest and participation.

There are a variety of programs that could be drawn upon to meet this need. We know of three models, each with a different primary focus, which could be employed nationally:

- *Project Citizen*. This is a national curricular program for middle, secondary and postsecondary students; youth organizations; and adult groups that promotes competent and responsible participation in local and state government (*http://www.civiced.org*).

- *Our American Voice*. This after-school program involves middle school students directly in the democratic process by employing an action learning model to help them develop the core knowledge, attitudes and abilities for citizenship. It enables students to understand the critical role they play as citizens in a democratic society. The program is run by the Barat Education Foundation (*http://www.ouramericanvoice.org*).

- *Kids Voting*. Kids Voting USA® gets students involved and ready to be educated and engaged citizens. Students learn about democracy through a combination of classroom activities and authentic voting experience and family dialogue (*http://www.kidsvoting.org*).[37]

In mid-June 2013, the American Academy's Commission on Humanities and the Social Sciences released a report, *The Heart of the Matter,* which focused national attention on the need to expand the educational envelope beyond STEM.

The Heart of the Matter devoted one of its five chapters to K-12 education and identified three overarching goals, including the "need to educate Americans in the knowledge, skills and understanding they will need to thrive in a twenty-first century democracy." It emphasized that "These goals cannot be achieved by science alone."[38]

This intensified focus brings a renewed national attention to this important area. Time will tell whether it produces tangible results in terms of citizenship and civic engagement.

Collaboration: National Service Not Military Service

Require mandatory national service for youth of a certain age.

A debate has erupted over the past few years regarding reinstating the military draft. Representative Charles Rangel (D-NY) introduced a bill for this purpose in 2011 and again in 2013.[39]

Proponents of the reinstatement include Thomas Ricks, a fellow at the Center for New American Security, and Lawrence Korb, a former assistant secretary of defense in the Reagan administration.[40] Their primary arguments center on the following three points: a draft would cause greater deliberation before entering a conflict, shorten the length of engagement due to public pressure and provide relief to an all-volunteer army during extended periods of combat.

Opponents of the reinstatement include Melvin Laird, secretary of defense under President Nixon, and Elliot Feldman, a special project officer and consultant in the Defense Department in the Reagan administration.[41] Their primary arguments center on the points that an all-volunteer force is highly professional and well trained, more cost effective than the alternative and it would be difficult to make the draft equitable.

Given the nature and consequences of the Iraq and Afghanistan wars in terms of blood and treasure, this is an important debate to have.

In our opinion, however, the debate is too narrowly framed. It should be about whether we should have a program of mandatory national service not military service.

We first proposed such an initiative in *Renewing*. If there were a requirement for national service for those youth of a certain age, military service could be one of just many options they could select.[42]

In 1961, President John F. Kennedy famously said, "Ask not what your country can do for you; ask what you can do for your country." In 1964, President Lyndon Baines Johnson called upon us to build a "Great Society." Note that President Johnson used the word "society" and not "country." In the mid-1970s, President Jimmy Carter asked that we sacrifice by reducing our gas consumption.

Since the early 1980s, requests for shared commitments or sacrifices have not been too visible on the country's radar screen. Until the past few years, the national refrain appears to have been "Ask what you can do for yourself."

Service to country seemed to belong to those in the armed forces, the well-off or the do-gooders.

We are not recommending that the draft be reinstated to correct this lack of personal investment and involvement in America. We believe, however, that some type of national service should be made mandatory. The service could take one of many forms, for example, military, community, or education.

During the 2008 campaign for the presidency, John McCain and Barack Obama both expressed a desire for more Americans to be engaged in national service when they shared the stage at Columbia University at a forum commemorating the seventh anniversary of the 9/11 attacks.[43] However, it is Jim Lehrer who speaks most articulately on this topic.[44]

As the commencement speaker at Harvard University in 2006, Mr. Lehrer stated "I have come with only one major commencement-like point to make . . . I believe we should consider adapting some form of national service. No, not a return to the military draft—something entirely different, and completely new for us. National service in its fullest meaning."

Jim proceeded to recall the lessons he learned about life and himself in the diverse company of his fellow Marines during his three years of service. He then observed why he felt national service was so necessary:

> I have never seen us more disconnected from each other than we are right now. . . . We are splintering off into segments, interest groups, lobbies, target audiences, blogs, boxes. . . . Our racial, cultural and religious differences—always our great strength—have become an instrument in our great disconnection. Our growing economic differences . . . are feeding this. Our politics at the moment actually seem to be encouraging it; and our otherwise terrific explosion in new media outlets for information and debate . . .

Have we as a nation become less disconnected and have things gotten less divisive over the past seven years since Mr. Lehrer's commencement address? Sad to say, we think not.

The Edward M. Kennedy Serve America Act of 2009 and other initiatives such as service learning projects for students moved us in a more collaborative and interdependent direction.[45] But the explosion of the Tea Party upon the scene, the dysfunction of the 112th Congress, the highly charged and negative tone of most of the presidential contest of 2012 and the Pew Research survey that shows the partisan "values" gap between us as citizens at an all-time high provide ample evidence that we have grown more divided rather than more united as a nation over the past six years.

In the Eleanor Roosevelt article cited earlier in this chapter, Ms. Roosevelt eloquently makes the case that the schools and parents are mutually responsible for developing citizens and a commitment to a set of common core values.

She observes, "If the elders look upon public questions from purely selfish angles, with a view as to how they will be affected personally, and not as to what are the needs of the country or the world, then it is safe to predict that youth will do the same. This teaching of citizenship in the schools must be supplemented by teaching and example in the home."

She concludes her article by stating, "As the great majority of our children are being educated in public schools, it is all-important that the standards of citizenship should be of the best . . . we should take a constant interest in all educational institutions and remember that on the public school largely depends the success or failure of our great experiment in government 'by the people, for the people.'"[46]

It is 2013. Our public schools today pay little to no attention to the cultivation of citizenship. They devote the majority of their time to STEM and teaching to the test. Soon, they may very well not be teaching the majority of our children.

Charter schools, home schools, private schools, other schools. Where do they stand and what do they do to promote the cause of citizenship, bringing us together and service to the country?

We are indeed at a pivot point for the "success or failure of our great experiment" in government. Schools and families must play an essential role in building citizenship and the character of the nation. So too should national service.

In his Harvard comment speech, Jim Lehrer said, "I believe what we need is a new hard real-world dose of shared experience."[47] We couldn't say it any better.

National service provides a basis for sharing and potentially bridging divides. In the United States today, service is somebody else's business.

We need to make it the nation's business—service to our country and our fellow citizens. That is the measure of true patriotism.

It is not about waving the flag or pledging allegiance. It is about standing up and doing what is required to make America the very best it can be. A program of national service provides the means for accomplishing that. That is why we are advocates for it.

We were heartened to see that *Time* magazine in the cover story for its July 1, 2013, issue continued to advocate for national service as well. Richard Stengel, managing editor, pointed out that *Time* had published a cover story calling for national service six summers ago but since then the "idea of national service has moseyed along without much progress."[48]

Stengel opined that the tempo was picking up. He noted that this summer, *Time* in collaboration with the Aspen Institute's Franklin Project and its chairman, General Stanly McChrystal, was convening a 21st Century National Service Summit.

Stengel in his editor's comments and Joe Klein in his cover article for this issue highlighted that national service is on the upswing. We agree with them. As with the issue of civic engagement, however, only time will tell whether this translates into a nationally mandated program of national service.

Participation: Voter Expression Not Voter Suppression

Reform our electoral process to promote and ensure maximum feasible participation by all eligible voters.

The 2011–2012 timeframe was an incredibly ugly one in terms of the attempts to restrict voter participation by tightening voting laws. According to New York University's Brennan Center for Justice, there were over 180 proposed laws passed in over 41 states. But as courts intervened, the new rules covered voters in only 13 states as many of the more onerous—and probably illegal—conditions were struck down.[49]

The most common new laws that stood up include reduced time for early voting, restricting the activities of groups doing voter registration, tightened voter identification requirements and tougher rules for ex-convicts. In spite of, or perhaps because of, these new laws, the voter turnout for the 2012 presidential election was good.

And the backlash to the attempt to suppress voter participation was substantial. Some states, such as Florida which had tightened its laws going into 2012, loosened them almost immediately after the election because of the negative publicity and feedback they received. Nationally, in early 2013, President Obama appointed a Commission on Election Administration to develop recommendations to improve the manner in which we conduct our elections.

As Bob Edgar, president and CEO of Common Cause, points out, this commission does not have to start from scratch. The problems in this area have been studied by numerous groups such as Common Cause, the Verified Voting Foundation, the Election Protection Coalition, and the Pew Election Initiatives. Edgar also recommends that Congress should hold hearings on the Voting Empowerment Act (HR 112, S3608) to modernize voting administration and penalize deceptive practices and should revive the Election Assistance

Commission to help states meet the voting quality standards that were established as part of the 2002 Help America Vote Act.[50]

So we just need to get on with it and put an effective and efficient system in place to maximize eligible voter participation. That's important for two reasons. Our current approach is anything but systematic. In early 2013, the Pew Charitable Trusts released a major new study that documented the wide variations from state to state and the sweeping nature of problems in the way things are done today.

In that study, Pew also ranked the 50 states on more than 15 criteria such as wait times, lost votes, and the use of absentee and provisional ballots. Surprisingly to some, the poor rankings were not restricted to a region of the country. The state ranked last based upon an analysis of the 2010 elections was Mississippi. The next two lowest ranked states were New York and California, in that order. As Adam Liptak of the *New York Times* reports, Heather K. Gerken, a law professor at Yale and a Pew advisor, observes, "Poor Southern states perform well and they perform badly. Rich New England states perform well and badly—mostly badly."[51]

An area in which most of the states and we as a citizenry perform "mostly badly" is in voter turnout and election participation. The average voter turnout in presidential election years from 1980 to 2012 was in the 50 percent range with a slight blip in 2008 to above 61 percent. The off-year participation in elections in that time frame ran around 40 percent. These are appallingly low percentages.[52]

On a 2007 international ranking of 172 democracies, the United States ranked 139th in voter participation. Other studies have ranked the United States as 28 to 40 among advanced or mature nations that vote democratically. A few countries like Australia and Belgium make voting mandatory. However, the majority do not.[53]

There are a variety of reasons people don't exercise their right to vote; they include apathy and alienation. One of those reasons should not be a Rube Goldberg voting system. That is what we have today. We need to fix it now or forever pay the price in terms of citizen trust and electoral representativeness.

Unfortunately, the Supreme Court moved us in the wrong direction in its June 2013 ruling, which struck down the part of the Voting Rights Act of 1965 that determines which states must get federal permission before changing their laws. The Court acknowledged that progress had been made in voting rights but that discrimination still existed. It then threw the ball back into Congress' court to come up with a new formula for making the determination as to which states should be subjected to federal oversight.

Immediately after the Court's decision, writing for the *Washington Post*, Karen Tumulty and Dan Balz observed this might very well leave the "law in limbo" due to the deeply divided nature of Congress.[54] What wasn't in limbo were the states like North Carolina, Texas and Mississippi who rushed to implement tougher voting requirements (e.g., voter IDs and fewer early voting dates) that had been stalled pending the Court's decision.[55]

By mid-2013, the national spotlight was being shone on national service and civic engagement, and it appeared that we might be taking two steps forward in those areas. In contrast, the Supreme Court's decision moved us at least one step back—and maybe many more.

Interdependence Day: Celebrating the "Us" in USA[56]

Establish a national holiday to recognize the diversity that is America and to promote a shared sense of unity and purpose.

It appears that we will be getting some form of immigration reform. It might seem that we have weathered the storm and we will have put our immigration "problem" behind us.

Unfortunately, this is not the case. Immigration reform addresses the legal issues but not the psychological problem underlying them.

That problem is the fragile status of the American community and our relations to each other as Americans. Given this condition, we believe that it's imperative to find a way to elevate that which unites us rather than to exaggerate that which divides us.

To accomplish this, we recommend adding a new holiday to the federal calendar—Interdependence Day. Its purpose would be to celebrate the "Us" in USA.

American holidays are held primarily to recognize past accomplishments and contributions as opposed to celebrating the present and future. This holiday should focus on who we are as a nation and recognize what we are becoming. The Statue of Liberty should be made central to this holiday. E pluribus unum should be its theme.

America is a nation of immigrants and continues to be so. The United States remains a unique vessel of being and becoming.

This day should be dedicated to celebrating the nation's diversity, progress that has been made, and the opportunities and challenges ahead. In 2009, the Statue of Liberty reopened certain viewing areas, and Ellis Island opened a new visitors' center. Interdependence Day could take these symbols in combination with others from around the country that demonstrate our common humanity and elevate the importance of what brings us together.

Interdependence Day would be an appropriate holiday at any time. Establishing Interdependence Day as a national holiday during this transitional period for the United States would be especially important.

Over the past few years, fueled by economic anxiety and insecurity, political partisanship and separatists, many Americans moved into isolated camps. Group turned against group. There was a rising tide of intolerance and xenophobia.

The tide took many forms and was manifested in many ways. Here are a few examples from 2010.

In April, Arizona passed a tough immigration law. A week later the bill was amended to ease concerns about racial profiling. (In spite of this, the Supreme Court invalidated most of the Arizona law in 2012.) Numerous states drafted or passed laws similar to Arizona's and polls at the time showed that a large majority of Americans supported them.

In the summer, a conservative Catholic group called Fidelis conducted a national survey of millions of Catholic voters. In the survey, Fidelis asserted that the Freedom of Choice Act would "require doctors to even kill live babies who survive a failed abortion" and that under the Fairness Doctrine "Catholic radio stations would likely be required to give equal time to atheists, Muslims, Hindus, Satanists, etc."

Throughout the course of 2010, the National Center for Constitutional Studies held over 180 sessions across the country to share its view of the Constitution and to frame the founding of the nation in a religious perspective. In one of these sessions, held in Springfield,

Missouri, Earl Taylor, president of the Center, reviewed the Constitution and all of its amendments.

During his discussion of the amendments, Taylor is reported to have stated that he felt the nation's leaders could have stopped at ten, claimed that Thomas Jefferson's slaves wouldn't have wanted to be freed because of the way he cared for them and opined that women's suffrage could have been enacted individually by the states.

This has been an incredibly divisive period. We need to confront this divisiveness head on by promoting national unity and a commonality of interest.

Interdependence Day would be a powerful means for accomplishing this.

The late John Wooden, the renowned coach of UCLA, said, "Sports do not build character. They reveal it." How we resolve our current debate and move forward in the coming years will reveal our American character. Our expectation, with Interdependence Day as a national holiday, is that we will do so, as we have in the past, as an independent and interdependent people striving together to create a more perfect union.

Pivot Point Report Card

Instructions

This report card is provided to allow you to reflect upon and assess the progress in this pivot point area. To use the report card:

1. Review the recommendations for the area.
2. Evaluate the progress made in the area to date and assign a letter grade using the system that follows: A–excellent progress. B–substantial progress. C–some progress. D–little progress. F–no progress.
3. Describe the nature of the progress and the rationale for your rating.

We will be posting our assessment for this area on an occasional basis. To see that assessment and to provide your input and feedback on the area, visit *http://www.workingthepivotpoints.com*.

Recommendations

- All for One and One for All
    - Education: From STEM to STERN
    - Collaboration: National Service Not Military Service
    - Participation: Voter Expression Not Suppression
    - Celebration: Interdependence Day

Grade

Reason

6 | Individual Economic Well-Being: The 100 Percent

There has been much analysis and discussion over the past two years about the increasing income inequality in the United States. Some advocate reducing the inequality and redistributing some of the wealth as a matter of fairness.

As noted in Chapter 3, we view it first and foremost as an economic and political issue. If the income distribution is highly skewed and there is a shrinking middle class, it retards the economy's ability to grow. Likewise, if citizens are in diminished circumstances, their belief in the political system, upward mobility and the American dream deteriorates and hurts the vitality of the democracy.

We are at a crossroads in the United States today. The American economy is restructuring into three groups: The have-a-lot-more, the have-not, and the have-a-lot-less. We need to reverse this in order to move beyond recovery of the economy at the macro level and renewal of individual economic well-being at the micro level.

During the 2012 election year, over and over again we heard about the 1 percent, the 47 percent, and the 99 percent. For America to be America, it is essential to ensure equality of opportunity for the 100 percent. In this chapter, we look at where we stand now, how people feel about it and what should be done to address the current conditions.

INCOME INEQUALITY: TRENDS AND TRAGEDIES

Thomas Piketty, economist at the Paris School of Economics, and Emmanuel Saez, professor at the University of California, Berkeley (Piketty-Saez), are unquestionably the experts on income distribution in countries around the world.[1] They have been studying incomes for more than two decades and provide special insights into income growth at the top end of the income spectrum.

Piketty-Saez' original research went through 2007 and showed a dramatic rise in the incomes of those at the top, with peaks in 2000 and 2007. In 2012, Saez updated that research with estimates through 2010 in an article titled "Striking It Richer: The Evolution of Top Incomes in the United States" and concluded that while the pre-tax income of the top 1 percent of households fell during the great recession, it and the share of income going to the wealthy rose strongly in 2010.[2]

In March, The Center on Budget and Policy Priorities analyzed the Piketty-Saez data in conjunction with Congressional Budget Office data sets and came to the following conclusions:

- The share of U.S. households' total income flowing to the top 1 percent rose to 19.8 percent in 2010. That is lower than 2007 and 2000 but still among the highest since the late 1920s.

- The average income of the top 1 percent rose by nearly 12 percent from 2009 to 2010 after adjusting for inflation. In contrast, the average income of the bottom 90 percent remained at its lowest level since 1983 in inflation-adjusted dollars.

- There is a tremendous range in growth in income and incomes even in the top 1 percent. In 2010, the average income for individuals in the 99th to 99.5th percentile grew 4.6 percent to an average income of $418,000, compared to growth for the top 0.01 percent of 21.5 percent to an average income of $23.8 million.[3]

Scott Winship of the Brookings Institution provides an interesting way of thinking about the difference between income earners in the top 1 percent and those below them. He suggests putting them on the 160th floor of Dubai's Burj Khalifa—the world's tallest building. He notes that "the richest household in the bottom

98 percent—earning $350,000" would be on the 93rd floor—67 floors below the top—and the household earning the median income of about $50,000 would be on the 13th floor. Based upon this, Winship observes, "the gap between the median household . . . and the 98th percentile is not dramatically greater than the gap between the 98th percentile and the 99th percentile."[4]

But, the gap between those on the lower floors and in the basement is huge and growing—as are the number of occupants. The Gini index is a measure developed to examine income inequality. It goes from zero where income is distributed proportionately among all households to one where one household has all of the income and the rest have none.

The Gini index value for the United States has been going up for several years. According to a report from the Census Bureau, in 2011 it rose to 0.475 from 0.469 for the nation—increasing in 20 states with no "statistically significant change" in the rest of the states. At the same time, the report showed median household income continued to decline from 2010 to 2011 and there was "great inequality among states as well as within them."[5]

Some would suggest that this inequality does not have much of an economic consequence and should be ignored. We disagree wholeheartedly and side with Professor Saez who states, "People say that reducing inequality is radical. I think tolerating the level of inequality the United States tolerates is radical."[6]

INEQUALITY TAKES MANY FORMS

The reason for being concerned about inequality is that it undermines a vibrant economy and democracy. Inequality is not just about income. It takes many forms in our nation as a whole and us as individuals.

In late 2011, the Bertlesmann Stiftung Foundation (Foundation) of Germany released a report titled *Social Justice in the OECD—How Do Member States Compare?* The Foundation combined a number of metrics from the Organization for Economic Development (OECD) for ratings in areas such as overall poverty, income inequality (Gini index), preprimary education, health and intergenerational justice to construct an overall social justice rating. The United States fared extremely poorly both on the individual ratings and the summative one.

It ranked near the bottom of the OECD countries (31 in total) on most measures and 27th overall, with only Greece, Chile, Mexico and Turkey lower. Countries that ranked slightly ahead of the United States on the overall social justice rating included Japan, Portugal, Slovakia, South Korea and Spain.[7]

It is definitely possible to quarrel with the Foundation's and the OECD's ratings. It's tough to quarrel, however, with the multifaceted and emerging face of inequality that started to emerge before the Great Recession and has gotten uglier after it. Let's look at a few of the forms that inequality takes and its consequences.

Health Inequality

In January 2013, the Institute of Medicine and National Research released a stunning and damning report on the state of American health care. The nearly 400-page report developed by a panel of experts compared health outcomes in the United State to those in 16 other rich countries. Among other things, the report revealed that in terms of life expectancy over the past 30 years American men ranked last and women second to last and Americans also had much higher rates of disease. This led the panelists to label their findings "the U.S. health disadvantage" and Dr. Steven Wolf, chair of the Department of Family Medicine at Virginia Commonwealth, to state, "Something fundamentally is going wrong . . . . And, it's getting worse."[8]

The report identified a number of factors that contributed to the sorry state of the health care outcomes such as poverty, educational level and a lack of health care coverage. It noted, however, that even college-educated Americans and those with higher incomes fared worse on many of the health care indicators than citizens of other countries. The panel also pointed out that the United States spent more on health care than any other in the survey and that in the 1950s, Americans scored better in life expectancy and diseases than the other countries in the survey.[9]

Unemployment and Underemployment Inequality

The official unemployment rate as reported by the Bureau of Labor Statistics (BLS) stays stuck at around 7.5 percent. The BLS reported in mid-2012 that the average length of unemployment was 40 weeks, the highest since 1948.[10] In a February 2013 *Washington Post* article titled "Weak Job Creation Has Become the New Normal," Robert Shapiro points out that since the recovery began in June 2009 the private sector has grown on average by 1.25 percent per year. This compares to growth in the expansionary periods from 1982–1989 of 3.7 percent and from 1991–2000 of 2.3 percent.[11] Combine this with the reduction in government jobs due to federal, state and local cutbacks and this does begin to look like the new normal unless there is an intervention.

In addition, because of the uncertain economic times, people are staying in jobs longer, working for lower wages and/or shorter hours. The Economic Policy Institute (EPI) highlights this in its book *The State of Working America, 12th Edition,* released on Labor Day, 2012. Based upon an analysis of 2011 data, EPI points out that the median hourly wage is lower than it was a decade earlier.[12]

Generational Inequality

The lack of job turnover has frozen the labor market, especially for those newer to the workforce. In 2012, on average there were about 23.4 million Americans un- and underemployed. According to Heidi Shierholz of EPI, 41 percent of those individuals (9.5 million) were under 30, compared to their labor force share of 27 percent. Shierholz says that "fully one-fifth" of those individuals who are working are underemployed.[13]

This is an especially problematic situation for the young person with a college degree who went to school assuming it would ensure them getting a job and/or advancement or promotion. Now, because of the increased cost of college and inability to find appropriate jobs, these graduates are faced with a "new normal" in which it is difficult to impossible to pay off debt or to build wealth in the manner in which their parents did. Reports released by the State Higher Education Executive Officers and the Urban Institute describe the dimensions of this dilemma in detail.[14]

Gender Inequality

Before the Great Recession, there was some concern about the shrinking percentage of males in the workforce. Since the recovery began, that concern has reversed. That's because, as Floyd Norris explains in a February 2013 *New York Times* article, between December 2009 and January 2013, 5.3 million new jobs were created and only 30 percent went to women.[15]

The proportion of jobs held by women went from 28 percent in 1948, peaked at 47.5 percent in January 2010, and in January 2013 stood at 46.8 percent. The sharpest declines in employment were in the 20–24 and 45–54 age groups. The largest increase in employment was for women in the 60–64 age group.

Asset Inequality

According to Phillip Longman of the *Washington Monthly*, the federal government spends more than $500 billion a year on policies to help individuals acquire or build assets. The three most expensive of these policies are mortgage interest deduction, the property tax deduction and preferential rates on capital gains and dividends. A Federal Reserve study indicates that 45 percent of these benefits flow to individuals with average income exceeding $1 million per annum, and that on average the top 1 percent get $57,673 in benefits compared to $3 in benefits for the poorest fifth of Americans.

A recent study by the Employee Benefits Research Institute (Institute) discloses that the average person is doing little to nothing to fill in that asset gap. Most Americans approaching retirement do not have a retirement account of any type. Among those who do, the median balance in 2009 was only $69,127. The Institute study found that 44 percent of Baby Boomers and Gen-Xers lacked the savings and pension coverage to meet even basic retirement-age expenses.[16]

In conclusion, this is not an exhaustive list of inequalities but we believe a representative one. It demonstrates that in some ways these inequalities impact all Americans but they impact those on the middle and bottom rungs of the ladder most severely. We turn our attention to them next.

THE INCREDIBLE SHRINKING MIDDLE CLASS

In August 2012, the Pew Research Center released a report with the telling title and subtitle *The Lost Decade of the Middle Class: Fewer, Poorer, Gloomier*.[17] The report took its title from the fact that real median income and real median net worth from 2001 to 2010 fell for those who Pew classified as middle class for purposes of its study: households with between two-thirds to double the median income—a range of approximately $40,000–$120,000 in 2011 dollars.

In 2011, the Pew survey found that the middle-income tier constituted 51 percent of all adults compared to 61 percent in 1971. In this same time frame, the upper-income tier rose to 20 percent from 14 percent and the lower-income tier rose to 29 percent from 25 percent.

Key findings from the survey include:

- Median household income (scaled for a three-person household) declined from $72,956 to $69,487 (–4.3 percent).
- Median net worth plummeted from a high of $152,950 to $93,150 (–40 percent).
- 85 percent of respondents said it was "more difficult" to maintain their standard of living than it was ten years ago.

In spite of these negative trends and perceptions, the survey participants still were relatively optimistic about "middle class mobility." Sixty percent felt their current standard of living is better than that of their parents at this stage of life compared to 67 percent in Pew's 2008 survey of the middle-income tier population. Forty-three percent expected their children's standard of living to be better than their own at the same age while 21 percent expected it to be the same.

The Pew survey findings for middle-class mobility are supported somewhat by a Brookings Institution Study released in 2012 titled *Pathways to Middle Class: Balancing Personal and Public Responsibilities*. That study showed that children born into middle-income families have a "roughly even chance of moving up or down once they become adults." An important part of that survey, however, is the fact that "those born into rich or poor families have a high probability of remaining rich or poor as adults.[18]

The American middle class is not only disappearing—its share of the wealth of the nation is also dismal in comparison to that of the middle class in other countries. Paul Buchheit provides substantial evidence on this in a July 1, 2013, article for the *Nation of Change*.[19]

His article presents a detailed chart comparing the United States to 29 other advanced countries on a number of factors including "total wealth," "mean wealth," "median wealth," the ratio of mean wealth to median wealth and percent of "total wealth."

The United States scores off the chart on total wealth with over twice the amount ($62.0 trillion) of its nearest competitor Japan ($28.1 trillion) and over three times that of China ($20.2 trillion). It also does relatively well on mean wealth with an average of $262,351, which puts it in the top third of the countries.

As Buchheit points out, "median wealth" is "probably the best gauge for the economic strength of the middle class." On that measure our performance is abysmal. America's median wealth is $38,786, which drops us to 18th out of 30.

More importantly, the U.S. ratio of median/mean wealth is 14.8, which ranks lower than any country other than Russia. And, the percent of total wealth held by those at the median income level is 0.6—worse than any country except for India and China. Based upon his analysis of all of this data, Buchheit concludes that "America's middle class is sliding out of the developed world and toward third-world status."

So the fact is that all things being equal, they are not. Inequality of opportunity is at work in the real-world American economy. And the fact remains that in 2013, as Jim Tankersley reported in his February 13 article for the *Washington Post*, "Two kinds of middle-class Americans are struggling today—people who can't find any work or enough work, and full-timers who can't seem to get ahead."[20]

A PERMANENT UNDERCLASS?

As the numbers show, being middle class is not as easy or rewarding as it once was. Being poor never was either, and things have gotten worse lately and from most prognostications could continue to do so into the future.

Poverty in the United States in 2013 is 15 percent. That's the highest in 20 years. Over 46.2 million Americans live below the poverty line, earning less than $11,170 for an individual and $23,050 for a family of four. In 2010, 27 percent of all children in the country lived below the poverty level, with African American children approaching 40 percent.[21] In a 2012 *Huffington Post* blog, Dean Baker, co-director of the Center for Economic and Policy Research, labeled poverty "the new growth industry in America."[22]

While the bottom is bad, potential mobility for a child to move from there up the ladder is bad as well. The Brookings and Pew Economic mobility research referred to earlier reveals that the chance for a child born into a family in the bottom quintile to move into one of the top three quintiles is only 30 percent.

This lack of upward mobility can be explained by a number of factors. One of the most interesting is the results of a recent study by Caroline Hoxby of Stanford and Christopher Avery of Harvard that showed that only 34 percent of high-achieving seniors in the bottom quarter of income distribution attended any one of the country's 238 most selective colleges. Top low-income seniors from the largest metropolitan areas did apply with some frequency to these colleges but students from rural and smaller metro areas like Bridgeport, CT; Memphis; and Sacramento did not.[23]

And as the bottom grows broader, those people who consider themselves as lower class grows as well. A 2012 Pew social trends survey found that almost one-third (32 percent) of Americans classified themselves as lower class (lower and lower-middle class) compared to 25 percent in 2008. In this time span, there was a significant increase in the percent of whites (from 23 percent in 2008 to 31 percent in 2012) and Hispanics (from 30 percent to 40 percent) who indicated they were lower class. Blacks who reported they were lower class stayed the same at 33 percent.

The Pew survey shows that the "hard times have been particularly hard on the lower class." Eighty percent of lower-class adults in the survey said they had to cut back spending in the past year, compared to 62 percent who say they are middle class and 41 percent in the upper class. The lower-class respondents also indicate that they were much less healthy and happy than those in the other two classes.

Finally, according to the Pew survey, "many in the lower class see their prospects dimming." About three-quarters (77 percent) say it's harder now to get ahead than ten years ago; only half (51 percent) say hard work brings success; and a full 35 percent say they think their children will be worse off than they are. Whites were especially pessimistic, with a full 42 percent reporting they expect their children's standard of living to be worse than theirs.[24]

CLASH WARFARE

Given the diminished circumstances of those in both the middle and lower classes, it might be thought that they would call for or engage in class warfare. They have not.

What we did have, however, during many of the political debates of the national election period of 2012 was the substitution of red hot rhetoric and hot button phrases for a meaningful discussion on the American condition and what is acceptable or unacceptable. We had sound bites rather than substance, personal attacks rather than policy arguments, and ideology rather than ideas.

While this form of "clash warfare" may have appealed to a minority of ardent supporters on both sides of the aisle, it did nothing to advance the national dialogue or to respond to the economic and social concerns of the majority of Americans. For them, class warfare was not the issue. Fairness and opportunity were.

As Andrew Kohut, president of the Pew Research Center, stated at the end of a piece that he wrote for the *New York Times* in early 2012, "While a December (2011) Gallup poll found few respondents wanting the government to reduce the income gap between the rich and poor, 70 percent said it was important for the government to increase opportunities for people to get ahead. What the public wants is not a war on the rich but more policies that promote opportunity."[25]

It is significant to note that the desire for enhanced government involvement was not a Democratic or Republican perspective. Approximately one-quarter of Republican and Republican-leaning registered voters had annual family incomes of under $30,000. A Pew Research Center survey conducted in early October 2011 found that 57 percent of this lower income group said that the government does too little for poor people.[26]

So the populous in general was in search of answers to important questions. Sadly, too many politicians preferred pandering to problem solving.

That was the bad news. The good news is that there is an emerging and growing body of literature and knowledge available for those politicians who are willing to move beyond "clash warfare"; do their homework, giving appropriate consideration to America's "class" problems; and then to decide how to work together to resolve them.

These writings range from Charles Murray's *Coming Apart: The State of White America, 1960–2010*, from the more conservative end of the spectrum, to Jacob Hacker and Paul Pierson's *Winner-Take-All Politics: How Washington Made the Rich Richer—And Turned Its Back on the Middle Class,* from the more liberal end. Both of these books are about class. Both agree that there is a widening gap between the wealthiest and the poorest in America. Their insights and explanations, however, differ.

Murray calls attention to and emphasizes the dramatic values and behavioral differences between what he labels the "new upper class" and the "new lower class." These include the percentage of employed individuals, marriage rates, in-tact families, amount of TV watched, obesity rates and community involvement.[27] Hacker and Pierson concentrate on the policy-making process; the nature of our institutional rules such as the filibuster; and the role of powerful organizations, such as big business and those representing the "elite," to describe and detail how we got to where we are today in terms of class in the United States.[28]

There are numerous other books that merit attention. To name just two more: Robert Frank's *The Darwin Economy: Liberty, Competition and the Common Good,* in which Frank provides an exploration of traditional economic theory and how it does or doesn't apply to the country's current circumstances,[29] and Dante Chinni and James Gimpel's *Our Patchwork Nation: The Surprising Truth About the "Real" America.*[30]

In their book, Chinni and Gimpel describe 12 community types (e.g., Evangelical Epicenters, Monied Burbs, Service Worker Centers and Tractor Country) that make up the nation. While not directly focused on class as some of the other works that we have cited, between and among the demographic portraits and patterns laid out in this book is a cultural narrative that will have a dramatic impact on the future of the nation. Let us put it this way, if one pays careful attention to *Our Patchwork Nation*, the devil is in the demographics.

We suggest these readings as a starting point for those citizens and candidates for office who are prepared to engage in a serious and substantive analysis of America's "class" issues rather than in superficial and shallow demagoguery. Our country deserves and needs concerned individuals and groups who are willing to confront the new realities of the nation's economic structure.

In spite of the gap—call it a chasm—between the haves and have-nots in our society, we Americans remain a resilient and optimistic lot. As Andrew Kohut noted in his *New York Times* piece, "In one recent Pew poll, 58 percent of respondents said they believed that people who wanted to get ahead could make it if they were willing to work hard."

Just working hard may no longer be enough, however. As Charles Murray asserts near the opening of *Coming Apart*, "But along with the continuing individual American success stories is a growing majority of people who run the institutions of America who do share tastes, preferences and culture. They increasingly constitute a class. They are also increasingly isolated. . . . This growing isolation has been accompanied by growing ignorance about the country over which they have so much power."[31]

Clash warfare or class warfare—neither choice should be acceptable. As we move forward in 2013 and beyond, those in power and our leaders have the power to obviate both alternatives through proactive and constructive actions. If they do not do so soon, the consequences will be inevitable and unintended.

THE NOT SO GREAT REDISTRIBUTION DEBATE

In addition to class, the 2012 national political debates also brought the topic of redistribution front and center.

Redistribution is a bad thing because it moves wealth from the makers to the takers. Conservatives and libertarians would probably think that way. Progressives and liberals would probably not.

This needs to move beyond an ideological or linguistic argument, however. Every now and then facts should intervene.

A common definition of redistribution is that it is reallocating wealth to reduce inequalities in income. The political argument during the presidential campaign hinged on the conception that it is taking money from the "deserving" rich and giving it to the "undeserving" poor. Both this definition and the conception are too narrowly constructed and also wrong-headed.

As David Firestone pointed out in his September 19, 2012, Taking Note blog for the *New York Times*, "the government has long redistributed wealth and . . . the country expects it to do so. . . . Government takes money from those who have it and uses it for the common good, whether that involves building roads or submarines, or handing some of it over to those who are desperate."[32] Harold Myerson in his September 25, 2012, *Washington Post* article broadened the scope of redistribution beyond government-supported programs observing that markets redistribute wealth continuously as do "Rules made by 'pro-market' governments."[33]

We agree with Firestone and Myerson and would expand the concept even further. The truth is that in the United States redistribution is a pervasive fact of life that permeates the American economy and rewards some more than others. Surprisingly, the 1 percent and the "other 47 percent"—not just the "47 percent"—are major beneficiaries of governmental largess and our many varieties of redistribution. Governmental entities, large corporations, farms, small businesses and all forms of organizations also benefit from the manner in which dollars and deductions are allocated to enable the increasing or sheltering of wealth. Let's look at some examples and evidence.

The government doesn't just do things to support the "desperate." It delivers exemptions, benefits and public goods of some type to all citizens. Michael Grunwald captures that condition beautifully in his feature article for the September 17, 2012, issue of *Time* aptly titled "One Nation on Welfare: Living Your Life on the Dole." Near the beginning of his article, Grunwald observes, "My handouts are not the handouts to the poor that fuel the America's political culture wars." He goes on to cite his various "handouts" including tax deductions for mortgage, home office, health and property taxes and federal subsidies for things such as flood insurance, transportation systems and beach preservation.[34]

Jared Bernstein reinforced Grumwald's perspective in his September 20, 2012, *Huffington Post* blog when he wrote "We almost all 'take' at some point and 'make' at another. Medicare and Social Security are social insurance programs to which we contribute during our working lives and receive benefits from in retirement. Are the beneficiaries of these programs makers or takers?"[35]

So when it comes to redistribution, it appears that we're all in this together—makers and takers. Actually we are not; there's a third category and that is what we call "shakers." The shakers are those people at the top of the economic food chain who have the rules tilted in their favor.

The best example of this favoritism is the manner in which capital gains are treated for taxation purposes. Until the fiscal cliff legislation passed in January 2013, the top federal rate for capital gains was 15 percent (it's now 20 percent), and in several states capital gains are not taxed at all. In contrast, the top marginal federal rate for an income earner is now 39.6 percent.

There probably aren't many high-income earners who will pay that new top rate. Even with these adjustments, it is easy to see whom the rules favor—the very wealthy who receive a high proportion of their wealth from capital gains.

Suzy Khimm highlighted the impact of capital gains treatment on income inequality in her January 2, 2012, *Washington Post* blog. Drawing upon a report from the Congressional Research Service, she notes, "Changes in income from capital gains and dividends were the single largest contributor to rising income inequality between 1996 and 2006." That's not to say that increasing capital gains would increase the earnings of the average worker.[36] In an economy in which the median income has declined for four consecutive years in 2011 and has fallen 8.1 percent since 2007,[37] however, it becomes clear that the wealthiest among us are being rewarded rather than penalized because of the current redistribution system.

The redistribution rewards are not restricted to individuals. As David Kocieniewski reported in his November 3, 2011, *New York Times* article, "280 of the biggest publicly traded companies faced federal income tax bills equal to 18.5 percent of their profits during the last three years—little more than half the official corporate rate of 35 percent and lower than their competitors in many industrialized countries."[38]

Then there are the billions of dollars that have been redistributed historically through the farm bill subsidies. As Robert Semple reported in the *New York Times* on June 2, 2012, between 1995 and 2010 about $200 billion (in 2010 dollars) was distributed. Of this 26 percent went to the top 1 percent of farms in terms of size and a mere 10 percent went to the bottom 80 percent.[39]

Finally, there is the redistribution of federal tax dollars back to the states. Based upon a review of 2005 federal spending, the Tax Foundation found that there were states that received much more than their state's contribution and others that got much less than they contributed. The top five states, in order, that received the most were New Mexico, Mississippi, Alaska, Louisiana and West Virginia. The five states that got back the least were New Jersey, Nevada, Connecticut, New Hampshire and Minnesota.[40]

Even though we said finally, the list could go on virtually ad infinitum and ad nauseum—the Troubled Asset Relief Program (TARP), the auto bailout, the continued protection of the banks, housing subsidies, private equity firms taking over troubled companies, offshoring, Wall Street gains and losses. These are all forms of redistribution. Redistribution is an everyday occurrence and it is at the heart of the American political and capitalistic system.

As we said earlier, in the redistribution scheme of things there are makers, takers and shakers. In the not so great redistribution political debates of 2012 there were also fakers. They were the folks who used a "hot button" word in an attempt to polarize voters even further and to divide rather than unite us. We need the makers and the takers. We may even need the shakers. The fakers we can do without for now and evermore.

HANDS ON, HAND UP, HANDS OFF

In addition to addressing the "class" question in an informed manner, we also need to have an intelligent national conversation about what to do regarding inequality and those in the greatest need.

That's true because America used to be a land where we took care of our own. Times are changing. Today, some would have the weakest and most vulnerable among us tighten their belts, lower their expectations and take care of themselves.

President Obama called the question on those individuals and on the shape and size of the nation's safety net in his second inaugural address. A debate was requested and it is an essential one for the future of our democracy and the American dream.

For far too long, as the words have piled up about the debt and deficit, those at the bottom and middle of the heap have been invisible or ignored. This new framing will make the ongoing discussion and dialogue regarding whom to protect and where to cut more transparent and should ensure that decisions are made based upon a full understanding of the current context and future consequences for the American economy.

America has always been known as a country of rugged individualists. Until the Great Depression the social contract was an illusory concept and social safety net services provided by government were slim to non-existent. Then, in 1935, Social Security legislation was passed and the country moved into the first of what we label three phases of government involvement: Hands-On, Hand-Up, and Hands-Off.

Hands-On Phase: The hands-on phase, which expanded government social services substantially, lasted for nearly one-half century from the mid-1930s to the end of the Carter administration. Programs implemented during that time frame, in addition to Social Security, included Medicare, Medicaid, unemployment insurance, the War on Poverty, equal opportunity, Aid to Families with Dependent Children and increased support for education.

Hand-Up Phase: The hand-up phase began with Ronald Reagan taking office in 1981 and declaring that "In this present crisis, government is not the solution to our problem; government is the problem." For the next 20 years or so, the emphasis was placed on personal responsibility and "shrinking the beast." The key talking points from this period came from Newt Gingrich and the Contract with America; the signature piece of legislation was welfare reform, which put "able-bodied" recipients to work; and Republican and Democratic administrations alike focused on cutting the size of government and reducing the scope of social services.

Hands-Off Phase: 9/11, the Bush administration's "compassionate conservatism" approach, and the great recession provided a brief interregnum between the hand-up and the hands-off phase—as did the first two years of the Obama administration. Because the Democrats enjoyed a substantial majority in both the house and Senate, they were able to pass "Obamacare" and an economic stimulus package without real bipartisan support.

The Republicans were already advocating "hands-off" in 2008 but their hands were tied. Then along came the Tea Party and the electoral landslide of 2010, which gave the Republicans definitive control of the House, and hands-off became a way of life. As we noted earlier, this is attested to by the fact that the 112th Congress passed a mere 220 laws in comparison to the more than 900 laws passed by the 80th Congress, called by President Truman the "Do Nothing Congress."[41]

This failure to legislate combined with the virtually singular focus on the governmental debt and deficit pushed the social contract to the outer edge of the radar screen for many elected Republican legislators—especially in the House.

The extent to which the debt and deficit dominated the perspective can be captured by two votes. The first was on the so-called fiscal cliff bill, which among other things made the Bush-era tax cuts for the middle class permanent and extended unemployment benefits. The bill passed the Senate with overwhelming bipartisan support and got some Republican support in the House with 85 voting for but 151 Republicans voting against it.

The second was the $50 billion relief bill for those communities and areas impacted by Hurricane Sandy, which the House approved on January 15, 2013, after several hours of contentious debate. The bill passed by a 241–180 vote with 179 Republicans voting against it and only 49 voting for it.[42]

These votes should not be viewed as isolated instances but as indicative of the divergent public opinion on the country's social safety net. As Bruce Stokes, Director, Global Economic Attitudes, Pew Research Center, pointed out in an excellent paper for the New America Foundation, our attitudes on the social contract are changing and "the current debate over debt reduction reflects Americans' conflicted, partisan, and often contradictory views on fairness, inequality, the role and responsibility of government and individuals in society and the efficacy of government action."

Some key findings from Stokes' paper include the following:

- Overall, public support for the "social safety net" has declined from 69 percent in 2007 to 59 percent in 2012.

- By a margin of 55 to 39 percent, voters in the 2012 election exit polls felt the U.S. economic system generally favors the wealthy. Only the Mitt Romney supporters (63 percent) felt the system was fair to most Americans.

- There is across-the-board support for existing universal entitlement programs (e.g., Medicare, Medicaid and unemployment insurance).

- There is significantly divided support on programs for the poor. In 2012, just 40 percent of Republicans felt that government had the responsibility "to take care of those who can't take care of themselves." That's down 18 points since 2007 and 22 points since Ronald Reagan's second term. In contrast, the view of Democrats has stayed relatively constant over time at about 75 percent.

- In early December 2012, nearly three-quarters (74 percent) of Americans felt the deficit should be reduced through a combination of spending cuts and tax increases. There were "substantial partisan differences" over the nature of the cuts. Republicans were about twice as likely as Democrats to support cuts in programs that help low-income people. Republicans are divided over whether to gradually raise the age for Social Security as opposed to 67 percent of Democrats who disapprove of any age adjustment.[43]

So, in spite of a general shift in the public policy-making arena from hands-on to hands-off, the public opinion on whether to be hands-on, offer a hand-up, or be hands-off varies by party affiliation, the type of program and the group or person getting assistance. This creates a decision-making conundrum and explains why the debt reduction axe could fall most heavily on domestic programs for those most at risk.

Stokes notes this in the conclusion to his paper when he writes, "In the effort to curtail the U.S. government debt, the support provided to the average Americans who are unemployed, poor, or in need of health insurance and pensions may be further reduced. Americans oppose such cuts in social services. But they also oppose most other efforts to reduce the debt, while supporting debt reduction in principle."[44]

The public's opinion must be factored into account in the debt and deficit debate. So too must the evidence. And that evidence is inescapable. As we have documented throughout this chapter America is rapidly becoming a nation where inequality of all types is on the increase and opportunity is on the decrease—especially for those on the lower and middle rungs of the economic ladder.

There is no doubt about the need for deficit and debt reduction. But that reduction must be done in a manner that keeps all hands on board rather than throwing those with the least influence overboard. This will require trade-offs among varying interest groups and priorities.

Government should not and cannot solve all problems. But government does have a pivotal role to play in ensuring a social contract for the nation that maintains the promise of America and the American dream for all.

All options should be on the table as part of the debt and deficit negotiations. Hands-off should not be an option, however, in the social contract debate.

LABOR'S LOVE LOST

An area in which there has been a dramatic shift that contributes to the conditions of inequality is the status of and attitudes toward unions.

"Look for the union label" was one of the catch phrases for the union movement in happier times. It used to be labor unions were something that many working-class Americans loved. It now appears that labor unions are something that many working-class Americans hate.

Where did the labor movement stand at the beginning of 2013? On January 23, the U.S. Bureau of Labor Statistics (BLS) released its *Union*

Members Summary for 2012, which showed that the union membership rate for wage and salary workers was 11.3 percent among all workers, with a total of 14.4 million union workers. Private-sector unionization was a mere 6.6 percent and public-sector unionization was more than 5 times that at 35.9 percent, but had fallen from 37 percent in 2011.[45]

In its 2011 *Union Members* release the BLS observed that "In 1983, the union membership rate was 20.1 percent."[46] Thus the overall decline in the membership percentage between 1983 and 2012 was almost 44 percent. That is a substantial shrinkage in those 29 years.

A more complete and revealing picture is provided by examining comparative historic data available at Unionstats.com maintained by Barry T. Hirsch and David A. McPherson. That data goes back to 1973 and shows that in the ten years between 1973 and 1983 private-sector union membership went from 24.2 to 16.5 percent (a decline of 32 percent) and public-sector union membership went from 23.0 to 36.7 percent (an increase of nearly 60 percent).

Public-sector union membership from 1983 to 2011 hovered in the 36 to 37+ percent range. In stark contrast, private-sector union membership tumbled from the 16.5 percent of 1983 to 6.9 percent in 2011 (a decline of almost 58 percent in that time frame, and a decline of over 71 percent since 1973).[47]

These statistics are stunning but they only tell part of the story about the current status of unions in both the private and public sectors. That story is in the backstories and not in the numbers.

Undoubtedly, the highest profile union story over the past two years was the battle between Governor Scott Walker (R) of Wisconsin and its public-sector employees. The battle began when Walker introduced legislation that the Wisconsin legislature passed to significantly change the collective bargaining process and powers of the union. The union in turn led an effort to have Walker recalled.

The recall election was held on June 5, 2012, and Walker easily beat his opponent Milwaukee mayor Tom Barrett (D). Walker's dual "union-busting" victories, along with the Republican Party Platform for 2012, which endorses, as Josh Eidelson points out in his August 29 *Salon* blog, "the enactment of a National Right to Work Law," do not augur well for the future of unions—either public or private.[48]

The resolution of the dispute between Caterpillar and its striking workers at its Joliet, Illinois, plant did not augur well either. As Steven Greenhouse reported in his August 18, 2012, *New York Times* article, "The fight . . . was considered a test case in American labor relations, in part because Caterpillar was driving such a hard bargain when its business was thriving." It was a "test" that Caterpillar won and the union lost as the workers, voting against the recommendations of their leadership, ratified a deal that gave Caterpillar almost everything that it was asking for. This included a six-year wage freeze for employees hired before 2005, a pension freeze for the senior two-thirds of the workforce and a "steep increase" in the portion of the health care insurance to be paid by the workers.[49]

If there is any one thing that symbolizes the sad state of the union movement currently, it is the fact that in 2012 the AFL-CIO put its National Labor College, which according to Eugene L. Meyer in his August 1, 2012, *New York Times* article, sits on "47 prime acres ripe for development just off the Capital Beltway," up for sale. Meyer reports that the college is being sold because of the "decline in organized labor's finances as well as the college's shift to mostly online courses." He quotes Greg W. Giebel, the school's first provost, on the sale, "It's a big failure on the part of the labor movement. It certainly is not what was intended as I knew it. The dream was we were to be the West Point of the labor unions."[50] That dream is dying.

Another dream that is threatened is the respect and regard that we as Americans hold for teachers, as highlighted by Frank Bruni in his August 18, 2012, *New York Times* article titled "Teachers on the Defensive." In that article Bruni writes, "In Chicago, Philadelphia, Los Angeles and other cities, Democratic mayors have feuded bitterly with teachers' unions and at times come to see them as enemies." Bruni points out that at the United States Conference of Mayors meeting in June, the Democratic mayors joined with the Republican ones in a "unanimous endorsement of so-called parent trigger legislation," which would "abet parent takeover of underperforming schools, which may then be replaced with charter schools or private entities."[51]

There is no question that unions are under siege on all fronts and their future looks increasingly murky. There are a multitude of reasons for this as Eduardo Porter pointed out in his excellent July 18, 2012, *New York Times* article. These include an ideological shift dating back to Ronald Reagan and Margaret Thatcher that caused employers to confront rather than work with unions, globalization, technological changes in the nature of work, the movement toward a more "free agent" and part-time workforce, a loss of public trust and resentment of non-union employees toward union employees.[52]

The list could go on. Probably the overriding problem of unions has been that they have not changed with the times and their leadership has not been advocates for change. Porter makes this point continuously through his article and concludes, "Union leaders understand this—to a point. They are slowly beginning to experiment with new models of organization. Time is not on their side, however. If they fail to embrace radical change, in 80 years unions may not be around at all."

We hope Mr. Porter's most dire prediction proves incorrect. As Jared Bernstein noted in a posting right after the BLS released its 2012 union membership results, "There's no question that de-unionization is related to the decline in job quality and increase in inequality faced by many in today's workforce."[53]

America's unions played an essential role in the development of our democracy and helped create the strongest middle class in the history of the world. We believe that unions can play a role in building America's future and ensuring a vital middle class. We know, however, that hoping and believing will not make it so.

What will be required will be union leaders with the vision, tenacity and courage to make their unions relevant to the 21st century. Ed Crego's father, Ed, was chairman of the union for Commonwealth Edison Company in Illinois. When he passed away in 1982, Jim O'Connor, the chairman and chief executive of the company, came to his funeral and said to Ed Jr., "Your father gave his enemies 110 percent." The unions need that 110 percent today. They need it to make new friends and allies and to regain that loving feeling.

We understand that a transformation of the union movement and a labor renaissance will be a long time coming—and may not occur.

Those suffering the conditions of inequality have needed and still need rapid responses. This brings us to our pivot point recommendations to promote enhanced individual economic well-being for those in the lower and middle class.

PIVOT POINT RECOMMENDATION: RENEW THE AMERICAN DREAM

Each of us has a personal definition or conceptualization of the American dream. Our definition follows:

> The American dream is the opportunity each and every citizen has to realize one's personal potential and to achieve success, generally measured as economic security. The fundamental elements of that dream are getting educated and working hard in order to have a good job that pays decent wages, provides adequate benefits, puts food on the table, a roof over one's head and allows for retirement with dignity.

Given this definition, the dream is definitely at risk for far too many citizens. They are doing their part. But the country is not holding up its end of the bargain. To reverse this we need to renew the dream by promoting opportunity and equality. The key ingredients for accomplishing this are:

- Job creation
- Wage enhancement
- Asset building
- Social safety net development

Job Creation

We presented our recommendation regarding job creation in chapter 3 of this book. We emphasize and reiterate here that the program to stimulate job creation must be a shared venture between the public and private sector. The public sector should take the lead in providing financial support for major interventions such as infrastructure repair and development and the private sector should be given incentives such as targeted job tax credits to stimulate their job creation.

Wage Enhancement

Adapt President Obama's proposal of a minimum wage of $9.00/hour tied with an automatic increase tied either to the cost of living or indexed to inflation.

When President Obama made this proposal in his State of the Union address he received rebukes from both the right and the left. Those on the conservative side criticized the increase as a job killer and harmful to small business. Those on the progressive side such as Senator Tom Harkin and Ralph Nader saw the increase as insufficient and too small to be meaningful.[54]

As might be expected, there are research papers that support both sides of the argument. David Neumark of the University of California at Berkeley and William Wascher of the Federal Reserve say the wages reduce employment primarily for young and low-skilled workers.[55]

Arindrajit Dube of the University of Michigan and John Schmitt of the Center for Economic and Policy Research see little to no effect from a wage increase. Schmitt notes in his paper, "Economists have conducted hundreds of studies of the employment impact of the minimum wage. Summarizing those studies would be a daunting task, but two recent meta-studies analyzing the research conducted since the early 1990s conclude that the minimum wage has little or no discernible effect on the employment prospect of low-wage workers."[56]

As we look at the advocates and researchers on both sides, in our opinion the risk-reward ratio tilts toward doing something rather than nothing. That's because we continue in a jobless recovery with wage stagnation for those who are employed.

Moreover, research done by the National Employment Law Project in 2012 shows that the majority of the jobs that were lost were in the middle range of wages ($13.84–$21.13/hr) but the majority of the jobs that have been created since the recovery began are in lower wage jobs ($7.69—13.83/hr). Unions that in the past have been instrumental in ensuring "good" wages or increases for their members have lost both their members and bargaining power. Finally and most important for us, wages historically have been around 50 percent of GDP. They have been on a steep decline since 2001 and hit a record low of 43.5 percent in 2011.[57]

In our opinion, we need a raise in the minimum wage as one of the means to prime the consumption pump. If we do not, those at the lower end of the employment continuum will still find it harder to make ends meet and not be able to contribute to a recovery.

Asset Building

Create incentives/mechanisms for Americans to do asset building and to protect asset value.

As noted earlier in this chapter, the majority of average Americans have done little in terms of asset building. Reid Cramer, director of the Asset Building Program at the New America Foundation, working with others who specialize in this field, has developed a number of "signature proposals" that should be considered as part of a national policy package. They include the following: Make childhood savings accounts universal. Get behind auto-IRAs. Make savings easy and automated. Bank the unbanked at low to no cost.[58]

As we also noted, the typical "middle class" American has had a significant decline in net worth over the past decade. In the main, this was attributable to the loss of savings that were in the market and to reduced home valuations. The government should consider taking one-time compensatory actions such as extending the earned income tax credit (EITC) to middle income earners and providing a tax credit to homeowners who have continued to make timely payments on "underwater" mortgages.

The EITC currently covers working families with children with incomes below $36,900 to $50,300, depending on the number of children, and poor people with incomes below $13,900 ($19,200 for a married couple). EITC coverage was expanded to cover more earners by the Recovery Act of 2009. This expanded coverage was extended through 2017 under the American Taxpayer Relief Act enacted in January 2012.

We recommend expanding the Taxpayer Relief Act to the bottom one-quarter to one-third of middle-class earners for a short period of time—say two to three years. The Center for Budget and Policy Priorities reports that research indicates that the current recipients of EITC "mostly use the EITC to pay for necessities, repair vehicles that are needed to commute to work, and in some cases, obtain education or training to boost their employability and earning power."[59]

We believe these new EITC earners would do the same, thus reducing financial stress on themselves and helping to grow the economy. We believe the same would hold true for all "underwater" mortgage holders who have mortgages up to a certain amount—say $200,000—who received a one-time tax credit "write-off" that would allow them to deduct a portion of what they are paying above their current value of their home on their federal taxes.

HUD currently has programs such as the Home Affordable Modification Program, which helps homeowners who can secure refinancing to lower their monthly mortgage payments to 31 percent of their verified monthly gross; the Principal Reduction Alternative, which encourages servicers and investors to reduce the amount owed on homes that are worth significantly less than what is owed; and the Home Affordable Refinance Program, which is available to owners who are current on their mortgage and can't secure financing through traditional means.[60]

This tax credit alternative would be available to all "qualified" homeowners and would not require negotiating or refinancing with an intermediary. In our opinion, it would be far simpler to administer and much more effective as a method for middle income taxpayers to get some "return" on an asset that is overvalued.

Social Safety Net Development

Maintain existing poverty programs and develop and implement innovative methods to increase their reach and effectiveness.

There is a joke—of sorts—that goes something like "America fought a war on poverty—and poverty won." We don't believe that to be true.

The war on poverty has not been perfect—far from it. But in our opinion, it has been far more successful and much less expensive from a cost-benefit standpoint than two other wars (namely Iraq and Afghanistan) of much shorter duration.

Robert Greenstein, president of the Center on Budget and Policy Priorities, makes an excellent case for the results of our current safety net programs. He explains that when all of the programs (e.g., cash welfare, food stamps, earned income tax credit [EITC]) are looked at together, they cut the number of poor people nearly in half—by more than 40 million. Greenstein emphasizes these programs do more than reduce poverty. They ensure children who had access to food stamps in early childhood were healthier as adults. The EITC creates more work opportunities for single parents and leads to improvement in children's school performance.

Having made this case, Greenstein concludes, "So, we should move aggressively to identify, test and evaluate a variety of new approaches and to institute and spread effective initiatives, to help more children advance, and poor adults surmount barriers to success in the labor market."[61]

We concur with Mr. Greenstein. This is not a time to cut bait. It is a time to teach people to fish and to give them better nets.

The Rationale for Attacking Inequality

As we said at the opening of this chapter, we are not for attacking inequality because it is a moral imperative but because it is an economic one. Joseph Stiglitz, Nobel laureate in economics, is the person who makes this case most articulately and persuasively.

He did so at length and in detail in his powerful book *The Price of Inequality*, which was published in mid-2012.[62] He addressed our current dilemma directly in his January 20, 2013, *New York Times* article "Inequality Is Holding Back the Recovery" in which he states without any equivocation that "Economic inequality leads to political inequality and a broken decision-making process."[63]

Jerry Muller, professor of History at the Catholic University of America reinforced the serious need for addressing inequality in a significant and substantial way in his article titled "Capitalism and

Inequality" in the March/April 2013 edition of *Foreign Affairs*. Muller asserts, "For capitalism to continue to be made legitimate and palatable to populations at large, therefore—including those on the lower and middle rungs of the socioeconomic ladder, as well as those near the top, losers as well as winners—government safety nets that help diminish insecurity, alleviate the sting of failure in the marketplace, and help to maintain equality of opportunity will have to be maintained and revitalized."[64] In other words, eliminating inequality is in everyone's best interest.

Finally, we should address inequality, because of its downside and the need for better risk management. That's the argument that Anant Thaker and Elizabeth Williamson make in a paper originally written while they were enrolled in Harvard Business School titled *Unequal and Unstable: The Relationship Between Inequality and Financial Crises*.[65]

In their paper, Thaker and Williamson state that evidence suggests three primary mechanisms reinforce each other so that extended periods of increased income inequality help to cause financial crises:

- Sharp increase in debt-to-income ratios among lower- and middle-income households looking to maintain consumption levels as they fall behind in terms of income

- The creation of large pools of idle wealth, which increase the demand for investment assets, fuel financial innovations and increase the size of the financial sector

- Disproportionate political power for elite financial interests, which often yields policies that negatively affect the stability of the financial system

Case made. Case closed. That appeals to the rational and analytical side of our brains. There's another reason for reducing the conditions of inequality that comes from and appeals more to the intuitive and emotional side of our brains. And that is the inescapable need for hope as the basis for persevering when the cards seem stacked against you.

HOPE DIES LAST

Hope may not be a strategy. Nonetheless, hope is a necessary but not sufficient condition for surviving tough times and achieving great things.

Hope may not make something so. But a lack of hope makes accomplishing anything virtually impossible. Hope is the fuel of strivers and doers. If hope disappears, progress ends.

Hope is essential. It is what keeps us going against what appear to be overwhelming odds and adversity.

The late Studs Terkel, America's greatest oral historian, understood this when he named his last book *Hope Dies Last*.[66] Ed Vulliamy makes this point in his review of the book for *The Observer* in 2004 when Terkel's book came out by noting, "Hope has never trickled down, writes Terkel. It has always 'sprung up'—and he gets his title from Jessie de la Cruz, a founder member of the farmers union, who insisted, 'If you lose hope, you lose everything.'"[67]

America is a nation founded on hope. Think about the ragtag bunch of patriots who decided to take on a seemingly unbeatable British Army in red coats with only their wits, wills and muskets. It was this singular act of hope that allowed the Founding Fathers to proclaim in our Declaration of Independence, "We hold these truths to be self-evident, that all men are endowed by their Creator with certain inalienable Rights, that among these are Life, Liberty and the pursuit of Happiness."

America is the land of hope. Think about the millions of immigrants who have been drawn to our shores because of the country's pledge and the promise made to them by the inscription on the Statue of Liberty, "Give me your tired, your poor, Your huddled masses, yearning to breathe free, The wretched refuse of your teeming shore, Send these, the homeless, tempest tossed to me, I lift my lamp beside the golden door."

America is in the business of hope. Think about the millions of entrepreneurs who started and succeeded in their own enterprises. We are among them and we know this could only have been possible in a country such as ours.

America is dedicated to perfecting hope. Think about the civil rights movement: Rosa Parks not giving up her seat on that bus, those kids who integrated that high school in Little Rock, Arkansas, and the demonstrators like Congressman John Lewis who marched and were assaulted in Selma, Alabama.

America is committed to innovating hope. Think about the polio vaccine, putting a man on the moon, the internet, the vaccines for the AID's virus and communications satellites.

America is the world's best hope. Think about World Wars I and II, Ronald Reagan saying "Tear down that wall," the government's countless humanitarian initiatives, the endless generosity of the American people in response to natural disasters and George W. Bush's AIDS assistance to the African nations.

To sum it up, we have just described elements of the American dream. Hope is the stuff of that dream and realizable aspirations. Hope is central to the concept that makes America exceptional but does not completely define the essence of American exceptionalism.

We understand that hope is not a strategy—as Rick Page advised us in his 2004 marketing and sales best seller with that title. As businesspeople, we know that you need a plan and proper execution for success. But as businesspeople, we also know that you need passion and persistence because there is no guarantee of an initial or easy victory. One only need look at Steve Jobs' track record to recognize that.

Here is the simple truth: a strategy by itself is just about as meaningless—we think even more so—as hope. While they don't teach hope in business school, perhaps they should. That's because hope is the emotional glue that holds us together both individually and collectively during stressful periods.

Even though the American economy is recovering—albeit slowly—these are still stressful and trying times. We need to move from that begrudging process of recovery to renewal in the belief in America and the American dream.

How important is hope to that renewal? Here's what Ronald Reagan had to say, "I do not believe in a fate that will fall on us no matter what we do. I believe in a fate that will fall on us if we do nothing. So, with all the creative energy at our command let us begin an era of national renewal. Let us renew our determination, our courage, and our strength. And let us renew our faith and our hope."[68]

We have spent the past few years impaled in partisan political conflict aimed at blocking problem solving, collaboration and compromise. This conflict has increased citizen cynicism and skepticism and reduced hope.

Now, more than ever, we need to emphasize rather than ignore hope. We say that as lifelong Cubs fans who know that hope springs eternal. We also know unequivocally that hope dies last. Strategies die first.

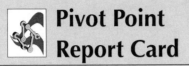 **Pivot Point Report Card**

Instructions

This report card is provided to allow you to reflect upon and assess the progress in this pivot point area. To use the report card:

1. Review the recommendations for the area.

2. Evaluate the progress made in the area to date and assign a letter grade using the system that follows: A–excellent progress. B–substantial progress. C–some progress. D–little progress. F–no progress.

3. Describe the nature of the progress and the rationale for your rating.

We will be posting our assessment for this area on an occasional basis. To see that assessment and to provide your input and feedback on the area, visit *http://www.workingthepivotpoints.com*.

Recommendations

- Renew the American Dream
  - Job creation
  - Wage enhancement
  - Asset building
  - Social safety net development

Grade

Reason

7 | Global Competition: Up Against the BRIC Wall

THE FIRST CHAPTER OF *RENEWING THE AMERICAN DREAM*, TITLED "Competitive Advantage for the Twenty-First Century," begins as follows:

> The United States has stood alone atop the world stage for nearly a quarter of a century. It has enjoyed a competitive advantage on almost all fronts. Now as we stare into the second decade of the twenty-first century, America's primacy is challenged. Whether on the playing field or the battlefields, in the board room or in the anterooms, nothing seems the same anymore.

And indeed it wasn't. As we came out of the Great Recession, the United States was confronted by a new set of emerging competitors: Brazil, Russia, India and China—a BRIC wall if you will. For most of 2009 and 2010, all these countries seemed to be outperforming us substantially in economic development terms. Then, in 2011 and 2012, the BRIC wall hit a wall of its own.

COMPETITIVENESS ASSESSMENT

Let's take stock and determine how things stand now. Where exactly is the United States in the race today? To determine that it is useful to do a competitiveness assessment on the United States as a nation and each of the countries in the BRIC wall.

The World Economic Forum (Forum or WEF) produces an annual report on global competiveness. We draw on the Forum's *Global Competitiveness Report: 2012–2013** to conduct the assessment—first at a top line level and then drill down for a country by country analysis of strengths and weaknesses.[1]

In its most recent report, the WEF evaluates 144 economies on a Global Competitiveness Index. The Index has three subindexes that contain "twelve pillars of competitiveness" as indicated in the following table.

Basic Requirements Subindex	Efficiency Enhancer Subindex	Innovation and Sophistication Factors Subindex
Pillar 1: Institutions Pillar 2: Infrastructure Pillar 3: Macroeconomic Environment Pillar 4: Health and Primary Education	Pillar 5: Higher Education and Training Pillar 6: Goods Market Efficiency Pillar 7: Labor Market Efficiency Pillar 8: Financial Market Development Pillar 9: Technological Readiness Pillar 10: Market Size	Pillar 11: Business Sophistication Pillar 12: Innovation

The Forum ranks each of the economies from 1 to 144 overall, on each of the subindexes, on each of the pillars, and on each of the individual components that are used to construct the pillars. For purposes of this competitiveness assessment, we examine the overall ranking and the rankings on the subindexes and pillars comprising them.[2]

---

*The survey covers 2011—the most currently available data. The new survey for 2013–2014 will be available in September 2013. We will update this assessment at our pivot points website based upon those results.

Overall Competitiveness Assessment[3]
Overall, the United States and the BRIC wall countries rank as follows:

Country	Rank
United States	7
China	29
Brazil	48
India	59
Russia	67

All of the six top-ranking economies in this year's report are much smaller than the United States. They are Switzerland, Singapore, Finland, Sweden, Netherlands and Germany.

Basic Requirements Subindex Competitiveness Assessment[4]
This subindex has four pillars: Institutions, Infrastructure, Macroeconomic Environment, and Health and Primary Education. The rankings on the index follow.

Country	Rank
China	31
United States	33
Russia	50
Brazil	73
India	85

This is the only subindex on which the United States does not rank first. That is primarily due to the fact that China receives a very high ranking of 11 on the Macroeconomic Environment pillar compared to the U.S. ranking of 111. In contrast, the United States scores 14 on Infrastructure compared to China's 47.

Efficiency Enhancers Subindex Competitiveness Assessment[5]
This subindex has five pillars: Higher Education and Training, Goods Market Efficiency, Labor Market Efficiency, Financial Market

Development, Technological Readiness and Market Size. The rankings on the index follow.

Country	Rank
United States	2
China	30
Brazil	38
India	39
Russia	54

The United States has a clear advantage on this index. It ranks 1 on the Market Size pillar and no lower than 23 on any pillar (Goods Market Efficiency). All of the BRIC countries rank in the top ten on the Market Size pillar. But with the exception of India, which scores 21 on the Financial Market Development pillar, none of them scores below 40 on any of the other pillars and most of the rankings for all of them are 50 or higher.

Innovation and Sophistication Factors Subindex Competitiveness Assessment[6]

This subindex has two pillars: Business Sophistication and Innovation.

Country	Rank
United States	7
China	34
Brazil	39
India	43
Russia	108

Again, the United States enjoys a clear edge on this index. It scores 6 on Innovation and 10 on Business Sophistication. The highest ranked BRIC countries are Brazil ranking 33 for Business Sophistication and China ranking 33 for Innovation. Russia nearly falls off the chart with a rank of 119 on Business Sophistication.

STRENGTHS AND WEAKNESSES ANALYSIS

In summary, the United States has a fairly substantial comparative advantage against the BRIC nations on most of the pillars of competitiveness. The question now becomes what are the relative strengths and weaknesses of these countries and the United States revealed by the 2012–2013 survey, which covered the year ending in 2011. We look at that next.

Brazil Strengths and Weaknesses[7]

Brazil had a population of almost 200 million people with a GDP per capita (US$) of $12,789 and a 2.91 percent share of the world's total GDP. Brazil entered the top 50 for the first time in the WEF's rankings, moving up five positions to 48.

Brazil's strengths cited in the Global Competitiveness Report include its large internal market, fairly sophisticated business community, access to financing and improvements in macroeconomic conditions. Its weaknesses or challenges include trust in politicians, government efficiency and excessive government regulation (144 ranking out of 144).

Significantly, entrepreneurship and procedures and time to start a business "remain among the highest in the sample" (130 and 139, respectively). Taxation was ranked 144 out of 144 and perceived to be "too high and have distortionary effects."

Russia Strengths and Weaknesses[8]

Russia had a population of about 150 million with a GDP per capita of $12,993 and a 3.02 percent share of the world's GDP. It dropped one position in this year's survey from 68 to 67.

Russia's strengths cited in the report include large domestic market, fairly good infrastructure, high level of educational enrollment and a "sharp improvement" in the macroeconomic environment, up from 44 to 22 because of low government debt and a budget that has moved into surplus.

Its weaknesses were numerous, with Russia ranking above 100 and in the 120s and 130s on a number of items including public institutions, inefficiencies in goods, financial markets, trust in the financial system, inefficient anti-monopoly policies, lack of business sophistication and low rates of technological adoption.

India Strengths and Weaknesses[9]

India had a population of more than 1,250 billion with a GDP per capita of $1,676.1 and a 5.65 share of the world's GDP. India ranked 59 in this year's survey—this is a drop of three places from the previous survey. India has lost ten places from its peak at 49 in 2009.

The report cited no specific strengths for India because of its diminished status and reducing rankings on many of the competitiveness pillars and their components. It did state that inflation "returned to single digit territory" and that India has been "slowly improving" its infrastructure since 2006.

A number of weaknesses were cited, including insufficient energy and transport infrastructure, health and basic education (101 ranking); and public trust in politicians (106). The macroeconomic environment rank is 99 due to large and repeated public deficits, and India has the highest debt to GDP ratio among the BRICs.

China Strengths and Weaknesses[10]

China had a population of almost 1,370 billion with a GDP per capita of $5,414 and a 14.32 share of the world's GDP. It lost three places to fall to 29 in this year's ranking.

China still has significant strengths, including its "very favorable" macroeconomic situation (11), moderate budget deficit, high gross savings rate of individuals, and "relatively high marks" in health and basic education and enrollment in higher education.

The weaknesses that caused China's overall ranking to decline included deterioration on the following measures: financial market development (54, down 6), technological readiness (88, down 11) and market efficiency (59, down 14). The WEF expressed a special concern on "insufficient domestic and foreign competition as the various barriers to entry seem more prevalent."

United States Strengths and Weaknesses[11]

The United States had a population of over 325 million with a GDP per capita of $48,387 and a 19.3 percent share of the world's GDP. It continued its decline from number 1 a few years ago, falling two more spots this year to 7 from 5 in the past year.

The strengths cited for the United States were considerable, including sophisticated and innovative companies, excellent university system, flexible labor markets and the "sheer size" of the domestic economy. According to the survey, "these qualities continue to make the United States very competitive. In addition, the U.S. showed substantial improvement on the 'financial market development' pillar improving from 31 two years ago to 16 this year."

United States' weaknesses cited "which have deepened since past assessments" included business community critical of public and private institutions (41), trust in politicians (54) and government spending (76). The greatest weakness continued to be on macroeconomic stability (down to 111 from 90 last year).

COMPETITIVENESS SUSTAINABILITY: CHINKS IN THE BRIC WALL

As with the top line assessment, the comparative strengths and weaknesses analysis shows the United States in a very strong position vis-à-vis the BRIC wall countries.

For a variety of reasons, China still appears to be the major contender over the long run and Brazil is an up and comer. India is falling back into the pack. And, given its extremely poor ratings on the Efficiency and Innovation and Sophistication subindexes and many of their components, it is questionable why Russia was ever in the mix at all. That might be because, as Ruchir Sharma, head of Emerging Markets and Global Macro at Morgan Stanley, puts it, "Although deeply out of balance, Russia remains a member of the BRICs, if only because the term sounds better with an *R*."

Recognizing that nothing is forever, however, what does the competitive future hold for the BRICs? Sharma and the World Economic Forum do not paint a bright picture for them in general.

In his article for the November/December 2012 issue of *Foreign Affairs*, Sharma observes that "since 2009, Chinese growth is slowing sharply down from double digits to seven percent or even less . . . Brazil's annual growth has dropped from 4.5 percent to two percent, Russia's from seven percent to 3.5 percent, and India's from nine percent to six percent."

Sharma sees this slowdown as the natural order of things. He comments, that since 1950, for a given decade, one-third of the emerging economies have been able to grow at an annual rate of 5 percent or more; one-fourth for two decades, one-tenth for three decades; and only Malaysia, Singapore, South Korea, Taiwan, Thailand and Hong Kong for four decades. Based upon his analysis of this and other data, Sharma concludes, "The last decade was unusual in terms of the wide scope and rapid pace of global growth, and anyone who counts on that happy situation returning soon is likely to be disappointed."[12]

Looking forward rather than backward and inward rather than outward for their insights, the WEF has developed two other pillars that they claim will determine competitiveness over time: the Environmental Sustainability and Social Sustainability pillars.[13]

The indicators looked at in the Environmental Sustainability pillar follow.

Environmental Policy	Use of Renewable Resources	Degradation of the Environment
Environmental regulations (stringency and enforcement)	Agricultural water intensity	Level of particulate matter concentration
Number of ratified international treaties	Forest depletion (change in forest cover and forest loss)	CO^2 intensity
Terrestrial biome protection	Fish stocks' overexploitation	Quality of the natural environment

The indicators looked at in the Social Sustainability pillar follow.

Access to Basic Necessities	Vulnerability to Shocks	Social Cohesion
Access to sanitation	Vulnerable employment	Income Gini index
Access to improved drinking water	Extent of informal economy	Social mobility
Access to health care	Social safety net protection	Youth unemployment

The WEF assessed a country's performance on these two pillars and used them to adjust the scores on its Global Competitiveness Index (GCI) to establish a "sustainability adjusted GCI score." Brazil's scores stayed essentially the same. Russia, China and India's scores went down substantially to "reveal significant weaknesses in both dimensions of sustainable competitiveness."

Selected comments made on the BRICs' adjusted ratings by the WEF were:

- *Brazil:* Performs slightly better in overall environmental-adjusted sustainability than in social-adjusted GCI sustainability . . . the country's very high inequality remains an area of concern.

- *Russia*: Does particularly poorly in terms of environmental sustainability, with some of the poorest ratings globally for three indicators.

- *India:* Worst performer among the BRICs, with concerns in both areas of sustainability.

- *China*: Competitiveness performance is notably weakened once the sustainability measures are taken into account, especially in terms of environmental sustainability.

In case you were wondering, the United States' adjusted scores stayed basically the same. The report observed that the United States "shows middling results in both social and environmental sustainability." The social score was affected slightly by "increasing inequality and youth unemployment." But the WEF stated, "It is the score in environmental sustainability . . . that is a concern for the country's sustained prosperity."[14]

So there you have it, all in all not a bad—in fact, a very good—competitiveness report card for the United States. It is impossible to predict what grades the United States and the BRIC countries will receive on the Global Competitiveness Report that will come out in September of this year. Given the massive Brazilian protests that began in June 2013 and the dramatically changing economic dynamics of China and its national "business model" in terms of the balance between exports and imports, it is difficult to imagine these two current front-runners of the BRIC contingent scoring much better. Likewise,

India and Russia appear to have accomplished little to enhance their status and rankings.

THE CONTEXT FOR COMPETITION: IS GLOBALIZATION DEAD?

Before we proceed, there is one more area that we would like to examine before reaching our conclusions and making our pivot point recommendation.

That is what is going on in the economy and the competitive arena worldwide in 2013. The times they are a changing—just as they have been since the Great Recession began and will continue to do so through the remainder of this decade.

Here's a quick take on where things and the United States stand right now. The world remains in the economic doldrums and it looks like it will stay that way for quite a while.

In September 2012, the World Trade Organization (WTO) downgraded its forecast for world trade expansion to 2.5 from 3.7 percent, and also scaled back its forecast for 2013 to 4.5 from 5.6 percent.[15] In April 2013, the WTO cut its forecast for 2013 back even further to 3.3 percent. The United Nations Conference on Trade and Development (UNCTD) also painted a bleak picture in its Trade and Development Report 2012.

UNCTD saw problems on two fronts. It observed that some of the larger developing countries that had helped "stoke recovery in the world economy" after the economic meltdown of 2008 were "losing momentum. But it cited "the inability of the developed countries to return to a normal growth pattern" as the "immediate problem" that was threatening the global economy.[16]

Based upon his analysis, David Smick, founder and editor of the *International Economy* magazine, attributes this to the "cracking up" of the globalization model that has driven growth and expansion for 30 years. Smick sees this as dangerous because globalization has driven growth both worldwide and in the United States during this period. He realizes there have been "flaws" in globalization, but in general "it has been a wealth-creating machine."[17]

Robert Samuelson, columnist for the *Washington Post*, has also described the "slowing" and "declining" of globalization. He did not see this as a necessarily bad thing either for the world or the United States, however.

In terms of the world, Samuleson cited economist Fred Bergsten of the Peterson Institute, saying that this trend will make the world economy more balanced and should also constrain the erratic capital flows that have triggered past financial crisis thus promoting stability.

In terms of the United States, Samuelson declares, "To Americans, some aspects of deglobalization will seem delicious. That's because of factors like the manufacturing revival here and a recalibrating of the country's export-import equation."[18]

There is no question that the world economy is fragile and the American recovery remains sluggish. There are a number of green shoots for the United States. These include the manufacturing momentum, the apparent oil and gas boom and the continued strong performance of the financial markets. At the macro and corporate level, there are many reasons for cautious optimism.

Or maybe not even that cautious. In March 2013, the Business Roundtable announced that the chief executives of the largest U.S. companies were much more optimistic about sales than they were three months earlier. Seventy-two percent of its members expected sales to increase over the next six months compared to 58 percent at the end of the year. In spite of this, the executives were recalcitrant about hiring. Twenty-nine percent said they were going to increase hiring. That's the same percentage as in the past two Roundtable surveys.[19]

AMERICAN COMPETITIVENESS: GOOD TO GREAT

The evidence is clear. What we wrote near the beginning of the first chapter of *Renewing* still applies:

> The United States has been, and still is a champion. To stay a champion and to renew the American dream, however, we need to win the race for competitive advantage. The race will not go to the swiftest, but to the one who understands the critical requirements for success going forward, prepares properly, and perseveres.

The United States is uniquely positioned, to borrow a phrase of Jim Collins, to go from good to great. That will require doing the right type of in-depth assessment and developing the right plan to win the competitiveness race. Fortunately, a lot of good work has already been done in this regard. We highlight some of it here.

In early 2011, President Obama established the President's Council on Jobs and Competitiveness headed by Jeffrey Immelt, chairman of GE. The Council was created to provide nonpartisan advice on how to strengthen the economy and ensure the competitiveness of the United States and on ways to create jobs, opportunity and prosperity for the American people.[20]

In November 2012, the Council on Competitiveness, a group of corporate CEOs, university presidents and labor leaders, put out a paper called *A Clarion Call for Competitiveness*. The paper identified American strengths ("silver linings") and weaknesses ("dark clouds") and provided recommendations to "drive U.S. productivity, leadership in world markets, and raise the standard of living for all Americans."

The immediate recommendations were ensure lower cost, provide easy access to high-quality education and training, maintain federal investments in science and technology, and reform and simplify the tax code. Recommendations to achieve over the next ten years were create at least 21 million jobs, reduce unemployment to 5 percent, reduce government debt by $4 trillion, invest $2.2 trillion in infrastructure and double export.[21]

Michael Porter and Jan Rivkin, the co-leaders of the Harvard Business School's United States Competitiveness Project published an article in *The Economist* right after the election that presented the following eight recommendations for federal policy to be implemented in the next two to three years that would "restore American vitality" in key areas:

1. Ease the immigration of highly skilled individuals.

2. Simplify the corporate tax code.

3. Tax overseas profits only where they are earned.

4. Address trade distortions.

5. Simplify regulation.

6. Enact a multi-year program to improve infrastructure.

7. Agree on a framework for developing shale gas and oil.

8. Create a sustainable federal budget.[22]

These recommendations were based upon the results of a survey of "some 10,000" Harvard Business School alumni. Porter and Rivkin classified the survey responses into the four categories in the following table.

Weakness but Improving	Strength and Improving
	• Universities • Entrepreneurship • Firm management • Property rights • Clusters • Capital markets • Innovation
Weakness and Deteriorating	**Strength but Deteriorating**
• Tax code • Legal framework • Macro policy • K-12 education system • Political system	• Logistics infrastructure • Skilled labor • Communications infrastructure • Flexibility in hiring and firing

Porter and Rivkin comment that their eight priorities "are not all that America must do to restore its competitiveness (e.g., tackling K-12 education and health will take longer than three years)."

The recommendations, strengths and weaknesses cited here are not exhaustive and because of their sources they are not necessarily representative. They do, however, provide a starting point for initiating the type of thinking and planning that will be required for achieving competitive advantage in the future. This is where our pivot point recommendation comes in.

PIVOT POINT RECOMMENDATION: GLOBAL COMPETITIVENESS COMMISSION

We should establish a National Global Competitiveness Commission to develop a Competitive Advantage Plan for the United States. The Commission should be a commission similar to the 9/11 commission in its bipartisan nature and the unfettered scope of its reach but different than the Commission in its composition.

The group should be nonpartisan, not bipartisan. Its members should be drawn from national leaders with expertise and experience in business, politics, government, civic and community service, and academia. It should be led by representatives from the business, civic/community and governmental sectors. While the Commission should include a few former elected officials, they should be a minority of the membership.

The charge to the Commission should be to conduct a thorough and in-depth SWOT analysis and strategic assessment of the United States' current position, and to develop a comprehensive competitive advantage strategic plan for the United States. At a minimum, that plan should clearly spell out a vision, goals, strategies, strategic action programs, implementation requirements, facilitating factors, potential obstacles or barriers and critical success factors. The plan should also present a budget and cost-benefit analysis for its implementation.

Sufficient time should be spent to do the right planning, meaning 18–24 months. The Commission should present its plan to various stakeholder groups such as the government, U.S. Chamber of Commerce and the National Association of Manufacturers for review and comment. The final plan should be provided to the President and U.S. Congress for consideration and action.

The Commission should be paid for by a mix of public and private funds. It should also solicit volunteer-contributed time to assist in the research and analysis from organizations such as businesses, consulting firms and civic organizations.

As we noted earlier, the Commission will not have to start from scratch. The Competitiveness Council and Harvard's Competitiveness Project has done excellent work and analyses that can be used as a starting point. Other groups of all stripes and persuasions, such as the Heritage Foundation, Cato Institute, the New America Foundation, Center for American Progress, Brookings Institution and the Third Way have also done excellent work. This full body of knowledge should be reviewed and considered as input by the Commission in the analysis phase of its planning.

We need a holistic plan that positions the United States and its citizens for success going forward. In this regard, let us borrow the competitiveness definition provided by Professors Porter and Rivkin who say, "The United States is competitive to the degree that companies can compete successfully in the global economy while raising living standards for the average American. Companies must be able to compete, but employees have to prosper as well. One without the other is not true competitiveness and is unsustainable."[23]

We would add to the professors' definition by saying that it is not only the living standards but the number of jobs created as well that matters for competitiveness of the nation. As we have seen over the past few years, corporations have been prospering but wages have been stagnant and company growth has been jobless. This issue must be addressed as part of the nation's competitive advantage plan.

We currently have a rising tide that is raising many boats. The problem is that there are fewer and fewer people in those boats.

WE'VE ONLY JUST BEGUN

In conclusion, based upon our research and analysis, we end this chapter with a strong sense of optimism regarding American competitiveness and the future. That optimism is borne out by a special report in *The Economist* titled "An America That Works" that came out the week of March 18, 2013.[24]

This issue painted a very positive picture of the current economic circumstances of the United States. It reinforced the perspective in *The Economist*'s May 12, 2012, article, "Declinism resurgent" (subtitled: "The election campaign encourages America to feel worse about itself than it needs to"). That article observed that "America is prone to bouts of 'declinism' and asserts there are "grounds for optimism," which include a young workforce, skilled workers and the best universities in the world.[25]

We agree with *The Economist*'s take on this. In spite of legitimate concerns about where the country stands now, we are unequivocal in the opinion that it is still the best country standing. There are undeniable opportunities for improvement (e.g., continuing high un- and underemployment, wage stagnation and increasing income inequality), but the nation is rebuilding from a position of strength rather than one of weakness. There are substantial "grounds for optimism" in the short, medium and long term.[26]

The United States is doing very to extremely well in recovering from the economic crisis in comparison to the majority of the Eurozone and mature economies. Although somewhat constrained, the flow of innovation and entrepreneurial initiatives remains unparalleled worldwide. And the administration and the private sector have put these areas front and center for the next four years.

In the future, as the superheated growth of the emerging economies of India, China and Brazil continue to slow and their inevitable "growing pains" play out, the United States will become an even greater safe haven for investment. Over the next 30 years, as the multinationals achieve targeted market penetration and the wage differentials between presently developed nations and the developing nations shrink, the primary drivers for the spate of "offshoring" of American jobs will disappear.

Within that same time frame, the demographics that currently favor the Chinese over the United States will begin to switch. The United States will grow at a reasonable and attractive rate to support future economic growth and business development stateside. In contrast, because of the "one child" policy that China adopted in the late 1970s, China's population will decline precipitously and put a serious strain on its economy.

Finally, the *virtually* unrivaled natural resources of the United States—vast expanse of habitable land, tillable soil, large bodies of fresh water, oil and natural gas—and the absolutely *unrivaled* diversity of the country's human resources base will become the sources of America's future competitive advantage. Our ability to harness the country's natural and human resources helped make America what it is today and should enable us to prosper tomorrow.

There is no guarantee of a return on these "grounds for optimism," however. We are at a crucial pivot point.

What we do over the next decade will determine the future nature of America and the next "American era." Given this context, we are firmly convinced that this next era can be comparable to or better than the past one, if we are able to focus on:

- Renewal of the American spirit and dream and not just macroeconomic recovery

- Rebuilding all forms of capital (e.g., institutional, political and human), not just addressing financial capital and the debt and deficit concerns

- Unifying citizens and communities rather than dividing them into warring camps and pitting them against one another

One American era has ended. Will we have another? Yes, we can. Yes, we will. That's not a political slogan. It's a statement of faith in America. It is a conviction borne out of review of its current capacity and potential in both the domestic and international arenas. It is a reflection on the enduring tenacity, resilience and common sense of the American people. It leads to the conclusion that we've only just begun.

Pivot Point
Report Card

Instructions

This report card is provided to allow you to reflect upon and assess the progress in this pivot point area. To use the report card:

1. Review the recommendation for the area.

2. Evaluate the progress made in the area to date and assign a letter grade using the system that follows: A–excellent progress. B–substantial progress. C–some progress. D–little progress. F–no progress.

3. Describe the nature of the progress and the rationale for your rating.

We will be posting our assessment for this area on an occasional basis. To see that assessment and to provide your input and feedback on the area, visit *http://www.workingthepivotpoints.com*.

Recommendation

- Global Competitiveness Commission

Grade

Reason

8 | Manufacturing: Slip, Sliding, Away?

FOR MORE THAN TWO DECADES THE UNITED STATES HAS EXCELLED at creating low-value jobs that contribute little to building a sustainable economy and competitive advantage for the nation and its citizens. The country has been majoring in the minors.

A primary way that the United States can reverse this trend is to place a renewed emphasis on manufacturing and to make it central to the American economic agenda. The critical importance of manufacturing to the future of the United States cannot be overstated.

The recognition of this need is growing. President Obama placed a strong focus on manufacturing in his 2013 State of the Union address by proclaiming "Our first priority is making America a magnet for new jobs and manufacturing."[1] He reinforced this message in subsequent public meetings. Others have been "beating the manufacturing" drum for some time.

There is an emerging consensus that America cannot be America without a vital and vibrant manufacturing sector. In this chapter we discuss why, where we stand now and what needs to be done to revitalize American manufacturing.

As we will demonstrate, there has been no shortage of good ideas over the past two years. The problem has been that the 112th Congress was the place where good ideas went to die—especially as policy making went into suspended animation during the national election year.

We now have a new Congress and the chance to breathe life into those ideas, bring forward new ones and to begin constructive policy making again. It is time—past time—to start passing legislation and implementing a manufacturing agenda that will be transformative for the nation and its citizens.

THE MANUFACTURING IMPERATIVE

Once upon a time, America was the world's factory. That time will never come again. But recent results and research indicate that factories and products will and must play a pivotal role in manufacturing America's future.

Even with its relative decline as a contributor to GDP as an employer of American workers, the manufacturing sector remains a powerful force. Bruce Stokes notes in a posting published by the New America Foundation:

- The United States is the world's mightiest manufacturing economy, producing 21 percent of all goods made globally versus Japan's 13 percent and China's 12 percent.

- Manufacturing still employs more than 11 million jobs in the United States.

- For every dollar U.S. manufacturers spend directly, they foster another $1.40 in economic activity.

- Manufacturing workers have higher pay and more generous benefits—about 20 percent higher—than those in nonmanufacturing jobs.

- Manufacturing jobs have a direct linkage to high-level service jobs (as many as five per job) and create five to ten indirect jobs for each direct manufacturing job.[2]

Manufacturing fuels innovation.[3] It accounts for approximately 70 percent of all private-sector R&D spending. It drives exporting and productivity increases.

American manufacturing is clearly on the rebound. Between January 2010 and July 2012, manufacturing added approximately 500,000 jobs, the fastest growth in the sector since 1995.[4] In the "Made in the USA" cover article for the April 22, 2013, issue of *Time*, Rana Foroohar and Bill Saparito document the extent of the manufacturing recovery and attribute to it a number of factors including increasing costs abroad, companies getting low-cost energy, more productive local labor and cost-saving automation technology.[5]

Moreover, as Charles Fishman highlighted in his December 2012 *Atlantic* article titled "The Insourcing Boom," industry is also returning to the United States at an accelerating rate.[6] Companies such as General Electric, Whirlpool and Otis Elevator are bringing the manufacturing of many of their products back to the United States. Apple is soon to start making Macs in America again. In addition, manufacturers such as BMW and Volkswagen have opened new facilities stateside.

The Economist also featured American "reshoring" of manufacturing in a special report on outsourcing and offshoring in its January 19–25, 2013, edition. According to that report:

- An April 2012 Boston Consulting Group survey disclosed that 37 percent of those firms with annual sales above $1 billion are "actively considering" moving production facilities from China to America.

- A Massachusetts Institute of Technology study of 108 multinational firms found that 14 percent had "firm plans to bring some manufacturing back to America."

- And the Hacker Group, a Florida-based consulting firm that counsels firms on offshoring and outsourcing, projected that the "outflow of manufacturing will slow over the next two years" and "reshoring will double over the previous two years."[7]

THE STATE OF MANUFACTURING

It appears that the reports of the "death of American manufacturing" were definitely premature. In fact, for most of the 42 months of consecutive economic recovery after the Great Recession, the manufacturing sector was doing quite well.

Then in December 2012, the Institute for Supply Management (ISM) announced that in November the sector contracted to 49.5 percent on the Purchasing Managers Index (PMI) [50 percent is indicative of growth]. The 49.5 percent was a decline of 2.2 percent from the October PMI score and the lowest level since July 2009. In addition, the sector had experienced only "modest expansion" in the two months before the November reading.

This contraction was not a good sign for either the sector or the United States in general. Immediately thereafter, however, things started to look up again. The PMI registered 50.2 for December 2012, 53.1 for January 2013, and 54.2 for February—the fastest pace of expansion since June 2011.[8]

More importantly, ISM's December 2012 semiannual survey of the nation's purchasing and supply management executives showed they were bullish on the manufacturing sector for 2013. Revenue was expected to increase by 4.6 percent and capital expenditures by 7.6 percent.

Capacity utilization was down at year's end, standing at 77.5 percent compared to 81.6 percent in April 2012. Nevertheless, ISM reported the manufacturing survey respondents were "optimistic about their overall business prospects for the first half of 2013, and even more optimistic about the second half of 2013."[9]

In spite of that optimism, the performance of the manufacturing sector through the first half of 2013 was a checkered one. The ISM's reading of factory activity in May was 49.0—the lowest in four years. The reading went up to 50.9 for June.[10]

Even with these fits and starts and a few hiccups, manufacturing is definitely recovering. The industry and individual companies are prospering. Multinational corporations such as Eaton, Caterpillar, General Electric and Honeywell have consistently reported solid profits and performance increases. That's the bright side.

Unfortunately, there is a dark side to the manufacturing rebound. That's the fact that manufacturing business success in general has not begun to turn into significant job creation or economic stimulus here in the United States. Foroohar and Saparito make this point in their *Time* magazine article.[11]

The ISM reported that manufacturing employment fell to 48.7 in June 2013 and it was projected that the July jobs report would show that factories had cut jobs for the fourth straight month.[12]

The tide has begun to turn but there is no tidal wave yet. Here are some distressing numbers:

- According to the Bureau of Labor Statistics (BLS), the nation lost more than 30 percent of its manufacturing jobs from 2000 through 2010, going from employment of 17.3 million to 11.7 million.

- Manufacturing employment fell precipitously by over 2 million jobs in the two-year period from the time the recession began in December 2007 through December 2009.

- The manufacturing sector did add 500,000+ jobs from January 2011 to July 2012. But that represented less than 10 percent of the jobs lost between 1999 and 2009.

- The ISM survey projected employment in the manufacturing sector to grow by less than 1 percent in 2013.

- The BLS projects that manufacturing employment between 2010 and 2020 will be essentially flat with 11.5 million jobs in 2010 and 11.4 million in 2020.[13]

There are a variety of reasons why the manufacturing recovery has been a less job-generating one than might have been expected, and the future forecast is not optimistic. Some of the causes are structural and can be attributed to productivity improvements, technological changes and the nature of employment in advanced nations. Others can be traced to globalization, the potential—albeit a diminishing one—to reduce labor costs by moving jobs offshore, and the growing importance of and investment in other economies. Those factors in combination continue to tilt the balance somewhat for large global firms away from creating jobs in the United States to creating them elsewhere.

In addition, small to mid-sized manufacturing businesses continue to have difficulty in getting adequate access to capital to expand or hire new employees. Small business job creation overall plummeted by 23 percent from 2007 to 2011.

In a 2011 report, the McKinsey Global Institute projects that even in a high-job-growth scenario unemployment will not return to normal at approximately 5 percent until 2018. McKinsey states that "slowing the rate of manufacturing job losses since 2000 will also be critical in the high-job-growth scenario."

It should be stressed that there is no guarantee of achieving the McKinsey "high-job-growth" scenario. McKinsey's low-job-growth scenario projects unemployment remaining high with significant further contraction in manufacturing employment through 2020.[14]

We need to avoid McKinsey's low-job-growth scenarios and the further erosion of the nation's manufacturing employment base. This will not be an easy task.

THE STATE OF MANUFACTURING LEGISLATION

The truth is that while progress is being made and momentum is accelerating, we are still a long way from a full-blown renewal of American manufacturing and making America "a magnet for new jobs and manufacturing." Accomplishing that will require legislation and policy that is strategic, comprehensive, coordinated, practical and results-producing in the short, medium and long term.

The president's proposal to build a National Network for Manufacturing Innovation (NNMI), which he first unveiled in March 2012 and emphasized in his 2013 State of the Union address, signifies the intense focus being placed to ensure that manufacturing retains its preeminent role here and must be a central part of that framework.[15] Senator Sherrod Brown (D-OH) is taking the lead in creating the legislation for a network, which would be comprised of 15 regional manufacturing innovation institutes across the country based upon the pilot test institute in Youngstown, Ohio.[16]

In addition, looking back just a little, while there was no single piece of legislation in the 111th or 112th Congress that satisfied all of these criteria, Congress did introduce—and in some cases passed—legislation that began to address most of them.

Some of the more significant bills related to:

- A National Manufacturing Strategy
- The "Make It in America Agenda"
- A National Infrastructure Bank

National Manufacturing Strategy[17]

In April 2011, Senators Mark Kirk (R-IL) and Sherrod Brown (D-OH) and Congressman Dan Lipinski (D-IL) introduced bipartisan bills in the Senate and House to develop a National Manufacturing Strategy Act. These bills were patterned after Representative Lipinski's 2010 National Manufacturing Strategy Act, which passed the House by a margin of 379–38.

In a joint announcement, Senator Brown and Representative Lipinski stated the bills required the development of a manufacturing strategy in order to boost traditional and high-tech manufacturing, spur American job growth, and strengthen the middle class. Key elements of the House bill included requiring the president to establish a national manufacturing strategy board. Then, every four years, the board would conduct a comprehensive analysis of the manufacturing sector covering matters ranging from financing to trade to the defense industrial base. Based on this analysis and ample public input, the board would develop a strategy that includes specific recommendations to the president, Congress and industry.

Senator Brown's National Manufacturing Act of 2011 would have required the Commerce Secretary to conduct a comprehensive analysis and prepare a report on the nation's manufacturing sector within 180 days after the bill's passage. The report would have identified what goods are produced, where they are produced and in which sectors the United States is most competitive. It would have also set out a strategy to increase U.S. manufacturing jobs, identify emerging technologies to strengthen U.S. competitiveness and strengthen the manufacturing sectors in which the United States is most competitive.

"Make It in America" Agenda[18]

On May 4, 2011, Minority Whip Stenny Hoyer (D-MD) announced the Democrat's Make It in America agenda. The agenda is something that Hoyer had been advancing for almost one year. He first blogged about it in The Hill's Congress Blog on July 22, 2010, writing "the Democrats are launching the 'Make It in America' agenda: a manufacturing strategy based on the idea that when more products are made in America, more people will make it in America."

Hoyer's announcement refocused attention on the agenda, which is diverse and at different stages of development. Six Make It in America bills have been signed into law:

- *U.S. Manufacturing Enhancement Act:* Makes it cheaper for American companies to obtain materials they need to manufacture goods (PL 111-227).
- *Protecting American Patents:* Helps the Patent Office unclog its backlog by giving the agency greater access to more fees to accelerate the processing of applications (PL 111-224).
- *Preventing Outsourcing:* Closes tax loopholes that encourage companies to send jobs overseas (PL 111-226).
- *Small Business Jobs Act:* Expands lending to small businesses and offers tax incentives to help small businesses grow (PL 111-240).
- *Energy Jobs and Training for Veterans Act:* Provides grants for programs to provide on-the-job training, apprenticeship, work experience and long-term employment in the energy fields (PL 111-275).
- *America COMPETES Reauthorization Act:* Establishes innovative technology federal loan guarantees for small and medium-size manufacturers and invests in science, technology, engineering and math education (PL 110-69).

Representative Lipinski's National Manufacturing Strategy Act (H.R. 1366) discussed above was at the heart of the 2011 legislation. Working within this framework, the agenda itself addressed eight areas:

- Investing in infrastructure and the flow of commerce
- Keeping America competitive
- Supporting small businesses
- Smart tax policy
- Clean energy jobs
- Innovative educational policy
- Making it in America
- Smart regulations and efficient government

National Infrastructure Bank[19]

On March 18, 2011, Senator John Kerry (D-MA) filed legislation to create a national infrastructure bank to attract capital for major transportation, water and energy projects.

The BUILD Act (Building and Upgrading Infrastructure for Long-Term Development) would have authorized an independent not-for-profit institution patterned after the U.S. Import-Export Bank to develop projects and attract private investment in large-scale infrastructure projects. Co-sponsors of the Act included Kay Bailey Hutchinson (R-TX) and Mark Warner (D-VA).

The infrastructure bank would receive seed money of $10 billion from the federal government from existing sources by drawing on funds available. It was projected that the bank could leverage as much as $640 billion in private investments within the next ten years.

The Build Act specifically called for establishing an American Infrastructure Financing Authority (AIFA), which would provide loans and loan guarantees for projects that are at least $100 million in size ($25 million in rural areas) and of national and regional significance. The AIFA would provide no more than 50 percent of a project's cost.

The AIFA would have been a nonpartisan government-owned entity operated independently. It would receive strong oversight by Congress and the federal government through a board to be appointed by the president and candidates to be nominated by Congress. The CEO and professional staff of the AIFA would select the eligible projects and the board would review and approve them. The AIFA was expected to be self-sufficient within a few years through the collection of fees for its loans or loan guarantees.

MANUFACTURING IDEAS

Congress has not stood alone. Over the past few years, numerous groups and practitioners have also provided a wealth of ideas for renewing our manufacturing sector. We highlight a few of those that we consider noteworthy here.

Andrew Liveris

In 2011, Andrew Liveris, the chairman and CEO of The Dow Chemical Company, published a seminal book, *Make It in America: The Case for Re-Inventing the Economy.*[20] In his book, Liveris made a forceful and persuasive argument that manufacturing must be central to creating America's future and spelled out an agenda for achieving that future as the "world enters the golden age of manufacturing." Liveris' agenda included simplifying the tax code of regulations, moving toward energy independence, investing in research and development, building our "human capital" and rebuilding our crumbling infrastructure.

For us, the most powerful aspect of Liveris' book was not its prescriptions but his emphasis on a public-private partnership and business leaders taking a more active role "to rebuild this great country." He specifically called upon the business community "to work together across industries, to develop a common agenda for American commerce—a policy agenda that would be meaningful and beneficial to all business, regardless of sector or size."

Liveris' book received rave reviews from business and political leaders. It helped shape the renewed focus on manufacturing. President Obama named Liveris co-chair of his Advanced Manufacturing Partnership.

In that capacity, he led the development of a report titled *Capturing Domestic Competitive Advantage in Advanced Manufacturing*, which was endorsed by the President's Council of Advisors on Science and Technology (PCAST) and provided the framework for the President's Plan to Revitalize American Manufacturing, which was introduced in July 2012. The President's Plan was targeted on three categories: Enabling Innovation, Securing the Talent Pipeline and Improving the Business Climate.[21]

Brookings Institution

The Brookings Institution (Brookings) has always been a powerful force and thought leader in shaping public policy. Shortly after the presidential elections were held, Brookings issued three briefs as part of its federal policy initiative: Remaking Federalism/Renewing the Economy: Create a Nationwide Network of Advanced Innovation Hubs; Create a "Race to the Shop" Competition for Advanced Manufacturing; and Support the Designation of 20 U.S. "Manufacturing Universities."[22]

Ideas put forward in these briefs included create and build a network of regional advanced innovation hubs to perform highly collaborative applied and process research on key problems in manufacturing innovation, use the Race to the Shop competition to get the most transformative "bottom up" initiatives in manufacturing renewal and conduct a competition to identify multiple metropolitan initiatives each year worthy of scaling up.

These Brookings briefs make the clear link between innovation and advanced manufacturing. They provide solid recommendations for harnessing the nation's substantial intellectual capital to make manufacturing a key driver for restoring the country's economic growth in the mid and long term.

The Information Technology and Information Foundation

In December 2012, The Information Technology and Information Foundation (ITIF) issued a paper titled *Why America Needs a National Network for Manufacturing Innovation*, which was a perfect complement to the Brookings briefs.[23] ITIF's paper does an excellent job in Part I of documenting the need for a national network explaining how other countries such as Germany and Taiwan use such vehicles to accelerate the development and deployment of manufacturing initiatives.

In Part II, the paper sets forth five principles for setting up the network to be comprised of Institutes for Manufacturing Innovation (IMI). They include having each IMI focused on an industry-defined challenge, making the IMI's independent membership organizations led by manufacturers, and funding split approximately 50/50 between manufacturers and governmental resources.

MANUFACTURING RENEWAL RECOMMENDATIONS

We provided our own input for shaping America's manufacturing renaissance by presenting eleven manufacturing recommendations in *Renewing the American Dream*.

Progress has been made on all of the recommendations but none has been fully implemented.[24] Therefore, we reiterate them here.

Primary Recommendations

1. Develop and fund an industrial and innovation policy focused on driving research and development and on the rapid growth and restoration of manufacturing in targeted sectors.

2. Reform corporate tax policies and create strong incentives for American manufacturers to establish plants and manufacture products domestically.

3. Create vehicles for public-private financial support for targeted R&D and manufacturing/industrial initiatives. (Incentives and financing for "Entrepreneurs' Funds" should be established as part of this innovation and restoration of manufacturing leadership.)

4. Continue to expand funding and heighten public awareness of the importance of STEM (Science, Technology, Engineering and Math) and how basic workforce competencies and cutting-edge expertise in these areas can make our manufacturing sector second to none in the world.

Subsidiary Recommendations

5. Implement a major jobs program focused on creating manufacturing and construction jobs related to rebuilding America's crumbling and critically important infrastructure, including a new infrastructure for delivery of alternative forms of energy—solar, wind, biofuels, etc.

6. Develop an integrated education and training plan that rationalizes the nation's approach for developing a skilled manufacturing workforce.

7. Ensure the manufacturing technical training and support capabilities of America's community college network.

8. Ensure the level of financial and technical assistance required to make small businesses leaders in manufacturing.

9. Provide assistance to small manufacturing companies to help them reduce their health care costs.

10. Establish a trade agreement with China that is based on the principle of reciprocity.

11. Heighten public awareness of the importance of manufacturing and manufacturing careers.

THE MANUFACTURING NEED

That is the current context and conditions. As the foregoing attests, excellent recommendations have been advanced by organizations such as the Brookings Institution, the New America Foundation, the Alliance for American Manufacturing, the National Association for Manufacturing, the U.S. Business and Industry Council, the President's Advanced Management Partnership, the President's Council of Advisors on Science and Technology (PCAST) and others including academics and industry practitioners.

At the federal level, the executive and legislative branches have put forward numerous proposals related to manufacturing. Manufacturing-related initiatives of the Obama administration include the Advanced Manufacturing Partnership, Advanced Manufacturing National Program Office, Advanced Manufacturing Technology Consortia Program, National Robotics Initiative, Materials Genome Initiative and the National Network for Manufacturing Innovation.[25]

The need at this point, as we said in *Renewing,* remains "to implement a comprehensive and consistent set of policies and practices that put manufacturing front and center on the nation's radar screen as the basis for creating the American economy of the future."

In our opinion, even though PCAST did not call for one in its 2011 *Report to the President on Ensuring American Leadership in Advanced Manufacturing* (also referred to as *Capturing Domestic Competitive Advantage in Advanced Manufacturing*),[26] we believe that the nation needs an industrial policy/agenda that supports the growth of businesses and job creation in targeted manufacturing sectors. The critical importance of that dual need is highlighted by two papers from the McKinsey Global Institute.

In its 2011 paper, *An Economy That Works: Job Creation and America's Future,* McKinsey examines the slow pace of the economic recovery and cautions, "Waiting for the US job market to correct itself and depending on the solutions of the past will not hasten the return to full employment or set the stage for sustained job creation in the years to come. To create the jobs that America needs to continue growing and to remain competitive, leaders in government, business and education will have to be creative—and willing to consider solutions they have not tried before."[27]

In its 2012 paper, *Manufacturing the Future: The Next Era of Global Growth and Innovation*, McKinsey analyzes the different types of manufacturing and economies and advises, "The way it (manufacturing) contributes to the economy shifts as nations mature: in today's advanced economies, manufacturing promotes innovation, productivity and trade more than growth and employment."[28]

McKinsey also observes, "As advanced economies recover from the Great Recession, hiring in manufacturing may accelerate, and some nations may even raise net exports. Manufacturers will continue to hire workers, both in production and nonproduction roles (such as design and after-sales service). But in the long run, manufacturing's share of employment will remain under pressure as a result of ongoing productivity improvements, faster growth in services, and the force of global competition, which pushes advanced economies to specialize in activities requiring more skill."

The United States is in a worldwide competition not only for manufacturing but also for manufacturing jobs. That is why we absolutely need a job-centric industrial policy/agenda.

That agenda should be developed based upon the McKinsey findings and the best available recommendations. Our pivot point recommendations for consideration and potential inclusion in such an agenda follow.

PIVOT POINT RECOMMENDATIONS: BACK IN THE DRIVER'S SEAT

There can either be a *manufacturing recovery* that is relatively jobless—producing benefits primarily for companies—or a *manufacturing renewal* that generates benefits for the nation and its citizens.

The distinction between manufacturing recovery and manufacturing renewal is a critical one. At present, we have a disjuncture between "recovery" at the macro or industry level and "renewal" at the micro or individual level. We make this point here and throughout the book.

America helped put General Motors and Chrysler back in the driver's seat. It's time to do the same for manufacturing by implementing an industrial policy/agenda for the nation and its citizens with manufacturing as the centerpiece, placing an immediate and intensified emphasis on job creators and job creation.

With this perspective, we offer the following manufacturing "pivot point" recommendations for inclusion in a "jobs-centric" industrial policy/agenda:

- *Establish a national industry, innovation and infrastructure bank.*
- *Ensure a "job creation" linkage in all initiatives to strengthen and grow manufacturing.*
- *Enhance the financial and technical assistance available to small manufacturing businesses and entrepreneurs.*

National Industry, Innovation and Infrastructure Bank (3-I Bank)

As noted earlier, Senators Kerry, Warner and Hutchinson filed legislation to create a national infrastructure bank. The bank would receive seed money of $10 billion from the federal government and leverage private investments of as much as $640 billion for major transportation, water and energy projects.

We support the establishment of such a bank but recommend that its scope and mission be expanded to include support of all forms of infrastructure upgrading; the financing capability for "scaling" of manufacturing concerns of all types; and "seed" and start-up funding for new ventures and innovative businesses in the early stages of their life cycles.

The key drivers for the future growth of the economy must be Industry, Innovation, and Infrastructure. By creating a national 3-I Bank, the government can put those drivers to work through a public-private partnership in a "development" bank for the United States. We provide additional recommendations regarding the 3-I Bank in the innovation chapter of our book.

Job Creation Linkage

There are a multitude of proposals and excellent ideas that have been advanced in areas such as education, skills shortages and R&D that can and will be used to launch initiatives to help manufacturing recovery. To ensure they also *renew* manufacturing, all of these initiatives should include a "job creation" test and requirement.

For example, an area that businesses consistently say needs reform is taxation. We agree wholeheartedly with the need for reform. Given the jobless recovery, however, we recommend making a strong and direct linkage between tax policies and incentives and job creation. Specific recommendations in this regard include:

- Eliminate the payroll tax on new hires for a period of at least three years.

- Implement targeted jobs tax credits for new "high value" jobs (high-skill/high-wage jobs) created by a manufacturing company.

- Create a "re-shoring" tax incentive for U.S. companies with "high-value" jobs to bring those jobs back to the United States.

- Create a blended set of incentives, working in collaboration with states and local governments, to bring high-tech, advanced manufacturing companies from around the world to make the United States their location of choice.

- Make the R&D tax credit permanent and consider increasing it but tie it to jobs created and provide additional credits for commercializing and producing goods here in the United States.

- Allow the repatriation of profits made overseas but tie that repatriation to a pledge of a specific number of jobs to be created stateside with those profits. Establish a reporting system to monitor performance. If the jobs are not created, charge the companies for those taxes plus a penalty.

- Modify the accelerated depreciation of equipment to include a provision for the addition or retention of machine operators as part of the depreciation formula. If there are no human factors involved, implement a less accelerated schedule.

- Conduct an independent, in-depth study of the actual effective average tax rate paid by manufacturing companies and the number of new jobs that would be created by lowering the rate to 25 percent or increasing the R&D tax credit to 25 percent and making it permanent. Determine what to do regarding the corporate rate and R&D credit based upon the results of that study.

Small Business and Entrepreneurial Financial and Technical Assistance

Establishing a national 3-I Bank would enhance financial assistance for small manufacturing businesses and entrepreneurs. In addition, we offer the following recommendations:

- *Enhance the assistance available to enable small manufacturing businesses to participate more fully in exporting.*

As a result of the Obama administration's focus and support, new businesses are entering the export arena and those who are exporting are doing well. Small and mid-size businesses, however, still have a very small share of the total export pie—only about 4 percent.[29] There is a substantial opportunity to grow both the number of companies doing exporting and their share of the export market.

Additional direct financing to these businesses and development of an even more robust and comprehensive program of technical and marketing development assistance would contribute to achieving this growth. On the financing side, we recommend that the Small Business Administration (SBA) make direct "bridge" loans to small and mid-size companies to supplement the loan guarantees that are presently offered. These loans would be especially useful to "early stage" businesses. On the technical and marketing assistance side, we recommend that the SBA implement a comprehensive consulting export assistance package patterned after the services provided through and/ or implemented in conjunction with the Manufacturing Extension Partnership.

- *Attract and retain talented educated immigrants and entrepreneurs who will contribute to renewing the manufacturing sector.*

Carl Schramm, CEO of the Kauffman Foundation, points out that, "In the 10 years prior to 2006 . . . fully one quarter of the technology and engineering businesses were founded or co-founded by immigrants." The Small Business Administration reported that in 2008, immigrant entrepreneurs generated nearly 12 percent of all business income.[30]

The lesson from this is simple and straightforward. Immigrants have and will be critical as job creators and in the job creation process for the future. We need to continue to replenish the immigrant talent pool to keep America entrepreneurial.

To accomplish this, we should extend the visas for immigrants with advanced degrees in science, technology and mathematics rather than forcing them to leave when they graduate; provide tax and financial incentives to foreign entrepreneurs to bring their businesses to the United States; and implement a targeted program to reach out and repatriate high-value manufacturing and supply chain jobs that have moved overseas to countries like Brazil, Russia, India and China as part of the offshoring trend of the past decade.

MANUFACTURING THE FUTURE

During his re-election campaign President Obama set the goal of creating a million new manufacturing jobs during his second term. He has also identified repairing America's "broken" infrastructure as a source of good jobs. We agree with the focus on manufacturing and infrastructure job growth as key drivers for renewing our middle class.

Some question whether it is realistic to think that jobs of this type can be pivotal in restoring the American economy. We do not.

Jeff Immelt, CEO of GE and the head of President Obama's Jobs Council shares our positive perspective. Near the end of their *Time* article, Foroohar and Saparito quote Immelt as follows: "Will U.S. manufacturing go from 9% to 30% of all jobs? That's unlikely. But could you see a steady increase in jobs over the next quarter and years? I think that will happen."[31]

So do we. Manufacturing and manufacturing jobs by themselves will be insufficient to redress our current situation. The absence of both, however, will ensure a continued rise in income inequality and the deterioration of the American dream.

After World War II, manufacturing jobs drove the creation and growth of the American middle class. Without those jobs in an appropriate number, there can be no middle class. Without the middle class, there can be no American dream. Without the American dream, America will be engaged in a race to the bottom instead of the top.

In conclusion, over the past two years, Congress has concentrated much of its attention on the debt ceiling and cutting the deficit. For the sake of working-class Americans, it should now give even greater attention to the factory floor and manufacturing America's future. It's time to stop tearing things down and to start building them up again.

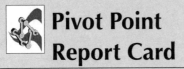 # Pivot Point
Report Card

Instructions

This report card is provided to allow you to reflect upon and assess the progress in this pivot point area. To use the report card:

1. Review the recommendations for the area.

2. Evaluate the progress made in the area to date and assign a letter grade using the system that follows: A–excellent progress. B–substantial progress. C–some progress. D–little progress. F–no progress.

3. Describe the nature of the progress and the rationale for your rating.

We will be posting our assessment for this area on an occasional basis. To see that assessment and to provide your input and feedback on the area, visit *http://www.workingthepivotpoints.com.*

Recommendations

- Back in the Driver's Seat
  - National Industry, Innovation and Infrastructure Bank
  - Job Creation Linkage
  - Small Business and Entrepreneurial Financial and Technical Assistance

Grade

Reason

9 | Entrepreneurs: I Have a Dream

Entrepreneurs are dreamers who dare. They are risk takers who create the businesses and jobs of the future.

Unfortunately in the United States, since the Great Recession, there have been a lot fewer dreamers and risk takers. This is one reason for our jobless recovery.

In this chapter we examine why there has been a precipitous decline in new business start-ups and small business job growth, and what can be done to prime the entrepreneurial pump.

NO FIRE IN THE BELLY. NO FUEL IN THE TANK

Historically, American small businesses have been strong engines for job creation. For the past few years, however, those engines have either been turned off or idling.

We need to start those engines again if we want to get on the road to meaningful economic growth and recovery. Given the current attitude and the performance of the small business community over the past few years, however, that will not be an easy proposition. Two polls released early in 2013 reveal the extent of the problem.

The January 2013 Wells Fargo/Gallup Small Business Index painted a more optimistic picture than its November Index, which had been at the most pessimistic level in two years. As the Wells Fargo news release notes, "The latest Index improved 20 points to a positive 9 (+9) . . . up from a negative 11 (–11)."[1]

In contrast, the National Federation of Independent Business' (NFIB) Small Business Optimism Index released in February 2013 was not as bright. The Index gained only 0.9 points, rising to 88.9. And, according to the NFIB, "Expectations for improved business conditions increased by five points, but remain overwhelming low—negative 30 percent—the fourth lowest reading in survey history."[2]

Setting optimism aside, the more important data in each survey relates to job creation—or the lack thereof. The NFIB survey states "Actual job creation and job creation plans improved nominally, but still not enough to keep up with population."[3] The Wells Fargo/Gallup survey reports, "More small business-owners say they let employees go than hired them on average over a new hiring index of –10 in January . . . This is similar to the –12 recorded in November, the –9 a year ago, and the –12 of January 2011, but up from the low of –27 in January 2010."[4]

The top responses that the participants in the Wells Fargo survey gave for not hiring were:

- Don't need additional employees at this time (81 percent)
- Worried about the revenue and sales to justify new employees (74 percent)
- Concerned about the status of the U.S. economy (66 percent)
- Worried about the potential cost of health care (61 percent)

There is a message in that bottle and it's essentially the same one no matter the reason. Unlike their big business brethren, small business owners tend to lack confidence and be pessimistic about the future.

As Catherine Rampell noted in her February 2013 *New York Times* article "Small Businesses Still Struggle and That's Impeding a Recovery," there is a huge "gulf in optimism between large and small companies".[5] There are reasons for that.

SMALL MAY NOT BE SO BEAUTIFUL

In a front page *New York Times* article on March 4, 2013, with the Dow Jones industrial average at a near record high, Nelson D. Schwartz quoted Ethan Harris, co-head of global economics at Bank of America Merrill Lynch, as saying, "So far in this recovery, corporations have gained an unusually high share of the income gains. The U.S. corporate sector is in a lot better health than the overall economy. And, until we get full recovery in the labor market, this will persist."[6]

Drawing upon research by Citigroup economists, in January 2013, *Bloomberg* reported that "Payrolls at firms with fewer than 500 employees accounted for less than 50 percent of the total workforce for the first time in 2008, and have barely recovered since . . . After hovering close to 50 percent, small businesses' share of gross domestic product began dropping in 2001 to reach about 45 percent in the latest available research."

The Citigroup research disclosed that in spite of their problems small businesses still account for 60 percent of job creation in the United States. But that compares to 61 percent in the ten years through 2007, 65 percent in the decade ending in 1997, and 77 percent in the decade ending in 1987.[7]

Commenting on the difference in the performance of the large business community versus the small business community, Bloomberg observed, "While corporate profits are at record levels as a share of GDP, small businesses are still struggling to make a profit."

"Struggle" seems to be the operative word for the condition of small businesses currently. We devote the remainder of this chapter to providing additional information on where small businesses stand now and what can be done to help them in that struggle.

SMALL BUSINESS SCORECARD

The negative attitudes and poor job creation numbers tell the story behind the country's sluggish economic recovery. Small businesses still represent about half of the private-sector economy and more than 99 percent of all businesses.

In its *Small Business Economy 2012* report, however, the Small Business Administration (SBA) observed that "While the small business economy is growing, the effects of the most recent downturn are still being felt. The number of business births and their associated employment remain below pre-downturn levels and employment gains have been muted compared with previous downturns."[8]

The report goes on to state, "The future of the small business sector depends on factors including the improving personal financial balance sheets of consumers after more than three years of sluggish expansion." Selected business indicators the SBA highlighted included:

- The number of employer firms has fluctuated from just under 5 million to about 6 million over the past quarter century. Firms without employees increased from 14 million in 1992 to more than 22 million in 2010. (We note that the number of employing firms declined by almost 200,000 between 2008 and 2010).

- Small businesses with fewer than 500 workers outperformed large firms in net job creation in three of the four quarters of 2011— similar to an overall pattern that has existed since 1992 in periods when private-sector employment rose.

In commenting on small business financing, the report said, "The credit market environment remained supportive of small business financing, but small businesses continued to face an uphill battle." Selected financial data the SBA highlighted included:

- Total net borrowing and lending in credit markets declined somewhat in 2011 after a substantial increase from 2009 to 2010. Decline in government and household borrowing were offset by increases in nonfinancial business borrowing.

- The number of small business loans outstanding increased, although the value of loans declined—indicating a smaller average loan size in 2011.

- Lending to businesses by finance companies contracted by 1.6 percent in 2011.

- Funds raised by venture capital firms and their disbursements increased in 2011. The amounts of funds committed and disbursed were comparable to those in 2004.

Based upon our review of this data and the accompanying tables, we would agree with the SBA's assessment that "small businesses continued to face an uphill battle." And we would add that the hill they must climb remains a very steep and tall one.

Our review of business turnover (employer births vs. employer deaths) between 2008 and 2010 reveals the following:

Year	Employer Births	Employer Deaths	Difference
2010	533,945	593,347	−59,402
2009	518,500	680,716	−162,216
2008	597,074	641,400	−44,326

On the *Morning Joe Show* on MSNBC on July 2, 2013, Steve Rattner displayed three charts using Bureau of Labor Statistics data that told the small business story over almost a 20-year time period from 1993 through 2012.[9] Here's what those charts showed:

- Small business births consistently outpaced deaths by around 25,000 from 1993 until 2001 when births and deaths were about the same. Then, births ran ahead of deaths from 2002 to 2008, when the bottom fell out for small businesses, and they have been struggling to recover ever since.

- From 1993 to 1997, small businesses with less than 250 employees contributed 50 percent or more of the nation's employment. That has changed dramatically with employment by small businesses with less than 250 employees declining fairly steadily every year so that by 2011 these businesses accounted for only 47 percent of employment.

- From 1994 until 1999 small business start-ups created 30+ percent of the nation's jobs. Since 2000, with the exception of 2003, their job creation has consistently been below 30 percent. Their percentage contribution fell off the cliff in 2003 and in 2012 stood at approximately 22 percent.

The small business deaths are sad. But it is the births and the nurturing of those employers born most recently that will matter the most for the future of the economy.

START-UPS AND ENTREPRENEURIAL JOB CREATION

That's because business start-ups and newer companies that are growing rapidly are especially important for job creation. In 2009, the Ewing Marion Kauffman Foundation (Kauffman Foundation), a foundation devoted to entrepreneurship and small business, reported that from 1980 to 2008, all net job growth had come from businesses less than five years old.

In the same vein, in December 2012, Citigroup issued a report stating, "firms have continued to account for over 60 percent of job creation. But the key engine of job growth has not so much been the gradual expansion of small firms over time, but *young* firms." Citigroup went on to clarify, "It is the process of large numbers of entrepreneurs starting businesses and having a fraction of those businesses grow rapidly that is the prime driver of new employment in the U.S. economy."[10]

Not only do small businesses and entrepreneurs create most of the new jobs in the economy during "good times," there is evidence that they have been the job creators following the past two recessions. In 2009, the Kauffman Foundation also looked at the start-ups during recessions and bear markets and came to several interesting conclusions:

- Recessions and bear markets do not appear to have a significant impact on the formation or survival of businesses.
- Well over half of the companies on the 2009 *Fortune* 500 list, and just under half of the 2008 *Inc.* list, were started during a recession or bear market.
- Job creation from start-ups is much less volatile and sensitive to downturns than job creation in the economy as a whole.[11]

That was good news from the Kauffmann Foundation. The bad news came four years later in its State of Entrepreneurship Address released on February 5, 2013, to coincide with its annual entrepreneurship conference.

The Address reported that "After three decades of relatively steady levels of entrepreneurial activity, the number of new businesses dropped sharply in 2008 and 2009, and has yet to rebound. A close look at available data indicates, however, that the rate of American entrepreneurship began to drop even before the Great Recession. . . . Despite these troubling trends, pockets of intense entrepreneurial activity exist in places such as Silicon Valley, Boston and New York City."[12]

THE FEDERAL GOVERNMENT, ENTREPRENEURS AND SMALL BUSINESS

The federal government has not been blind to the problems and needs of the small business person and entrepreneur. In the years leading up to the Great Recession, the government wasn't doing too much for this sector.

The Kauffman Foundation reported that the SBA's budget was cut 28 percent in the period from 2000 to 2008. According to Senator Mary Landrieu (D-LA) "The agency's funding was cut more than any other agency in the last 8 years."

To its credit, the government has taken many steps since 2009 to improve its focus on the entrepreneur and the small business community. Let's look at what has been done over the past four years.

The 2009 stimulus bill provided $730 million to the SBA for expanded lending to small businesses. That was only about 1 percent of the total stimulus package of $789 billion. But it was assumed that the SBA funds would leverage tens of billions in private-sector financing for small businesses. In 2009, then–Commerce Secretary Gary Locke announced the establishment of an Office of Innovation and Entrepreneurship and a National Advisory Council to support the work of the Office.[13]

The Small Business Jobs Act of 2010 extended the enhanced SBA loan provisions and offered billions more in lending support, tax cuts, and other opportunities for entrepreneurs and small business. It included a provision of $30 billion in low-cost capital for smaller community banks. The Jumpstart Our Business Startups (JOBS) Act of 2012 permits "crowdfunding" and use of the public capital markets for investing in emerging growth companies.[14]

At the beginning of 2012, President Obama made Karen Mills, the administrator of the SBA, a member of his cabinet, thus elevating the profile of the agency. During her four-year tenure, Ms. Mills, who had announced her departure from the SBA pending a replacement, turned the SBA around, which according to *Businessweek* "had languished under the George W. Bush administration."[15] Under Ms. Mill's leadership, "the SBA supported more than $106 billion in lending to more than 193,000 small businesses and entrepreneurs, including two record years of delivering more than $30 billion in loan guarantees."[16]

That brings us to 2013. What was done in the first quarter of the year that impacts small business? There was no direct legislation passed but small business and job creation was definitely impacted by the resolution of the fiscal cliff and the implementation of sequestration.

The fiscal cliff bill was a mixed bag for small business. It had positive features such as an extension of the R&D tax credit, expensing of up to $500,000 in capital expenditures, and accelerated depreciation of qualified new equipment. On the other hand, as Scott Shane writing for entrepreneur.com comments, "three of its major components discourage small business job creation: the end of the payroll tax holiday, higher marginal tax rates on the wealthy and the increase in capital gains tax rates."[17]

The sequestration does not look like a mixed bag for small business. It looks like an unmitigated disaster placed on top of an already gloomy economic forecast. It's far too early to tell the final impact. But here were some of the economic indicators before the sequestration took effect.

The Congressional Budget Office (CBO) budget outlook released in February 2013 projected that the U.S. economy was not expected to return to its full potential until 2017. The CBO saw unemployment staying high for some time: at around 8 percent throughout 2013, declining to 6.8 percent in the fourth quarter of 2015, and not getting down to 5.5 percent until the fourth quarter of 2018.[18]

According to Lori Montgomery of the *Washington Post*, the CBO estimated that the sequester would "shave about 1.25 percentage points off economic growth this year to cost the nation about 1.5 million jobs."[19] A White House press release stated that "the automatic cuts triggered by a sequester would reduce loan guarantees to small businesses by up to $902 million."[20]

It's far too early to tell the final impact. There has and will be jockeying to try to ease the economic pain. But make no mistake about it. There will be blood because of the sequestration. It's just a question of whose, where and when. There will also be unintended consequences by the harm that has been caused.

We think this harm can be corrected by doing some good. We recommend that the good be focused in two categories: entrepreneurial support and small business assistance.

Based upon its research, which disclosed that the key drivers of job growth are "entrepreneurism and the rapid growth of young firms," Citigroup recommended that "public policy should be geared more toward encouraging small business creation rather than to supporting the small business sector per se." We agree with the need to stimulate entrepreneurship but not to the exclusion of providing relief to the mom and pop small businesses who must contribute to the economic recovery by retaining and adding workers in a slow and steady manner.

GROWING THE GAZELLE COMPANIES

There is already an intensive focus on entrepreneurship that has been stimulated and facilitated to a great extent over the past few years by the work of the Kauffman Foundation. In March 2010, it released a study titled *High-Growth Firms and the Future of the American Economy.*[21]

That study found that in any given year, the top 1 percent of firms account for 40 percent of jobs created. Within that category, fast growing *"gazelle"* companies (three to five years old)—which constitute less than 1 percent of the 1 percent—account for approximately 10 percent of the net new jobs. The average company in the top 1 percent creates 88 net new jobs a year compared to the two to three net new jobs of the average firm in the economy as a whole.

Based upon these findings, the Kauffman Foundation recommended that policymakers should "foster the creation of more high-growth firms." The report made three recommendations to drive job creation:

1. *Create more companies*—thus expanding the pool from which high-growth companies will emerge.

2. *Remove barriers*—such as accessing financing, excessive regulation and excessive taxation that prevent existing companies from achieving high-growth.

3. *Focus on universities and immigrants*—by removing barriers to commercialization of university research and expanded or enhanced visa programs.

Three years after this report, there are significant public and private initiatives underway directed at supporting entrepreneurs and the "gazelle" companies. These include:

- The SBA making "strategic investments that focus on increasing access to capital for high-growth businesses, strengthening entrepreneurial skills training and building regional entrepreneurial ecosystems (through clusters and growth accelerators)."[22]

- The JOBS Act, which will accelerate capital formation for start-ups and emerging businesses. In its 2013 State of Entrepreneurship Address, the Kauffman Foundation stated, "The United States took a significant step toward changing the regulatory environment for entrepreneurial finance in the spring of 2012 with the passage of the Jumpstart Our Business (JOBS) Act, which included provisions for equity crowdfunding."

- The Kauffmann Foundation devoted its entire 2013 entrepreneurial meeting to reviewing three categories of policy recommendations for financing entrepreneurial growth: equity (including crowdfunding, angel investors and venture capital), public markets and debt.[23]

- The Start Up America Partnership (Partnership), which was created by AOL co-founder Steve Case and the Kauffmann Foundation to provide technical assistance and support to early stage companies. The Partnership, which was started in January 2011, already has 12,000 members in 30 states and expects to add another 10 states in 2013. The Partnership brings these start-up firms together to network, share and learn from one another.[24]

Frank Islam has many lessons from his experience as an entrepreneur that are relevant for high-growth start-ups and gazelle companies. Frank built his information technology firm, QSS Group, Inc., from less than $45,000 and one employee to almost $300 million and 2,000+ employees in just 13 years. Over that period, Frank's firm was consistently on the *Inc.* 500 list of fastest growing companies. In 1999, Ernst and Young named Frank Maryland Entrepreneur of the Year and in 2001 the SBA named him Small Business Person of the Year.

Frank was able to achieve this because he adhered rigorously to his set of core management principles, which included:

- *Distinctive Core Competence*: Integrate a blend of engineering, science, and information technology skills in the firm. IT firms in D.C. were a dime a dozen. Frank knew that his firm would stand out with the right skill set and by emphasizing the engineering and science qualifications as its differentiators.

- *Laser-Beam Customer Focus:* Get one key client. Treat the client extremely well and use that as the basis for building the business. From 1994 to 1999, NASA was QSS's only client. QSS got the first assignment with NASA because of Frank's scientific background and the experience he gained in working as an executive at Raytheon.

- *Niche Differentiation*: Expand outward from the core client business to those with similar characteristics and needs. QSS's first work outside NASA was with NOAA (National Oceanic and Atmospheric Administration) and the FDIC. After that, QSS added the Department of Defense, HUD, and other agencies.

- *Perfection in Performance:* Past performance is critical in getting governmental contracts. Frank knew that many IT firms were late on deliverables and sometimes did poor project management and shoddy technical work. He vowed that his firm would stand apart from other firms in his competitive arena and established "Performance as Promised" as QSS's corporate motto. It was more than a motto. It was the way QSS did business and a springboard for getting additional business.

Frank also placed a strong emphasis on top team recruitment and selection and sharing the wealth as part of his formula for success. Finally, unlike many entrepreneurs, Frank wasn't a control freak who was involved in every detail of the business. He trusted the key decision maker he had recruited to run the business while he concentrated on marketing and sales and financial management. As Frank put it, "I hired the very best. I knew my role was to hold them accountable and get out of the way and let them do their jobs."

Frank is not a member of the Start Up America Partnership. But he has mentored a number of businesses in Maryland and Virginia and sits on the boards of business schools at George Mason University, the University of Maryland and his alma mater, the University of Colorado. He is also on the board of Advanced Institute Studies at Johns Hopkins University and the American University in the Emirates, Dubai.

So there is a wide and increasing range of assistance available for and accessible to the high-growth gazelle company—the 1 percent. There is much less for the old line, main street and smaller start-up businesses—the 99 percent. That is why we devote our pivot point recommendation to them.

PIVOT POINT RECOMMENDATION: HELP THE MAINSTREAM AND MAIN STREET

The real question is what to do for the mainstream small businesses that are not growing today and are still threatened by a fragile economy. The surveys of these businesses consistently reveal concerns regarding taxation, regulation and the new health care legislation. They will also be the businesses most negatively affected by any decline in demand or consumption because of the ending of the payroll tax holiday. In addition, as Bloomberg reports, these businesses are still having difficulties in securing loans and capital due to the consolidation of the banking industry and tightened lending standards.

These conditions suggest a long-term and short-term course of action. In the short term, Congress should pass legislation similar to the Small Business Jobs and Tax Relief Act, which would have given businesses tax credits for hiring new employees.[25]

In the long term, Congress should request a systematic and rigorous examination of each of the areas that appear to be problematic to determine their actual effect on the small business' bottom line and impact on job creation. This study should be used to develop bipartisan legislation to create positive incentives and/or eliminate those provisions or practices that are retarding small business performance.

Finally, SBA should develop a plan to put itself back into the direct lending business. We made this proposal in *Renewing*.

After the Great Recession started, the House twice passed legislation calling for SBA direct loans; in the Senate Ben Cardin (D-MD) and Robert Menendez (D-NJ) introduced bills for direct loans as well. The bills didn't become law at that time apparently because the SBA felt that they would require substantial increases in staffing and new computer systems and cost "billions of dollars in administrative funds."[26]

The SBA can make direct loans to businesses, homeowners and renters after a disaster. In February 2013, the agency reported that it had approved more than $1.1 billion loans just three months after Superstorm Sandy devastated the Northeast. The majority of those loans—over 15,000—went to homeowners. Slightly more than 800 loans, worth $84.9 million, went to businesses.

The approval rate for the business loans was approximately 8 percent. This compared to an approval rate of 3.1 percent ten weeks after Hurricanes Katrina and Rita clobbered the Gulf Coast.[27]

The bottom line regardless of the comparative performance is that the SBA has proven that it can make direct loans in times of disaster. It seems to us that the Great Recession was and continues to be an ongoing disaster for the small business community in general in terms of its ability to get access to capital.

The SBA's lending statistics in its Small Business Economy Report bear that out. So does Citigroup's research. In its report released in December 2012, based upon its analysis, Citigroup found that:

- Since 2004, commercial and industrial loans to large firms are up by 75 percent, while loans to small businesses are "little" changed.

- Small financial institutions (less than $1 billion in assets on their balance sheet) now account for just 20 percent of business loans smaller than $100,000, compared to almost 40 percent a decade ago.
- The "sustained and sizable decline" of small banks as providers of credit is "very likely" a factor in the downturn in the share of credit provided to small firms.

Citigroup also observed that "poor sales" was seen as the single most important problem through the depths of the financial crisis and states that "confidence among small firms remains remarkably weak." It's easy to understand that lack of confidence when consumer demand remains low, credit is tight, and it's harder than ever to find somewhere to get a loan.[28]

If the SBA were to become a lender of first rather than last resort by going into the direct lending business in a thoughtful way, it could help to restore that small business confidence and put pressure on small financial institutions to get back into the small business lending business at the same time.

As we said in *Renewing*, "Those 'small businesses' that are bigger than micro-businesses but smaller than major corporations are left without an advocate or support system. There should be a substantial increase in direct loans now that banks have reduced their lending. . . . We are concerned about the whole guaranteed loan concept—especially when you are protecting up to 90 percent of the lender's exposure. We know how it benefits and protects the lender. We're not certain what it does in terms of adding value for the new business or borrower."

MAKING THE CASE FOR SMALL BUSINESS

The Federal Reserve's pumping of money into the financial system and keeping interest rates low has helped drive the stock market and corporate profits to all-time highs. High-growth and gazelle companies are on most policymakers' and financiers' radar screens. The majority of small businesses who have survived the Great Recession to this point are not underwater but they are definitely treading it, and their interests are submerged.

In 2012, the Bureau of Labor Statistics released an experimental data set on private-sector jobs that showed the following total change in employment in the period from April 1990 through March 2011:

- Small companies (1–49 employees) = +10.5 percent
- Medium companies (50–499 employees) = +13.1 percent
- Large companies (500 or more employees) = +29.2 percent

That touched off a great debate of sorts among the wonks about who were the true job creators: small business or big business. Citing the work of John C. Haltiwanger and his colleagues, Jared Bernstein, a senior fellow at the Center on Budget and Policy Priorities and former economic advisor to Vice President Biden from 2009 to 2011, notes "once you account for the outsize contributions by new and young companies, they found 'no systematic relationship' between net job growth and company size."

Bernstein goes on to state that, "The size of a company is largely irrelevant to job creation." We agree with him. The fact is that to get out of this "jobless" recovery companies of all sizes—small, medium and large—will have to be job creators. New and young companies can't do it by themselves—especially because, as Bernstein points out, these companies have been creating fewer jobs over the past decade than before.

We also agree with Bernstein when he writes, "Many (small businesses) face distinctive hurdles compared with large businesses: they have tighter profit margins and thus less room for mistakes, they have diminished access to credit markets, and even with creditworthy borrowing records, many say they are not getting the loans they need."[29]

This situation demands remedy and more assistance to small businesses. It should not be ignored.

It's not well known but the fiscal cliff bill included a tax break for NASCAR "motor sports racing track facilities." That will ensure that the NASCAR drivers have safe speedways on which to start and run their engines. We need to give the same types of breaks to our nation's small businesses so they can restart their engines. When they do the American economy will begin firing on all cylinders again.

 **Pivot Point
Report Card**

Instructions

This report card is provided to allow you to reflect upon and assess the progress in this pivot point area. To use the report card:

1. Review the recommendation for the area.
2. Evaluate the progress made in the area to date and assign a letter grade using the system that follows: A–excellent progress. B–substantial progress. C–some progress. D–little progress. F–no progress.
3. Describe the nature of the progress and the rationale for your rating.

We will be posting our assessment for this area on an occasional basis. To see that assessment and to provide your input and feedback on the area, visit *http://www.workingthepivotpoints.com.*

Recommendation

- Help the Mainstream and Main Street

Grade

Reason

10 | Immigration: Don't Fence Me In

Almost immediately after the national elections were concluded, immigration reform again became a topic for conversation and potential legislation. Illegal immigrants had been at the center of debates and much of the discussion during the Republican presidential primaries.

With their hard-line, hard-headed and hard-hearted stances on things such as building a fence to keep illegal immigrants out of the United States and deportation of those who are in the United States, the Republican candidates for the presidential nomination boxed themselves in and built a fence between their eventual nominee and the country's emerging Hispanic population. This resulted in President Obama getting 70+ percent of the Latino vote to Governor Romney's nearly 30 percent.

This and other setbacks caused the Republicans to reevaluate and to begin presenting proposals for dealing with the illegal immigrant problem. That problem is only the tip of the immigration iceberg, however.

We do need to solve the immigrant issues that were created by too porous a border and a lack of enforcement. But, as importantly, we need to put an enhanced immigration system in place that contributes to the renewal of America not by building fences but by building bridges that ensure that we continue to attract and retain the highly skilled and talented immigrants who have been a wellspring of American growth and development.

IMMIGRANT NATION

America has always prided itself on being a nation of immigrants. The Statue of Liberty provides eloquent testimony to that with its inscription, which reads, in part:

> Give me your tired, your poor,
> Your huddled masses yearning to breathe free,
> The wretched refuse of your teeming shore.
> Send these, the homeless, tempest-tost to me,
> I lift my lamp beside the golden door!

The achievements and the contributions of immigrants to the nation's success are legion. Famous first-generation American immigrants, to name just a few, include Albert Einstein, physicist from Germany; I. M. Pei, architect from China; Joseph Pulitzer, newspaper publisher from Hungary; Felix Frankfurter, Supreme Court justice from Austria; Madeline Albright, Secretary of State from Czechoslovakia; Hakeen Olajuwon, basketball player from Nigeria; and Saint Francis X. (Mother) Cabrini, nun from Italy. The list could go on and on. Add second-generation immigrants to the list, it could go on almost forever.[1]

In spite of these accomplishments and its orientation, however, the United States has not always been the most hospitable place for immigrants. Over time, nearly every new ethnic group has been viewed with concern.

As Darrell West notes in his seminal book *Brain Gain*, near the end of the 19th and beginning of the 20th century the worries were primarily about those of European stock: individuals from countries like Scotland, Ireland, Germany and Italy. By the mid-20th century, they were about immigrants from places like Asia, Africa, Central America and Mexico.[2]

Border controls and quotas were established early in the 20th century, and during the Great Depression the political leaders almost stopped immigration completely. So the focus on immigration is not something of recent origin.

What made matters different since approximately 1980 was the growth of both the legal immigrant pool and the expansion of the illegal pool. As West points out, this brought about new legislation such as:

- The Immigration Reform and Control Act of 1986
- The Immigration Reform and Immigration Responsibility Act of 1996[3]

In addition, after 9/11, administrative decisions were made to tighten the legal immigration process and to punish those who were here illegally. Between 2000 and 2010, "more than 2 million undocumented aliens" were expelled from the United States. The Obama administration was spending over $18 billion annually on border security.

Nonetheless, during the 2012 election cycle, because of the large number of illegal aliens still here—11.2 million—and concerns about the impact of more aliens entering the country during the jobless recovery after the Great Recession, immigration remained a hot button topic. Little attention was paid to the significant role that immigrants play today in building the American economy and social fabric.

IMPORTING TALENT

Vivek Wadhwa highlighted the contributions of these immigrants to the country's economic success in his 2011 *Democracy Journal* article, "Our Best Imports: Keeping Immigrant Innovators Here."[4]

According to his 2006 study of more than 2,000 technology firms started in the previous ten years, "25.3 percent had a chief executive or lead technologist who was foreign born." The percentage of start-ups in various technology sectors is stunning: semiconductors, 35.2 percent; computers/communications, 31.7 percent; software, 27.9 percent; and innovation, 25.9 percent. Wadhwa estimated that "in 2005 immigration-founded tech companies generated $52 billion in revenue and employed 450,000 workers."

Wadhwa's research disclosed that the "vast majority" of these companies' founders didn't come to the United States to start businesses. Over 50 percent of them came to study. Three-quarters of them have degrees in the science, technology, engineering and math fields.

Frank Islam fits this profile of the immigrant entrepreneur perfectly. Frank grew up in a middle-class family of five siblings in India. Frank left India at the age of 15 to pursue the American dream. He got his B.S. and M.S. in computer sciences from the University of Colorado at Boulder. He worked at two major information technology firms in Washington, D.C., before purchasing the QSS Group, Inc., which, as we noted in the preceding chapter, he grew from a workforce of 1 to more than 2,000 employees and revenues of approximately $300 million in a little more than a decade.

The SBA reports that in 2008 immigrant entrepreneurs generated nearly 12 percent of all business income in the United States. Darrell West notes that, "Between 1996 and 2008, immigrants were twice as likely as native-borns to start new businesses." Based upon his analysis, West concludes, "The costs immigrants impose are not zero, but those side effects pale in comparison to the contributions arising from the immigrant brain gain."[5]

Claudia Kolker informs us that these contributions are not just intellectual or economic in her interesting book, *The Immigrant Advantage*.[6] They are also emotional and social. Kolker explains that because of supportive customs such as Vietnamese "money clubs" that help people save and Mexican cuarentenas—a 40-day period of rest for new mothers—many immigrants "tend to be both physically and mentally healthier than most native-born Americans."

There is substantial evidence that immigrants bring talent and gains on a wide variety of fronts. Given this, it would seem we would have been embracing those positive contributors and doing all that we can to enable them to use their "immigrant advantage" to enhance the United States' competitive advantage. Unfortunately, this is not the case for our current immigration system.

EXPORTING TALENT

In October 2012, the Kauffmann Foundation released a study which found that the number of high-tech immigrant-funded start-ups nationwide has stagnated or declined from 25.3 percent to 24.3 percent since 2005, with an even more precipitous drop in Silicon Valley from 52.4 percent to 43.9 percent. Dane Stangler, director of Research and Policy at the Foundation, commented, "For several years, anecdotal evidence has suggested that an unwelcoming immigration system in the United States has created a 'reverse brain drain.' This report confirms it with data."

The research was conducted by Vivek Wadhwa and compares the findings for the period from 2006 to 2012 to those of his similar study covering the period from 1995 and 2005.[7] The study disclosed that immigrant entrepreneurs are still substantial contributors to the economy and that immigrant founders of engineering and technology companies employed roughly 560,000 workers and generated an estimated $63 billion in sales from 2006 to 2012.

It also revealed that while immigrant entrepreneurship has "stagnated" in general and declined for founders from most other countries, the rates of Indian and Chinese start-ups have increased since 2005. The increase was most notable for founders from India with an increase of 7 percent and a full 33.2 percent of all start-up companies being Indian.

Mr. Wadhwa has written a book that draws upon the research titled *The Immigrant Exodus: Why America Is Losing the Global Race to Capture Entrepreneurial Talents*.[8] Based upon his analysis, he concludes, "The U.S. can reverse these trends with changes in policies and opportunities, if it acts swiftly. It is imperative that we create a startup visa and expand the number of green cards for skilled foreigners to work in these startups."

IMMIGRATION STRAIGHTJACKET

There is virtually no disagreement regarding the need to reform our current immigration system to make it more effective and efficient. The system—and we use that term loosely—is a defective one with many flaws. One of its most problematic features is the manner in which it allocates visas.

As Darrel West argues, one of the major flaws of our current system is that it is "tilted too far in favor of family reunification over other important national goals."

West traces the origins of the family priority to the Hart-Celler Immigration and Nationality Act of 1965 (Act). That Act, which had a civil rights and humanitarian orientation, abolished quotas by country of origin and had three distinct features:

1. It nearly doubled the immigration ceiling from 150,000 to 290,000 with 170,000 visas for the Eastern hemisphere and 120,000 visas for the Western hemisphere.

2. It gave preference to family unification over employment-based requests.

3. It exempted the spouses, children under the age of 21 and parents of naturalized citizens from any numerical limits.

When the Act was passed, it was not thought that it would have a dramatic effect on the size or nature of the immigration pool. This was wrong on both counts. By 2008, the number of visas went from 290,000 to over a million. In 1970, 60 percent of the visas were for occupational preferences. By 1978, occupational preferences had fallen to 17 percent. By 1996, only 12 percent of visas issued were for occupational reasons; 66 percent were for family reunification and 22 percent for humanitarian reasons. In 2008, 15 percent of visas were employment-based; 64 percent were family-related and 19 percent were humanitarian in nature.[9]

The immigration reasons changed substantially and so did the immigrant population. Over this same time period, there was an increase in immigrants from Latin America, Asia and Africa. This shift caused "fear and resentment" and, along with the illegal immigrant problem, led to acrimonious ongoing public debates for several years regarding how to handle the immigration situation.

These narrowly focused debates prevented a rigorous and thorough examination and review of the manner in which the immigration system is operated. And they concentrated most of the attention and discussion on Mexico.

MEXICAN IMMIGRATION TODAY: A TRICKLE OR A STREAM?

As frequently happens, it appears that the problem the debaters were trying to solve was not of the same magnitude it once was. At least, that's what a 2012 study by the Pew Research Hispanic Center titled *Net Migration from Mexico Falls to Zero and Perhaps Less* showed.[10]

The study revealed that:

- There has been a sharp downward trend in net migration that began about five years ago.

- In 2011, there were "some 6.1 million unauthorized Mexican immigrants" compared to "nearly 7 million" in 2007.

- Authorized immigrants "rose modestly" from 5.6 million in 2007 to 5.8 million in 2011.

The Center stated, "The standstill appears to be the result of many factors including the weakened U.S. job and housing construction markets, heightened border enforcement, a rise in deportations, the growing dangers associated with illegal border crossings and the long-term decline in Mexico's birth rates."

Even though the net migration was at a "standstill," the question of what to do with the illegal immigrants is still significant and one that must be addressed. Pew reports, "Just over half (51%) of all current Mexican immigrants are unauthorized, and some 58% of the estimated 11.2 million unauthorized immigrants in the U.S. are Mexican." Those are huge numbers requiring bipartisan problem solving. Fortunately, the election results of 2012 helped to bring a new perspective and a willingness to work together on immigration to Congress.

REFORM—SENATE STYLE: AN IDEA WHOSE TIME HAD COME

Near the end of January, the Gang of Eight (Gang), a bipartisan group of U.S. senators, released a five-page document outlining the broad parameters of a "sweeping" proposal for immigration reform. These senators were Republicans Jeff Flake (AZ), Lindsey Graham (SC), John McCain (AZ) and Marco Rubio (FL). Democratic senators were Michael Bennet (CO), Dick Durbin (IL), Robert Menendez (NJ) and Chuck Schumer (NY).

The proposal set out "four basic pillars": (1) "tough but fair path to citizenship . . . contingent upon securing our borders," (2) reforming immigration with a greater eye toward our economic needs, (3) workplace verification and (4) setting up a system for admitting future workers. It also provided a speedier path (modeled after the Dream Act) to citizenship for children brought here illegally.[11]

The proposal made it clear that the implementation of a new border security system was necessary before the "pathway to citizenship" could be initiated. That system includes an increase in the number of unmanned aerial vehicles and agents at the border, new rules for tracking people here on temporary visas, and a commission of Southwestern political and community leaders to make sure the required new enforcement measures are in place.

President Obama endorsed the proposal two days after it was announced in a speech in Las Vegas. He set out three principles for immigration reform: border security, a path to citizenship for current undocumented immigrants and making immigration easier for immigrants trained in science and technology.[12] He built upon a theme from his State of the Union address in which he called for "real reform" of the immigration system in order to "attract the highly skilled entrepreneurs and engineers that will help create jobs and grow our economy."

After the president's pronouncements, the Gang immediately went to work on turning their proposal into legislation. By early March, significant progress had been made in a number of key areas such as the pathway to citizenship requirements; a border enforcement provision, including biometric ID cards for those here on temporary visas; and increasing the number of green cards for higher skilled workers in science and technology.

The toughest issue revolved around how to implement a lower skilled worker program to bring in immigrants when Americans were not available or willing to take jobs. The Gang's plan called for a "sliding scale" approach that would bring in more immigrants when there was job growth and fewer during tough economic times.[13]

The Chamber of Commerce and the AFL-CIO had agreed to a set of principles in late February that had concessions from both sides. The agreements included creation of a new worker visa that wouldn't keep workers in an indefinite "temporary status"—a "guest worker" provision that had scuttled immigration reform legislation in 2007, and streamlining business' ability to hire foreign workers.[14]

In mid-April, after more than two months of negotiation, the bipartisan group of senators brought forward their proposed immigration bill. The sticking point had been the relation between tougher border measures and starting the path to citizenship for illegal immigrants. The compromise the senators came up with was to allow the Department of Homeland Security a ten-year period to make plans and use resources to fortify border enforcement and to achieve specific goals within five years before allowing any illegal immigrants to apply for permanent resident green cards.[15]

Immigration reform was finally an idea whose time had come. The eight senators who demonstrated leadership through their collaborative and cooperative behavior to make this happen should be commended. They proved the naysayers wrong and surprised many. As E. J. Dionne wrote shortly after the Gang introduced their proposal, "We've become so accustomed to the politics of obstruction that there is still such a thing as legislative craftsmanship."[16] Yes, there is, and these senators proved they were masters of their craft.

There was just one problem for the bill at this juncture. It was the group of eight's and not the full Senate's. As Marco Rubio said in an interview on NBC's *Meet the Press* on the Sunday before the draft bill was introduced, "It's not a take-it-or-leave-it offer. It is a starting point for reform."

And indeed it was the starting point and not the finish line. The Senate successfully passed an immigration bill on June 27, 2013, with a solid majority vote of 68–32. All Democratic and fourteen Republican senators voted for passage. None of the GOP senators in floor leadership positions voted for it.

What got the 1,200-page bill with a $50 billion price tag to the finish line with expanded Republican support were amendments authorizing 20,000 additional border patrol agents, constructing 700 miles of fencing along the Southern border and ensuring that immigrants could not claim Social Security benefits for the time they were here illegally.[17] The bill also received a boost from a Congressional Budget Office Report released during the Senate debates estimating that the bill would increase revenue by nearly $200 billion through 2023 and cut deficits by an additional $700 billion from 2024 through 2033.[18]

In spite of the margin of passage, the debate on the bill was sometimes heated and contentious. The Senate itself only voted on 10 of more than 500 amendments filed to the bill. On the other hand, after the bill was passed, majority leader Senator Harry Reid's (D-NV) office pointed out that the Senate Judiciary Committee "considered 212 amendments and adapted more than 40 Republican-sponsored amendments during its markup in May."[19]

A BUILDING CONSENSUS—BUSHWHACKED

The bipartisan group of senatorial legislators who came together to pass this comprehensive immigration bill were aided and abetted by shifting public opinion that was looking more leniently at immigration and leaders from across the board who came out after the elections speaking affirmatively in support of immigration reform.

The most unified support came from Silicon Valley executives and the Technology CEO Council. In early February, the Council, which represents companies such as Dell, Intel and Motorola, had meetings on Capitol Hill to lobby for the immigration bill to include a strong focus on high-skilled individuals. Steve Case, one of AOL's founders, testified at the first Senate hearing on immigration reform.[20]

Thomas Donohue, president of the U.S. Chamber of Commerce, and Richard Trumka, president of the AFL-CIO, were probably the oddest couple to embrace the need for immigration reform. They issued a joint statement toward the end of February calling for a visa system for lower-skilled immigrant workers while protecting American workers. The Chamber and the AFL-CIO set out three general goals for such a system: ensuring that American workers would get "a first crack at available jobs," a flexible visa program that would adjust to respond to the nature of the economy and greater transparency in determining the market need for temporary workers.[21]

Another unusual assemblage was the "high profile" bipartisan group brought together by the Bipartisan Policy Center headquartered in Washington to support changing the nation's immigration law to include a path to citizenship. The group is co-chaired by Republicans

Condoleezza Rice, former Secretary of State, and Haley Barbour, former Mississippi governor; and Democrats Ed Rendell, former governor of Pennsylvania, and Henry Cisneros, former Secretary of Housing and Urban Development. When the group was announced in early February, Ed Rendell said it would "aim to keep up momentum behind overhauling immigration and serve as a sounding board for policy makers."[22]

Jeb Bush slowed down that momentum a little in early March when he released his book *Immigration Wars: Forging an American Solution.* In the book, former Florida Governor Bush advocated a complete overhaul of the nation's immigration politics but cautioned against a pathway to citizenship for illegal immigrants.[23]

The surprising thing about this position is that it appeared to contradict the position that Bush took during an interview with Charlie Rose of CBS in June 2012. At that time, he stated, "You have to deal with this issue. You can't ignore it, and so either a path to citizenship, which I would support . . . or a path to residency of some kind."[24]

As Bush made the talk show rounds, he acknowledged the differing stances and even went further to recant the book's position. According to Michael Shear of the *New York Times*, "But Bush quickly found himself backpedaling from that position. In fact, he told a series of interviewers that he could easily support granting citizenship in the context of a comprehensive approach to immigration reform."[25]

It seems to us that Governor Bush was for a pathway to citizenship before he was against it and then for it again. The House members of Congress did not demonstrate that same maneuverability.

REFORM—HOUSE STYLE: WHAT'S THIS ABOUT COMPREHENSIVE?

While the Senate reached the finish line with a comprehensive bill, the House didn't appear to be willing to give a bill of this type serious consideration at the starting line.

In early February, conservative House Republicans argued against granting a path to citizenship to illegal immigrants. In late February, Republican Senators John McCain, Jeff Flake and Lindsey Graham met with a group of these Republicans including Steve King (IA) and Raul

Labrador (ID) who opposed any pathway to "update key house members and get their advice on this important effort."

In early March, House GOP leaders held "listening sessions" for members to educate them about existing policies. At that time, *CQ Roll Call* reported that "House immigration negotiators are working on a plan that could allow undocumented immigrants to eventually qualify for citizenship—but doing so in the way that roughly follows current rules."[26]

Jake Sherman and Kate Nocera of *Politico* reported that in addition to the main House bipartisan talks on immigration being led for the Republicans by Mario Diaz-Balart, a Cuban American from Florida, there were GOP "working groups" looking at issues ranging from border security to dealing with illegal immigrants already in the country.

Sherman and Nocera stated that "All this behind-the-scene activity shows a new intensity around immigration in the House and could be a harbinger for reform." They further observed, "Top lawmakers and aides in Boehner's chamber describe a process that would have the House pass a number of small-bore immigration bills with broad support. Those bills would lead to a formal conference negotiation with the Senate, when it passes its comprehensive bill."[27]

In April, House Judiciary Committee Chairman Bob Goodlatte (R-VA) announced that his committee was not going to wait for the comprehensive reform package from the bipartisan group but would start considering single-issue immigration bills. At the time, Goodlatte said, "I am very interested in seeing what those bipartisan groups produce but we are also going forward with the work we've been doing in committee. We were holding hearings on it all year long, we've been working on legislation, so I think soon you'll see legislation."[28]

Immediately after the Senate passed its bill, House Speaker John Boehner (R-OH) in a press conference announced that the House would not pass any immigration reform legislation—including a bill coming out of conference—that does not have the support of a majority of Republican and Democratic members. Boehner also reiterated his position that the House would not take up and vote on the Senate Bill.

What the House will produce in terms of immigration legislation, however, remains an open question. According to Russell Berman of *The Hill* in an article written after Speaker Boehner's press conference, "A series of individual bills moving through the Judiciary Committee have not gained Democratic support, and Boehner offered encouragement to a bipartisan group of negotiators that appear to have stalled again on legislation that has been in the works for years."[29]

According to Berman as well, the issue of the House passing a more comprehensive bill turns on "the timing of granting legal status to the nation's estimated 11 million illegal immigrants." The major flaw the conservative Republicans see in the Senate bill is that it grants provisional status to illegal immigrants "before border security and enforcement enhancements are implemented."[30]

Another factor that might inhibit considering comprehensive legislation in the House including any pathway to citizenship is its configuration. As Jonathan Weisman observed in his June 26, 2013, *New York Times* article, "If anything, the politics of a gerrymandered House where Republicans have much more to fear politically from the right than from the left could push many Republicans to oppose a conservative alternative to the Senate's plan."[31]

To sum it up, the odds of getting something resembling comprehensive from the House appear to be slim to none. That's unfortunate because at a minimum, we need comprehensive.

Much has been written about the need for a "comprehensive" approach to immigration reform. According to Audrey Singer of the Brookings Institution, "A comprehensive approach typically includes border security, worksite enforcement . . . changes to the admission process to admit more immigrants that are economically suited to the U.S. market . . . a policy that deals with the estimated 11 million people living in the United States without legal status."[32]

In our opinion, the issues that Ms. Singer identifies should absolutely be addressed as part of an immigration reform approach that is "comprehensive"—but more importantly as one that is strategic. Our pivot point recommendation for achieving strategic immigration reform follows.

PIVOT POINT RECOMMENDATION: STRATEGIC IMMIGRATION REFORM

Talented and skilled immigrants have been a driving force in building the nation's intellectual, human and financial capital. But our immigration system and policies are neither designed nor structured to magnify those contributions. They need to be.

The current approach to immigration is tactical and reactive, including many of the proposals for and provisions in the legislation under consideration. They deal primarily with the past and problem situations.

We need to change the immigration paradigm. This can be accomplished by developing a strategic and proactive immigration system that is focused on the future and unleashing the economic potential that immigrants can bring to creating that future.

A conceptual model that might be employed to correct this deficiency and to construct an enhanced system that emphasizes using immigration as an engine to contribute to the growth of the economy and job creation might be a five-level framework such as the following:

- Entrepreneur with existing business
- Entrepreneurial start-up
- Advanced/High skills
- Mid skill
- Low skill

These categories could be used in combination with factors such as country of origin, size of the country, and familial relationship to develop a methodology for rationalizing immigration decision making and aligning it the nation's economic, skill and job development needs.

In 2010, Vivek Wadhwa offered a number of excellent specific proposals for achieving this strategic alignment, including raising the number of H-1B visas for workers and graduate students with specialized knowledge, increasing the number of EB-1 through EB-3 visas for skilled workers and inviting foreign entrepreneurs to set up shop here. In his 2012 book *The Immigrant Exodus*, Wadhwa amplified on these recommendations, suggesting eliminating the current cap that permits only 7 percent of green cards for any one country (including huge ones like China and India) and allowing spouses of H-1B visa holders to work. He suggests doubling, tripling or even quadrupling the number of green cards.[33]

Darrell West provided recommendations similar to Wadhwa's and also got into the nitty-gritty of making the system work better in *Brain Grain*. He recommended accomplishing this by doing things such as: tightening verification through E-verify with an appeals process, modernizing visa processing through digital technology, narrowing the definition of relatives to immediate families, linking immigration levels to the economic cycle and establishing an independent commission to oversee the immigration system.[34]

In conclusion, the United States is at a critical juncture in terms of its immigration system and policies. We have moved beyond immigrant bashing and partisan politics to having a meaningful discussion and dialogue on immigration issues.

If we seize this moment for strategic rethinking and reform, the country and its citizens will get a significant ongoing return on that investment. If we squander it by focusing too narrowly and operationally, we will all pay the price both now and in the future.

A DISSENTING VIEW ON "HIGH-TECH" IMMIGRANTS

We would be remiss if we did not acknowledge that not everyone supported expanding the pool of immigrants trained in science, technology, engineering and math (STEM). Ross Eisenbrey, vice president of The Economic Policy Institute, took the contra-position in his *New York Times* article "America's Genius Glut."[35]

Mr. Eisenbrey asserted that we do not have a shortage of high-tech workers. Points that he makes in his article include the following:

- With just 5 percent of the world's population, the United States employs a third of its high-tech researchers, accounts for 40 percent of its R&D, and publishes over a third of its science and engineering articles.

- The United States has too many high-tech workers: more than 9 million have STEM-related degrees but only about 3 million have a job in the field—because pay levels don't reward their skills.

- Unemployment for high-tech workers is low—3.7 percent—but that is still twice as high as it was before the Great Recession.

- The number of foreign graduate students in science, engineering and health fields grew by more than 50 percent between 1990 and 2009.

- The United States granted permanent residence to over 300,000 workers and temporary work permits to hundreds of thousands more during the 2000s.

Mr. Eisenbrey stated the reason why companies are pushing for more high-tech workers is "simple." As he puts it, workers with H-1B visas are "more or less indentured, tied to their job at whatever wage the employer decides to give them. Moreover, too many are paid at wages below the average for their occupation and location: over one-half of all H-1B guest workers are certified for wages in the bottom quarter of the wage scale."

Mr. Eisenbrey presents an interesting case. We believe, however, the way to deal with his objections should be through a straightforward process of fact checking.

This could be done by conducting an independent supply and demand study to determine in what areas there is a need to expand H1-B visas. Wage differentials should be examined as part of that study. A study of this type would ensure that H-1B visas are not used as vehicles to bring cheap labor (and not necessarily higher skills) to the table in a manner that would result in fewer jobs for qualified American citizens.

DIFFERING VIEWS ON COSTS AND BENEFITS

As noted earlier in this chapter, the CBO study that showed the immigration reform bill being considered by the Senate would reduce the federal deficit helped the bill's passage there. Annie Lowrey, in her June 2013 *New York Times* article, points out that there are studies that support the CBO's findings. For example, the American Action Forum and the Center for American Progress foresee a reduction and the Heritage Foundation and the Center for Immigration Studies see an increase in the deficit.[36]

Here's our take on it. There have been numerous studies over the past several years that have looked at the economics of immigration reform. In general, they show that a comprehensive approach will be beneficial to the economy but that lower-skilled native-born American workers may be hurt by the reform.

The *CATO Journal* published a paper on "The Economic Benefits of Comprehensive Immigration Reform" by Raul Hinojosa-Ojeda, founding director of the North American Integration and Development Center at UCLA. Based upon his modeling, using ten-year GDP projections prepared by the Congressional Budget Office, he found that comprehensive reform would increase U.S. GDP by 0.84 percent per year. Over the ten-year period, this would generate "at least $1.5 trillion in added GDP." Former CBO official Arlene Holen estimated in a Technology Policy Institute paper that adding more skilled workers would bring in $100 billion over a decade.[37]

In a paper based upon its analysis of the proposed Comprehensive Immigration Reform Act of 2007, the Congressional Budget Office (CBO) presented some contradictory findings. The CBO stated that over a ten-year period from 2008–2017 implementing the Act would increase federal revenues by $48 billion with an increase in direct spending of only $23 billion. On the other hand, the CBO estimated that discretionary spending would go up by $43 billion "assuming appropriations of the amount or otherwise needed to implement the legislation."

The CBO concluded that "the legislation would exert a relatively small net effect on the federal budget over the next two decades, since additional expenditures would be mostly offset by additional revenue."[38]

The bottom line is—as with most forecasts—the bottom lines differ depending on what data is being used and who is doing the analysis. Our general conclusion, however, as we have documented in this chapter, is that high-skilled immigrants contribute to innovation, business development and job creation.

So too do low-skilled immigrant workers who, as University of California economist Gordon Hanson found, are much more willing to move to find work, such as farm labor, than native-born Americans, thus contributing to the economic development of regions that need additional workers for growth. These immigrant workers also may be willing to do work native-born workers do not want to do.

In an important Brookings paper, Darrell West makes the case that high- and low-skill immigrant workers are both essential to help address worker shortages at either end of the employment spectrum. West astutely points out these workers *complement* rather than compete with American workers by "filling in specialized roles" where there are job openings. This keeps jobs here in the United States and thus contributes to regional economic development and the future growth and prosperity of the nation.[39]

One of the frequent complaints about low-skilled immigrant workers is that they reduce wages for native-born Americans. Drawing upon two recent Hamilton Project papers, Michael Greenstone and Michael Looney of the Brookings Institution state this is not the case. Instead, these workers "typically boost American workers' overall standard of living by increasing American wages and lowering prices for consumers."[40]

Dylan Matthews, writing for the *Washington Post's Wonkblog*, compared and contrasted the findings of economic researchers who came to different conclusions on whether low-skilled immigrant workers have a positive or negative impact on wages. Based upon his review of competing data, Matthews concludes that "the typical native-born worker probably benefits." He observes that "In the long run, the economy adjusts such that the overall effect is minimal but the short term figures are still a cause for concern."[41]

In commenting on Matthews' observation, Jared Bernstein observes, "I think it's fair to say that the near term matters more to people as opposed to economists." Bernstein goes on to state, "If you are among those . . . who are 'substitutable' for low-wage immigrant labor, you will feel this competition, significantly, in your job offers and your paycheck."[42]

Christopher Matthews makes a similar point in his posting for business.time.com where he notes, "the benefits of increased immigration will be spread out among the entire population, while the costs will be borne by a relatively small group of individuals who will feel the effects acutely."[43]

To sum it up, comprehensive immigration reform will have substantial costs and benefits. As Eduardo Porter of the *New York Times* noted, though, "the chances are good that it would cost the government money."[44]

In our opinion, however, the overall benefits for the economy in general will far outweigh the costs. That is why we recommend embracing a comprehensive approach of the type being considered.

It ensures that we are not engaged in an expenditure that yields little return on investment to the American public. In this regard, we agree with Jared Bernstein when he writes, "We are spending $18 billion a year on immigration enforcement already, and I doubt there are big returns for more border enforcement."

There will be big returns on a comprehensive immigration reform package. There will be even more if the package is a strategic one and includes the appropriate provisions for dealing with the needs of those less educated, lower-skilled workers who will be most at risk and pay the highest price personally because of immigration reform. We provide our pivot point recommendations for that group in our chapters on income inequality and education.

Pivot Point
Report Card

Instructions

This report card is provided to allow you to reflect upon and assess the progress in this pivot point area. To use the report card:

1. Review the recommendation for the area.

2. Evaluate the progress made in the area to date and assign a letter grade using the system that follows: A–excellent progress. B–substantial progress. C–some progress. D–little progress. F–no progress.

3. Describe the nature of the progress and the rationale for your rating.

We will be posting our assessment for this area on an occasional basis. To see that assessment and to provide your input and feedback on the area, visit *http://www.workingthepivotpoints.com.*

Recommendation

• Strategic Immigration Reform

Grade

Reason

11 | Education: Up in the Error

Massive open online courses (MOOCs) became the rage of the educational community during 2012. The MOOCs feature professors from prestigious institutions such as Stanford, Harvard and the Massachusetts Institute of Technology delivering presentations with thousands of "students" logging on for a single session.[1]

These electronic versions of the old college lecture hall will become an alternative delivery system and will undoubtedly compete with the brick-and-mortar providers in the educational space—or should we say the "entertainment" space.

But, in the near to mid-term, we think that MOOCs will do little, if anything, to revolutionize education. That's because the needs and problems of education in the United States are systemic and not digital. There are issues and concerns related to outcomes, quality and cost across and throughout our educational "system" from higher education through our primary and secondary schools to preschool education.

In this chapter we examine all levels of the "system" beginning with higher education and working our way backward down the rungs of the educational ladder. We analyze the current state of various "educational reform" initiatives and conclude with our pivot point recommendation for a holistic intervention at the local level and in the early years of education.

HIGHER EDUCATION, STUDENT LOANS: VICTORS AND VICTIMS

As June 2012 drew to a close, after much wrangling, Congress passed a transportation bill that included extending the current 3.4 percent interest rate on government-subsidized student loans for one year.[2]

This was clearly a short-term but much-needed victory for students. That's because, based upon two reports that came out in July, it appears that the primary victors over the past decade have been some of the institutions making these loans and the victims have been many of the students who received them.

On July 20, 2012, the Consumer Financial Protection Bureau (CFPB) and the Department of Education (DOE) released its report titled *Private Student Loans*. Its Executive Summary states that "From 2005–2007, lenders increasingly marketed and disbursed loans directly to students… the percentage of loans made to undergraduates without school involvement or certification of need grew from 40% to over 70%."[3] The Summary highlights that there is more than "$150 billion in outstanding private student loan debt" and "cumulative defaults on private student loans exceed more than $8 billion." In commenting on this situation, in the press release distributed with the report, Secretary of Education Arne Duncan said, "Subprime-style lending went to college and now students are paying the price."

On July 30, 2012, Senator Tom Harkin (D-IA), chairman of the Senate Health, Education, Labor and Pensions Committee, released a majority report based upon a two-year study of for-profit higher education.[4] Tamar Lewin noted in her July 29 *New York Times* article that the report asserts "taxpayers spent $32 billion in the most recent year on companies that operate for-profit colleges, but the majority of students they enroll leave without a degree, half of those within four months."[5]

Lewin went on to report, "Students at for-profit colleges make up 13 percent of the nation's college enrollment, but account for about 47 percent of the default on loans. About 96 percent of students at for-profit schools take out loans, compared with about 13 percent at community colleges." Lewin quotes Senator Harkin on this matter as follows, "In this report, you will find overwhelming documentation of exorbitant tuition, aggressive recruiting practices, abysmal student outcomes, taxpayer dollars spent on marketing and pocketed as profit, and regulatory evasion and manipulation."

In a press release on July 29 responding to the report, The Association of Private Sector Colleges and Universities (APCSU) stated, "The report twists the facts to fit a narrative, proving that this is nothing more than continued political attacks on private sector colleges and universities." The *Harkin Report Backgrounder* that the APCSU distributed with its press release stressed that the private-sector colleges and universities "can open doors to many of the 13 million unemployed and 90 million underemployed by providing a skills-based education" and that these institutions "offer predominantly non-traditional students a means to improve their financial situation." The APCSU also challenged some of the claims in the report such as the default rate on loans (47 percent in the Harkin Report versus 24 percent in FY 2009 in the *Backgrounder*).[6]

That was then mid-2012. This is now mid-2013. One year later in June Congress failed to extend the interest rate for student loans. As a result, on July 1, 2013, it increased from 3.4 percent to 6.8 percent.

This will have an enormous impact on students. It will affect approximately 7 million borrowers who participate in the Stafford loan programs. It will increase the cost to the average college student by $2,600 and add $4,000 in interest costs if the student borrows the maximum allowed and pays it back in ten years.[7]

In June 2013, the One Wisconsin Institute (Institute) released a study showing that the impact extends far beyond the individual student. According to the Institute the "trillion dollar student loan debt crisis" presents a "clear and present danger for families and American economy."[8]

That's true because the Institute's survey revealed that individuals who were still paying back loans were significantly less likely to engage in economic activity such as home ownership and purchasing new vehicles as opposed to used ones that would stimulate the economy.

Congress did reduce the interest rate later in the year before the increase took effect. Nonetheless, the costs to both students and the American economy will remain high.

The important overriding fact is that the student loan issue and debate are only facets or symptoms of a much larger problem, which is that the country's higher educational system is in serious need of reform.

ATTAINMENT, ACCOUNTABILITY AND AVOIDANCE

That's not just our opinion. It was the opinion of the higher educational establishment as well. On October 17, 2011, six presidential higher education associations announced the convening of a new national Commission on Educational Attainment (Attainment Commission or Commission). The press release on the Attainment Commission stated, "The Commission's goal is to chart a course for greatly improving college retention and attainment, and, in turn, restore the nation's higher education pre-eminence."[9]

E. Gordon Gee, president of The Ohio State University, was chair of the Commission. In a May 12, 2012, *New York Times* article, Andrew Martin reported, "At a time of diminished state funding for higher education and uncertain federal dollars, Mr. Gee says that public colleges and universities need to devise a new business model to pay for the cost of education, beyond sticking students with higher tuition and greater debt."[10]

We were heartened when the Attainment Commission was formed. We were even more heartened to hear President Gee call for the development of a new business model for higher education.

We were dismayed, however, to realize that there had been a similar commission to this new one just a few short years ago in 2005. That commission, named the National Commission on Accountability in Higher Education (Accountability Commission), was formed by the State Higher Education Executive Officers to "stimulate conversations and make recommendations addressing the issue of accountability in higher education."[11]

The Accountability Commission was chaired by former Governor Frank Keating of Oklahoma and former Secretary of Education and former Governor Dick Riley of South Carolina. In remarks made to the

American Council of Education on February 15, 2005, in advance of the release of the Accountability Commission's final report on March 10, 2005, Paul Lingenfelter, executive director of the State Higher Education Officers, stated that "The Commission Report highlights three areas where performance must be improved, student success, research (capacity), and productivity (and cost effectiveness)." Near the opening of his speech, Mr. Lingenfelter observed, "the word 'accountability' makes us uncomfortable in higher education."

In the relatively plush economic times of 2005, the "accountability" discomfort could be avoided and the Accountability Commission's report could be ignored or put on a shelf somewhere to gather dust. In these post-recession times—with much worse economic conditions than then—that should not have been acceptable.

Unfortunately, it does not look like this will be the case. The Attainment Commission released its "report," which was originally due in the fall of 2012 in January 2013. The report was not only late. It also didn't present a business model and was devoid of details.

The report was delivered as an open letter rather than a plan. It provided three general recommendations: Change campus culture to boost student success. Improve cost-effectiveness and quality. Make better use of data to boost success. It also included some broad strategies and examples for consideration in each category.[12]

Writing for *Insidehighered.com*, Libby Nelson noted, "In the report, and in a call with reporters Wednesday afternoon, the college leaders cautioned frequently against 'one-size-fits all-solutions.'" And, they stop short of embracing some of the more controversial changes by other proponents of the "completion suggestion" such as the Gates and Lumina foundations often suggest."[13]

THE NEED FOR CUSTOMER-CENTERED REFORM OF HIGHER EDUCATION

We agree with the Accountability Commission that there can be no one-size-fits-all answer. On the other hand, we also agree with President Gee on the need for new business models.

We would add to that the need for universities to view their students as customers. Higher education students are in school to learn.

But the vast majority of them are there not only to graduate but to get a job or promotion where they can earn an appropriate return for the investment of their educational dollars.

This concept of return on investment is a pivotal one because, as Charles Blow notes in his 2012 *New York Times* article, "As college tuitions rise and state and local funding falls . . . students are taking on staggering levels of debt. And many can't find jobs that pay well enough to quickly pay off that debt."[14]

In March 2013, the State Higher Education Officers released a report disclosing that in constant dollars, state and local appropriations per full-time student had gone from a high of $8,670 in 2001 to just $5,896 in 2012.[15] At the same time according to a *CNN Money* report in September 2012, over the past decade, annual tuition costs at a community college have gone up by 40 percent and a whopping 68 percent at four-year public universities.[16]

The Attainment Commission did not have to provide "one answer." But it could have brought forward a range of new "business models" and actionable approaches to address this problem and to enable higher education to do a much better job in *creating value* for its customers—i.e., its students.

The report could have presented strong and implementable recommendations in the following critical areas that impact the value equation for those students: college costs, graduation and placement rates, return on investment, career education and skill development, teacher preparation, technology and education, and enhancement of the nation's primary and secondary education system. Here's some additional data on why improving the value equation in these areas is so critical.

Costs: Colleges Gone Wild. The Federal Student Aid division of the U.S. Department of Education in its *Strategic Plan FY 2012–2106* states: "The cost of attending public four-year institutions has grown at a rate of 6.5 percent per year from 2001 through 2010. The trend is similar in all sectors of post-secondary institutions. If this trend continues, the cost of a public education in 2016 will be well over twice the 2001 cost."[17]

How do the college costs stack up today? According to Michael Noer in his *Forbes* August 1, 2012 article "America's Top Colleges,"

"College is outrageously expensive." Noer highlights that "four years at an elite private school . . . costs more than a quarter of a million dollars. A degree from a more affordable state school . . . still costs around $100,000, even for 'in-state' students, who pay less in tuition."[18]

College costs have skyrocketed over the past half-century. In an October 23, 2009, *Inside Higher Ed* interview with Scott Jaschick, James Garland, former president of Miami University of Ohio and author of *Saving Alma Mater: A Rescue Plan for America's Public Universities*, observed, "Back in 1961 . . . (University of Minnesota undergrads paid) $213 yearly tuition. Last year (2008) Minnesota students paid $9,621 for the same experience, an increase of 4,400 percent."[19]

Graduation and Placement: Less Than Full Achievement and Disclosure. For students, it's not only getting into the higher education race, it's making it across the finish line and being rewarded appropriately for it. As various studies have shown, the results of higher educational institutions of all types are highly variable at best and awful at worst. Moreover, it's frequently hard to get sound data to judge those results—especially in terms of job placement.

In an April 9, 2012, article for *Businessweek*, Richard Vedder notes that "a goodly proportion (more than 40 percent) of those attending four-year colleges full time fail to graduate, even within six years."[20] The Harkin Report on for-profit higher education released on July 30 states that "more than half of the students who enrolled in those colleges in 2008–2009 left without a degree or diploma within a median of 4 months."[21]

In an attempt to provide better consumer information to prospective students, the Higher Education Act of 2008 included a number of new information requirements, including one to disclose "information regarding the placement in employment, obtained by graduates of the institution's degree or certificate programs." The American Enterprise Institute examined compliance with the employment placement requirement in its November 2011 report *The Truth Behind Higher Education Laws*, authored by Kevin Carey and Andrew Kelly. The authors indicated that "About two-thirds of the eligible colleges (101 out of 151) provided information about the employment of recent graduates." Carey and Kelly stated that 30 of those colleges "did not respond to the survey and did not have accessible employment information on their websites."[22]

Return on Investment: Fewer Dollars, Less Sense. One of the strongest arguments for getting a college degree is that the college graduate earns more than the high school graduate over a work life. As Mary Pilon notes in her February 2, 2010, article for the *Wall Street Journal,* the differences in projected earnings at that time ranged from a high of $1 million+ to a low of $279,893.[23] The Pew Research Center recently pegged that figure at $650,000 in a press release of May 17, 2012, which was based primarily on analysis of data in a report that Pew released in May 2011. The Pew press release reveals that "57% of Americans say colleges fail to provide students with good value for the money spent." In spite of this Pew reports, "86% of college graduates say it has been a good investment."[24]

Regardless of the exact size of the earnings difference, Richard Vedder in his *Businessweek* article asserts that "for many, attending college is unequivocally not the right decision on purely economic grounds." Vedder's arguments include: "Earnings vary considerably between majors." (The Pew research supports this, commenting, "The average figure masks wide variations in the financial returns to a college education, such as field of study.") "The number of college graduates far exceeds the growth in the number of technical, managerial and professional jobs . . . We have, for example, more than 100,000 janitors with college degrees, and 16,000 degree-holding parking lot attendants."[25]

Vedder in a July 20, 2012, posting for the Center for College Affordability, may explain why this is true: "Compare 2008 and 2010, looking at the average earnings of those working full-time year-round. For males with a high-school education, earnings rose 1.87 percent, while for those with bachelor's degrees, they *fell* 4.17 percent."[26] At least those people are employed. In his July 29, *New York Times* article "Is Algebra Necessary," Andrew Hacker points out that, "A January 2012 analysis from the Georgetown center found 7.5 percent unemployment for engineering graduates and 8.2 percent among computer scientists."[27]

The preponderance of the evidence leads to this inevitable conclusion—as college costs increase and if earnings do not increase proportionately, the return on investment or premium from a

college education will be lower. Moreover, as costs increase and employment is deferred, the payback period on the investment is lengthened.
No matter what calculations are being employed, the ROI for higher education in general appears to be getting much worse rather than better.

Career Education and Skill Development: Buyer Beware. The Obama
administration and its predecessor have placed great emphasis on use
of the community college system as an alternative for those students
who are vocationally oriented or need remediation or additional preparation before pursuing a four-year degree. Community and career
colleges are viable higher education options but not unqualified ones.
Many students who start programs do not complete them. The costs
can be high. And the students may be educated for jobs that don't exist.

The *Federal Student Aid Strategic Plan* points out, "The growth in
enrollments at proprietary and two-year institutions has soared in recent years (total growth of 31.6% between 2001 and 2009). This dramatic increase has produced its own unique set of challenges including
higher student default rates."[28] The Harkin Report highlights that at
for-profit colleges, "Among 2-year Associate degree seekers, 63 percent
of students departed without a degree."[29]

In a working paper issued in February 2012, The Center for Analysis of Postsecondary Education and Employment (CAPSEE) com-
mends the for-profits on the one hand, stating, "Short-run retention
is high and the for-profits do an admirable job of graduating students
from shorter certificate programs." CAPSEE then condemns them on
the other hand, stating, "But the for-profits also charge higher tuition
and fees than public sector alternatives, and their students are more
likely to end up unemployed and with substantial debts."[30]

Teacher Preparation: A Crisis in Competence. The quality of teacher
preparation and certification has been a concern in educational circles
for some time. Arne Duncan brought the issue front and center early in
his tenure as Education Secretary in a speech that he gave at Columbia
University in October 2009. In her October 22 *New York Times* article titled "Teacher Training Termed Mediocre," Jennifer Medina reported that
Secretary Duncan called for a "revolutionary change" in teacher training. Duncan related that based upon his conversations with hundreds
of teachers while serving as Chicago's school chief he universally heard

two complaints: (1) They did not get practical training they needed to manage their classroom and (2) they weren't taught how to use data to improve student learning.[31]

In June 2013, the National Council for Teacher Quality (NCTQ) issued a report, *Teacher Prep Review*, that added meat to the bones of Secretary Duncan's 2009 critique. The NCTQ reviewed teacher preparation practices at 1,130 colleges and universities that prepare 99 percent of the nation's traditionally trained teachers and was able to provide overall ratings for 608 of those institutions.

Based upon its research, the NCTQ declared that the teacher preparation has "become an industry of mediocrity, churning out first-year teachers with classroom management skills and content knowledge inadequate to thrive in classrooms with ever-increasing ethnic and socioeconomic student diversity." The NCTQ gave less than 10 percent of the rated programs three stars or more on a four-star scale and only four (Lipscomb, Vanderbilt, Ohio State and Furman University) got four stars.[32]

As might be expected, there has been some criticism and quarrelling with the NCTQ's findings and methodology. There should be no quarrelling, however, about the need to improve teacher preparation.

Technology and Education: Broad Band. Narrow Width. Over the past decade, and most especially since the Great Recession, online education has exploded. According to the Federal Student Aid Strategic Plan, "During 2006–2007 there were more than 11,200 college-level programs designed to be completed exclusively online. . . . More recent data shows that in 2009, nearly 30 percent of students took at least one online course, nearly three times the percent in 2002."[33] In addition, educational access to educational technology and tools of all types has increased substantially. There has been a phenomenal change in the manner in which education is being delivered. The more important question is whether the access to and utilization of technology is accelerating or enhancing learning both for adults and students at the primary and secondary levels.

The Department of Education in a September 2010 Meta-Analysis paper concludes, "Students in online conditions performed moderately better, on average, than those learning the same material through traditional face-to-face instruction."[34] In contrast, in a September 1, 2011, article, *Education Week* observes, "While there is much ongoing research on new technologies and their impact on teaching and learning, there is little rigorous, large-scale data that makes for solid research, education experts say." That same article reports, "organizations such as the consortium of School Networking, the State Educational Technology Director's Association, and the International Society for Technology in education, united on several occasions to voice their stance that investment in access and infrastructure was wasted without support for programs like EEET (Enhancing Education through Technology), which was designed to direct up to 40 percent of its funds to professional development needs."[35]

Secretary Arne Duncan appears to agree with this perspective. In an article written for the June/July 2011 issue of *Learning & Leading with Technology*, the magazine of the International Society for Technology in Education, he states, "But using technology is not an end in itself. The ultimate goal is to vastly improve the opportunity to learn, accelerate achievement and prepare students for success in the 21st century workforce."[36] Evidence suggests that in spite of some progress we are still quite a bit away from realizing that ultimate goal of using desktop and laptop to achieve the full potential of the shoulder top.

Primary and Secondary Education: Lessons from the Battlefield. The two major educational initiatives of the past decade were undoubtedly the No Child Left Behind Act of 2001 and the emphasis on Science, Technology, Engineering and Mathematics (STEM) educational programs. Now we are reconsidering them both. In the one case, it's a full-fledged retreat. In the other, it's a serious reexamination of scope and purpose. The "No Child" Act established strong federal requirements for states and schools, placing a strong focus on annual testing directed at promoting academic progress, and included penalties if performance was not satisfactory. The intent was to improve education, especially for the disadvantaged. That hasn't happened. As *Education Week* reported September 19, 2011, "By 2010, 38 percent of schools were failing to make adequate yearly progress." And in 2011, "several states did see failure rates over 50 percent."[37]

When it was signed into law in 2002, the Act had strong bipartisan support. Today it has few supporters. In a press release on February 29, 2011, the Department of Education announced that a total of 37 states and the District of Columbia had requested waivers from key provisions of No Child Left Behind in exchange for "locally designed plans to spur educational reform."[38]

STEM is still popular. Some have begun to question its universal necessity, however. Andrew Hacker makes the case against advanced mathematics forcefully and articulately in his "Is Algebra Necessary" article in which he comments, "Of course, people should learn basic numerical skills: decimals, ratios and estimating, sharpened by a good grounding in arithmetic. But a definitive analysis by the Georgetown Center on Education and the Workforce forecasts that in the decade ahead a mere 5 percent of entry-level workers will need to be proficient in algebra or above."[39]

Taken together all of these factors attest that our educational problem is multifaceted and the need for improvement is substantial. The bad news is that the journey to creating a customer-centered higher educational system will be a long and difficult one. The good news is that leaders within the higher education community have begun taking steps on that journey in all of the areas discussed here

EDUCATION REFORM IN MOTION

It's been said that necessity is the mother of invention. As we have shown, there is much necessity in higher education. This necessity has spawned "inventions" and innovations ranging from system changes at the federal, state and local levels to individual initiatives.

Even though the Attainment Commission's report was disappointing because of its lack of substance, it did highlight some of the efforts that warrant attention. We provide a Whitman's sampler of some of the other approaches that are being proposed, that are being discussed or are underway in the areas that can enhance the value equation for college customers (students).

Corralling Costs. As Andrew Martin reported in his May 14, 2012, *New York Times* article titled "Slowly, as Student Debt Rises, Colleges

Confront Costs," colleges have begun the cost control conversation but there has been little real substantive progress to date.[40] Jeff Selingo, editorial director of *The Chronicle of Higher Education*, reinforces Mr. Martin's perspective in his June 25, 2012, *New York Times* article stating "university leaders desperately need to transform how colleges do business."[41] Fortunately, there are numerous resources, such as James Garland's *Saving Alma Mater: A Rescue Plan for America's Public Universities,* that the leaders of higher education institutions can consult as they initiate their transformation journeys.[42]

Enhancing Graduation and Placement Rates. Public, private-sector and for-profit institutions are placing a renewed emphasis on graduation and placement. The "Open Letter to College and University Leaders: College Completion Must Be Our Priority" from the National Commission on Education Attainment shone a light but did not bring much heat to bear on the reform in this regard. Again, fortunately, there are other works such as Bowen, Chingos and McPherson's *Crossing the Finish Line: Completing College at America's Public Universities* that can be looked at as resources to improve performance in this area.[43]

Ensuring Value. Some institutions already excel at value creation. For the first time ever, in its college rankings released on August 27, 2012, the *Washington Monthly* included "a cost adjusted graduation rate performance ranking." The three institutions at the top of this list were University of Texas at El Paso, North Carolina A&T State University and Texas A&M University. New regulations and protections are being put in place to try to elevate the level of value delivered nationally.[44] In 2011, the U.S. Department of Education passed "Gainful Employment" regulations that, according to the Center for Analysis of Postsecondary Education and Employment, "will require most for-profit programs and certificate programs at public and non-profit institutions to pass at least one of three metrics to remain Title IV eligible." The Department of Education has also partnered with the new Consumer Financial Protection Bureau to provide tools to student borrowers to enable them to easily understand student loan debt and repayment requirements.[45]

Building Job Skills and Academic Competence. This was an area of important focus and concentration for the Bush administration and has been even more so for the Obama administration, as Kevin Manning noted in his August 7, 2012, *Huffington Post* article, "President Barack Obama's 'Skills for America' initiative is a step in the right direction."[46] By encouraging partnerships between community colleges and industry, students will be able to connect their educations to careers, many in new and emerging industries. Valencia College won the 2011 Aspen Prize for Community College excellence for its leadership in developing a "focused curriculum" targeted and tailored to the needs of industry.[47] Another community college model worth noting is the City University of New York's (CUNY) Accelerated Study in Associate Programs (ASAP), which is focused on low-income students and emphasizes workshops and intensive advising and tutoring. According to HCM strategists, ASAP is graduating students at "three times the rate of the average CUNY community college."[48]

Improving Teacher Preparation. Probably the most radical reform underway is in the area of teacher preparation and licensing. The Bill and Melinda Gates Foundation is shining a bright light on "Effective Teaching" as noted on the Foundation's website by "investing in bold research and reform efforts to better understand what makes a teacher effective and to rethink the way we recruit, retain and evaluate teachers in our schools in order to improve student outcomes."[49]

The Stanford Center for Assessment, Learning and Equity has developed a new model called the "Teacher Performance Assessment" that will be tested across the country over the next few years. In a July 30, 2012, article Al Baker of the *New York Times* reported, "New York and as many as 25 other states are moving toward changing . . . in favor of the more demanding approach that requires aspiring teachers to prove themselves through lesson plans, homework assignments and videotaped instruction sessions."[50] In spite of the number of states moving toward the new standards, there is still criticism and resistance by some educators about changing the teacher training, evaluation and certification process.

It can't be just about assessment though, it has to be about improving the preparation process itself. Over the past few years, diverse groups ranging from the American Association of Colleges for Teacher Education to the Center for American Progress have weighed in to describe innovations and better ways to teach teachers. We are not qualified to assess if there is a "best" way. We are qualified to know that "continuous improvement" is the hallmark of healthy organizations and professions and must be the same for teacher preparation.

Making the Connections. The U.S. Department of Education named August "Connected Educator Month."[51] In recognition of this, on August 1, 2012, Katherine Schulten—who blogs for the *New York Times* learning network—asked 33 educators to share their learnings and recommendations for sharing with their counterparts.[52] The educators provided hundreds of references proving the extraordinary value of these peer-to-peer connections in developing true learning communities that can be effective counterweights to top-down decision making that has frequently caused education to career from one fad to another. As we noted at the outset of this chapter, MOOCs (massive open online courses) represent a new way of connecting students worldwide to curriculum and faculty from elite institutions. MOOCs are in their infancy. Over time, they could be transformative or they could merely be a variation on the online delivery theme. Time, talent and technology will tell.

Passing the Test. No Child Left Behind has been left behind—and its successor appears to be the common core standards. These standards, which define the "knowledge and skills that students should have in English language arts and mathematics within their K-12 educational careers," were developed as a state-led initiative of the National Governor's Association for Best Practices and the Council of Chief State School Officers and launched in June 2010.[53] The standards had been adopted by 45 states and 3 territories by mid-2012. Thus a uniform set of standards has gained initial acceptance across the nation. The great debate, however, revolves around the testing related to those standards. As the readers' letters in "Sunday Dialogue: Improving Our Schools" in the July 22, 2012, issue of the *New York Times* demonstrates, there is great fear within the educational community that the standards are driven by an obsession with testing rather than focused on improving student performance or dealing with root causes of performance problems such as poverty and poor parenting.[54]

So that was the higher education report card in 2012–2013. If we were giving grades, most of them would be "incompletes." That might be disappointing to some but not to us. The attention being paid and the dialogue and discourse in all of these areas—even if some is in the early stages—are signs that reform is in motion and the higher educational system is "unfreezing."

Staying the same is not an option. That's not our opinion. It's that of President Gee of Ohio State whom Andrew Martin quoted in his May 14, 2012, *New York Times* article as saying, "The notion that universities can do business the very same way has to stop."[55] It has to stop because we are at a pivot point for the future of higher education in this country.

The Organization for Economic Cooperation and Development (OCED) supported this perspective in its report, *Skills Beyond School*, released in June 2013. As the New America Foundation (The Foundation) highlighted in its invitation to a July 10 event it hosted for the OCED, the report "makes clear that unless decades-old problems of quality, coherence and transparency are addressed, the United State will not continue to lead the world in postsecondary outcomes."[56]

The Foundation also pointed out in its invitation that research shows that a decade from now one in three jobs will require a Career and Technical Education (CTE) qualification. The OCED report on CTE "finds that rising tuition costs, widely varying quality standards and the growth of for-profit and online alternatives have introduced sizeable risks and complexities into the American higher education market."

Jeff Selingo referred to the period between 1999 and 2009 as the "industry's 'lost decade.'"[57] It appears the industry has begun to work the pivot points and there is forward momentum. If higher education, its allies and customers can continue to plot and chart the course that has and is being laid out, they have the potential and opportunity to make the period between 2009 and 2019 the industry's "found decade."

We need to find solutions for the U.S. educational problems and "system" at all levels, not just in higher education. We look at the other areas in the remainder of this chapter.

AMERICAN STUDENTS VERSUS THE WORLD

Over the past several years, an area that has received considerable attention is the relatively poor "average" performance of American students on international standardized tests compared to those from other places.

The most recent results for the 2011 exams of elementary and middle school students conducted by the International Association for the Evaluation of Educational Achievement showed U.S. students performing above average on math and science. But some experts said that these rankings, along with those that test students at a later age, show a problem in the American educational system because the average performance of the American student declines in later years.

In these most recent exams, fourth-grade U.S. students ranked sixth in reading, seventh in science and ninth in math. At the eighth grade, U.S. students ranked 12th in math and 13th in science. This compares to America's earlier rankings on exams of 15-year-olds conducted by the Program for International Student Assessment (PISA) in 2009, which found that out of 34 countries, the U.S. students ranked 14th in reading, 17th in science and 25th in math.[58]

The question is do the average scores and rankings on these international tests matter? We would say yes as a matter of national pride but not very much otherwise.

That's because these averages and aggregates conceal as much as they reveal. This is especially true, as is the case here, where we are comparing apples, oranges and grapefruits—or, in this instance, countries of different size, with significantly differing populations of test takers. Furthermore, the tests have little to no explanatory or predictive value regarding U.S. global competitiveness.

In the most recent elementary and middle school exams for fourth graders in math, the countries that ranked ahead of the United States were Singapore, Korea, Hong Kong, Chinese Taipei, Japan, Northern Ireland and Belgium. The highest scoring countries in the PISA rankings in math and science included Japan, Finland, Singapore and South Korea.

Is that problematic? We think not given the frames of analysis. As Gerald Bracey, former director of research and evaluation and testing for the Virginia Department of Education from 1977 to 1986, pointed out in two separate writings, based upon his review of the PISA results and related analysis:

- In science, the United States had 25 percent of all high scoring students. Among nations with high average scores, Japan accounted for 13 percent of the highest scorers; Korea, 5 percent; Taipei, 3 percent; Finland, 1 percent; and Hong Kong, 1 percent.

- Well-resourced schools showed excellent results.

And on recent elementary and middle school tests, states did much better than the average and the U.S. performance in a number of areas. For example, in fourth grade math, North Carolina performed better; in fourth grade reading, Florida and five other states performed better; and in eighth grade science, Massachusetts performed better.

Then there's the question of what this means in terms of economic development and educational effectiveness. On economic development, Bracey states, "test scores, at least average test scores, don't seem to be related to anything important to a national economy."[59] On educational effectiveness, the Brown Center Report on American Education cautions against attributing better test scores to a particular policy, relying on rankings to gauge a country's academic standings, and pointing to small high-performing nations and assuming that their policies should be adopted. (On this last point, the report notes, "On any test, the entire distribution must be considered, not just scores at the top."[60])

So, average test scores don't matter, right? Wrong. They do matter as indicators of problems within socioeconomic or demographic groups. Bracey makes this point in commenting on the PISA results for 15-year-olds, when he observes, "Poorly resourced schools serving low-income communities of color do far worse."

Clauz von Zastron, the chief operating officer of Change the Equation, a Washington, D.C.–based group that advocates for math and science education, makes a similar observation on the recent elementary and middle school outcomes. He says, "They (our most impoverished students) were holding even with the international average in some grade levels, fourth grade, but in eighth grade they've dropped below."[61]

DOOMED BY DEMOGRAPHICS?

This achievement gap is not restricted to performance differences on international tests. Large gaps exist among groups of students identified by socioeconomic (SES) factors such as race, ethnicity, family income, or native language.

As the Brown Center points out in its report, "closing achievement gaps related to SES is a prominent goal of federal policy, included in the No Child Left Behind Act, Race to the Top, and the Blue Ribbon Schools selection criteria." In our opinion, these SES gaps matter because they affect education level, potential for individual advancement and achievement, and the prosperity and growth of the nation.

The Brown Center (Center) notes that there has been interest in and debate about the size, nature and causes of these test gaps dating back to the Coleman Report of 1966 and the subsequent Harvard-based inequality studies. The Center itself did an analysis comparing the results on the two National Assessment of Educational Progress (NAEP) tests that are integral parts of the Nation's Report Card: The Main NAEP and the Long Term Trend (LTT) NAEP.

It found that the Main NAEP "consistently reports larger SES gaps." The Center notes this is important because the "magnitude of such gaps play an important role in policy." The Center then cautions that this was a "preliminary study" and "More work needs to be done on the topic."

The size of the gap matters in testing and policy terms. But the fact that a large gap exists matters much more in economic and human development terms.

There is no dispute that there is a gap. The Brown Center reports, "Researchers and policy makers are well aware that significant test score gaps exist between SES groups."[62] And due to the increase in poverty and changing nature of the educational system, in spite of best intentions and efforts, those gaps may be becoming gulfs.

In 2011, Misty Lacour, Southern Arkansas University, and Laura D. Tissington, University of Western Florida, did a literature review looking at the effects of poverty on academic achievement. They concluded there was overwhelming evidence that poverty directly affects academic achievement due to the lack of resources available for student success.

These resources include income, source of income and the mother's education level. Lacour and Tissington observed, on the other hand, that "Student achievement, particularly for at-risk students, is affected by the values and beliefs of the family and community."[63]

In another study, Savaltore Saporito, College of William & Mary, assigned poverty rates from the 2000 census of school attendance data for 21 of the largest school districts and looked at the number of poor students in each school. He found that the percentage of poor students in public schools was greater than in their corresponding "catchment areas" and the difference was even greater for children living in minority neighborhoods. According to Saparito, "These patterns reflect the withdrawal of wealthier children from public schools and into private, charter and magnet schools."[64]

CHARTER SCHOOLS: CURE OR CURSE?

The charter school movement is definitely changing the educational terrain. Is this a change for the better or the worse? The answer appears to be it all depends where and when you look and to whom you are talking.

On February 23, 2013, the *New York Times* published an editorial talking about the "better charter schools in New York" but referred to the national movement as "disappointing." Nina Rees, president and chief executive of the National Alliance for Public Schools responded to the editorial, taking exception and highlighting a number of facts including the movement has added 1,700 schools and a million students over the past five years with 610,000 on a waiting list; 500 charter schools have closed since the Stanford study of 2009, which gave the movement mixed reviews; and in New Orleans over 75 percent of the students are in charter schools with the number of students attending a failing school down threefold since Hurricane Katrina.[65]

There was a similar point/counterpoint to a March 1, 2013, *Washington Post* editorial focused on the successes of KIPP (Knowledge Is Power Program), a fast-growing national charter school network. The editorial cited a study by the independent firm Mathematica Policy Research (Mathematica) for 43 KIPP middle schools, which found that students in these charter schools showed significantly greater learning gains in math, science, reading and social studies than their peers in traditional public schools; that KIPP was not "creaming" to get the best student and not shedding its lower income students; and that three to four years' experience in a KIPP program translated into an 11-month gain in math and science, 8 months in reading and 14 months in science. One of the biggest differences that the Mathematica research discovered between the KIPP program and public schools is that it is an average of nine hours a day for 192 days a year versus 6.6 hours per day for the traditional program.[66]

In a web posting for School Finance 101 on March 1, Bruce D. Baker provided a rejoinder. He had some quarrels with the Mathematica "analyses and data presentation" but he focused his attention on the "big picture" lessons. They included the following: This is not about doing "things better" but doing the same things more and longer; the per-student cost difference is huge—the average KIPP school, depending on where it is located, spends about $4,800 to $5,000 more per student than its peers; and the scaling up costs to apply a KIPP approach across an entire city would be substantial: $688 million ($4,300 per student × 160,000 pupils) in New York City and $72 million ($2,000 per student × 36,000 pupils) in Houston.[67]

Stanford University's Center for Research on Education Outcomes (CREDO) should be the tiebreaker on the assessment of performance of charter schools. It has done the definitive research on them. When it presented its original findings in 2009, CREDO stunned the educational community and its observers by reporting that charter school performance varied widely, with some schools performing better than public schools, some the same, and some worse.

In January 2013, CREDO released a new report, *Charter School Growth and Replication,* which found that charter schools that start strongly are likely to continue to perform strongly and those that start off as low-performing schools usually continue that way. CREDO broke the schools into quintiles from high performing to low performing. It reported that, "80 percent of schools in the bottom quintile of performance remain low performers through their fifth year."[68]

CREDO's research presents a wealth of data and insights that can be mined to improve the performance of both charter and public schools. A primary focus of this new research was on charter management organizations (CMOs), a network of three or more schools built by a single operator.

Selected nuggets from the Executive Summary to the new report follow:

- On average CMOs are pretty average. There was a slight statistically different level in student learning compared to independent charter schools but nothing to brag or write home about.

- CMOs post superior results with historically disadvantaged student subgroups.

- The real story of CMOs is in their range of quality. Across 167 CMOs, 43 percent outpace the learning gains of the local TPS in reading, 37 percent of CMOs do the same in math. This is better for charter schools as a whole, where 17 percent posted better results than the TPS.

- CMO *new* schools on average deliver larger learning gains than independent charter schools but both lag the learning gains in the average TPS. These effects were consistent for reading and math.

- There appears to be no structural "new school" phenomenon for several years. Poor first-year performance simply cannot be overlooked or excused.[69]

In June 2013, CREDO released its National Charter School Study 2013 as the official follow-up to its 2009 study. The press release accompanying the study was titled "Charter Schools Make Gains, According to a 26-State Study."[70]

The best analysis of those "gains" that we have seen was provided by Tom Loveless in a Brown Center Chalkboard July 3 posting for Brookings titled "Charter School Study: Much Ado About Tiny Differences."[71]

In his posting, Loveless observes that at the beginning, "The new study showed charters doing better, outperforming TPS by .01 standard deviations in reading and scoring about the same as TPS in math." He asserts that the main finding of the CREDO studies is that "achievement between charters and TPS are extremely small, so tiny, in fact, that they lack real world significance."

Loveless follows that with an examination of standard deviations and statistical significance, which we won't go into here. But his conclusions are worth noting. There are "negligible charter-TPS sector differences uncovered by the 2009 and 2013 CREDO studies. The two sectors perform about the same."

The message in the bottle is a simple one. Charter schools are not a cure-all. In general, their highly variable performance tends to mirror, and in some instances lag, that of public schools. In our opinion, what is needed then is not a conversion of the public school system to a charter school system, but rather a collaborative system that produces the best outcomes for students—especially those who are "disadvantaged" in socioeconomic terms.

In December 2012, the Bill and Melinda Gates Foundation (Gates Foundation) gave $25 million in grants to seven cities to back public-charter cooperation in constructing approaches to benefit the students. In New York, four district schools and four charter schools will work together to develop a literacy program focused on the common core standards. In Denver, high-performing charter and public schools can apply for grants to serve as demonstration sites for teachers and administrators from struggling schools to visit and be paired with as mentors.[72]

The Gates Foundation is to be commended for funding this educational program that puts the kids' interest first. It promotes problem solving rather than turf protecting. It shows that what is new is not necessarily good and what is old is not necessarily bad. It shifts the discussion from yours or mine to ours.

EDUCATIONAL STATESMANSHIP

While the major educational fights about policy go on at the national level and the fight for school control goes on at the local level, because of the nature of the American educational system the true educational battleground and laboratory for experimentation is at the state level.

Because of the tough economic times, ongoing concerns about the quality of education, and philosophical and political differences, the fights at the state level that have received the most publicity over the past few years have related to topics such as reductions in force, increased class sizes, new approaches to teacher evaluation and collective bargaining.

The preponderance of coverage went to the states like Wisconsin and Ohio where Republican governors and unions clashed over their vision of what was right and labor rights. Less coverage went to states like New York where Governor Andrew Cuomo, a Democrat, quietly put in major educational reforms, and New Jersey where Republican Governor Chris Christie worked in tandem with Randi Weingarten, president of the American Federation of Teachers, to agree on a new teacher preparation and evaluation system that might serve as a model for other states and the nation.

As happens frequently, it's the things that don't get paid as much attention to that count. And what counts at the state level are not the sturm und drang surrounding them but the dramatic educational reforms that have been initiated or implemented over the past several years.

In its special report on American Competitiveness in March 2013, *The Economist* declared that "America's schools are getting their biggest overhaul in living memory." The major reforms include the adoption of common core teaching standards, permission for charter schools and tying teacher evaluation to students' performance. By the end of the first quarter of 2013, 46 out of 50 states had embraced the common core standards; 42 states had "bought into" charter schools; and about one-half the states had passed legislation related to teacher performance and student test scores.

In addition, *The Economist* reports that 17 states were offering vouchers for use in private school or tax breaks to those who donate to scholarship funds, 38 were putting in new pay structures and 19 had received Race to the Top grants for early childhood education.[73]

We're not saying that any of the measures is a panacea. In fact, in some ways that may be a placebo. As we noted above, charter schools are not an answer in and of themselves. But they are an effort to try to change the formula. So too are public schools and communities that place a priority on student performance and learning. (See our pivot point recommendation on this at the end of this chapter.)

There is no question that all of the states are attempting to do better with less. In spite of this, StudentsFirst, a group headed by Michelle A. Rhee, former school chancellor in Washington, D.C., issued a report at the beginning of the year that gave 12 states failing grades on their educational policies, with the two highest ranking states, Florida and Louisiana, only getting B- grades. These grades were based on an evaluation against a platform of policies such as overhaul of teacher tenure and using standardized test scores in teacher performance evaluations that StudentsFirst advocates.[74]

There is considerable debate in the educational community regarding the StudentsFirst group and the practices and policies it promotes. Our quarrel is with the report card itself. We think a state-by-state report card is a good thing. But that report card should be based upon performance or outcomes achieved rather than rigorous adherence to policies developed by some independent group.

The StudentsFirst report card takes only process into account. It reminds us of the Catholic school report cards that had comportment on one side and courses on the other. When it comes to reforming education we need to be grading achievement and attainment, not adherence or good behavior. This report card confuses means with ends. Adherence may have some relation to the end. But that ain't always necessarily so.

As a case in point, consider the Brown Center's findings on the common core standards. Based upon its analysis of a range of performance data, the Center foresaw the standards having "little to no impact on student learning." That's true because, as the Center notes, "Within state variation is four to five times larger than the variation between states." It goes on to observe, "Common state standards only target the differences between states not within them, sharply limiting common state standards' potential impact on achievement differences."

Just as with charter schools, common core standards in and of themselves are not the answer. Adapted to the particular circumstance and used appropriately, however, they can contribute to the solution. That's because, at the end of the day, the education drama plays at the local level. That brings us to our pivot point recommendation for education.

PIVOT POINT RECOMMENDATION: CREATE 10,000 UNION CITIES

David Kirp, professor of public policy at the University of California at Berkeley, has written a forthcoming book, *Improbable Scholars: The Rebirth of a Great American School System and a Strategy for American*

Schools. The book is about the highly successful transformation of the Union City, New Jersey, school system.[75]

Kirp summarized some of his major findings from that book on the Union City experience in a *New York Times* op-ed on February 10, 2013. They include:

- Start with pre-kindergarten, enroll almost every 3- and 4-year-old.
- Develop a solid "instructional core" focused on the skills of the teacher, the engagement of the students and the rigor of the curriculum that runs from pre-K through high school.
- In high school, tie everything to a single theme—pride and respect for "our house"—that resonates with the community culture of family, unity and respect.
- Build a district team and get significant participation and involvement to structure and lead the "turnaround."

Kirp celebrates the fact that Union City changed its existing system without outside intervention from groups like Teach for America or establishing charter schools. He states there are other "unsung" places that have had accomplishments similar to Union City.

Kirp notes, however, that there is "no quick fix." According to him, what is required is creating a "long-term strategy reaching from preschool to high school" and "learning from experience" and "tinkering" as the strategy is implemented.[76]

As we read Kirp's article and his concluding advice, a visual of a triangle came to mind. At the center of that triangle is the student, at the top is the family and at either tip are the schools and the community.

That triangle could be used as a broad framework for creating the "long-term strategy" to which Kirp refers. It could be used as the basis for bringing together all of the stakeholders within a district to create an integrated solution and shared ownership for educational transformation there. It would promote self-reliant planning and self-directed transformation. It would ensure that the transformation would be driven from the bottom-up rather than dictated from the top-down.

Each district's plan would be different. But there is one point that we think is critical from the Union City example and that is its adoption of almost universal pre-kindergarten for 3- to 4-year-olds. Based upon our review of the literature, there can be no better place to invest than in preschool.

As noted in a *Washington Post* article, "Educators see high quality early childhood as especially important to help close the achievement gap, which has been demonstrated to exist among children as young as 3 years old, and often reflects differences in socioeconomic status." According to that article, based upon a National Institute of Health study, early education for low-income children is estimated to generate $4 to $11 in benefits for every dollar spent.[77]

President Obama called for sweeping expansion of high-quality publicly supported preschool programs through a cost-sharing partnership in his State of the Union address. We are in complete agreement with the need for such an expansion so that the states and their school districts can get the financial support they need to initiate and implement this most essential part of transforming education at the local level.

The need and demand for such an initiative is demonstrated by the fact that at the beginning of 2013, only eight states—Florida, Georgia, Iowa, Oklahoma, Texas, Vermont, West Virginia and Wisconsin—provided pre-K education to more than half of their 4-year-olds. On the other hand, 35 states had applied for Race to the Top–like grants that were preschool related.[78]

In conclusion, high-quality education can be the great equalizer. It empowers people and is a key ingredient for success. We understand this as children who have come from families of relatively modest means and used our educational experiences at every level to prepare and propel us forward to achieve the American dream.

Frank Islam is passionate about and has made a commitment to support education so that others can achieve that dream as well. He funds scholarships at the University of Maryland, George Mason University and the University of Colorado. He also serves on the business schools at those institutions. In addition, Frank provides financial and intellectual support to Montgomery Community College in Maryland.

This is not just a philanthropic effort on Frank's part. He sees it as an investment in America's future—our youth who will be the leaders of tomorrow. Frank expressed his strong beliefs in this regard in a commencement address that he gave at George Mason University on May 17, 2013, when he said, "As I look out at those of you graduating today, I see me. I see the future of America. I see the future of the world."

Frank has put his money where his mouth is to help promote that future and those who will create it. Not everyone has or will.

We are in tough financial times and educational purse strings have gotten tighter. We would argue that this is not the time to pull back but to increase our educational investment. To paraphrase the ad, "You either pay me now or pay me later."

Failure to invest in early education and in proper support of a high-quality education for those who are the neediest among us has significant long-term costs. Lack of education is a breeding ground for failure and despair. If educational inequality wins, we all lose. This is a lesson we ignore at society's peril.

Pivot Point
Report Card

Instructions

This report card is provided to allow you to reflect upon and assess the progress in this pivot point area. To use the report card:

1. Review the recommendation for the area.

2. Evaluate the progress made in the area to date and assign a letter grade using the system that follows: A–excellent progress. B–substantial progress. C–some progress. D–little progress. F–no progress.

3. Describe the nature of the progress and the rationale for your rating.

We will be posting our assessment for this area on an occasional basis. To see that assessment and to provide your input and feedback on the area, visit: *http://www.workingthepivotpoints.com.*

Recommendation

- Create 10,000 Union Cities

Grade

Reason

12 | Innovation: Progress Is Our Most Important Product

THE UNITED STATES DID NOT INVENT INNOVATION. BUT IT MIGHT be said that innovation helped invent the United States.

From the American Revolution, to the Industrial Revolution, to the information technology revolution, American creative geniuses of all types have always pushed the outer edge of the envelope. As we move further into the second decade of the 21st century, however, it appears the envelope may be signed and sealed with not much to deliver.

In this chapter, we examine the innovation envelope to determine where America stands today and what will be required to make the country a winner in the "innovation wars." With no further ado, as they say at the academy awards, "May we have the envelope please?"

INNOVATION INHIBITION

Let's start by looking at the gloomier pictures and predictions, which see a significant slowdown in innovation and no major breakthroughs for some time. Two of the major proponents of this perspective are economists Robert Gordon of Northwestern University and Tyler Cowen of George Mason University.

Cowen came out of the box first in January 2011 with an e-book provocatively titled *The Great Stagnation: How America Ate All the*

Low-Hanging Fruit of Modern History, Got Sick, and Will (Eventually) Feel Better.[1] According to Cowen, the "low-hanging fruit" we ate that drove prosperity for "typical American families" were free land, technological breakthroughs, and smart, uneducated kids.

Citing Stanford economist's Charles Jones' research, Cowen reports that "Looking at 1950–1993, he found that 80 percent of the growth came from the application of previously discovered ideas." Looking at other data, Cowan asserts "the average rate of innovation peaks in 1873, which is more or less the beginning of the move to the modern world of electricity and automobiles."

Cowen concludes, based upon his analysis, that the primary factor driving the *Great Stagnation* today is the fact that "Recent and current innovation is more geared to private goods than public goods." In his opinion, that is what accounts for increasing income inequality, stagnant median incomes and the financial crisis of 2007.[2]

While he is highly critical of the country's current conditions, Cowen is cautiously optimistic in the long term. He sees three positive trends that may produce new low-hanging fruit in the future: the interest in science and engineering in China and India, the internet creating more revenue generation and the emphasis on greater accountability and quality in K-12 education in the United States.

Gordon's analysis is similar to Cowen's but his prognostications are far darker. In a paper issued in August 2012, he poses the question, "Is U.S. Economic Growth Over?" His answer is "yes."

Gordon's analysis reveals that the periods of slow and rapid growth in the United States have related to three industrial revolutions (IR): IR #1 (steam, railroads) from 1750 to 1830, IR #2 (electricity, internal combustion engines, running water, communications, chemicals, etc.) from 1870 to 1900 and IR #3 (computers, the web, mobile phones) from 1960 to present.

Gordon concludes that IR #2 was more important than the others and due to "spin-off inventions" was largely responsible for 80 years of relatively rapid productivity growth between 1890 and 1972. In contrast, IR #3 was quite short, promoting a "growth revival" between 1996 and 2004.

Gordon concludes that there have been no new breakthrough innovations recently and few spin-offs because of their one-time nature.

He goes further to assert that six "headwinds"—demography, education, inequality, globalization, energy and environment—will have a dramatic negative future effect on GDP and income distribution. He projects that it is likely that long-term GDP growth in the United States will be half or less the 1.9 percent experienced between 1860 and 2007 and "growth in consumption per capita for the bottom 99 percent of the income distribution could fall below 0.5 percent per year" for decades.[3]

PATENTS PENDING

Are Gordon and Cowen right? Is the American ideas machine broken?[4]

On August 18, 2011, the U.S. Patent Office issued its 8th million patent.[5] In September 2011, President Obama signed legislation dubbed the America Invents Act that mandated the first overhaul of the patent system since 1952.[6]

At the time the president signed that bill, the Patent Office was examining about half a million applications a year and due to underfunding had a backlog of 700,000 applications. This would make it seem that American ingenuity is alive and well.

Unfortunately, it's not that simple. Patent applications submitted and those approved are not necessarily the most useful metric for determining innovativeness.

That's because, as Joe Nocera wrote in his February 8, 2013, *New York Times* article, "America's patent system is a mess. The United States Patent and Trademark Office, understaffed and overwhelmed, issues too many needless patents. Patent trolls buy or create patent portfolios whose only purpose is to extort fees from the companies that actually make the things that the patents supposedly cover."[7]

President Obama acknowledged this problem in mid-February when he said patent reform needs to go further. He specifically cited the need to deal with companies who do not manufacture anything suing other companies for patent infringement. These cases are especially prevalent in the high-tech and software domains.[8]

When it comes to patents, it appears creativity is being exercised. But it's more by a bank of well-paid lawyers sitting in a room deciding whom to sue next rather than an inventor working diligently in his or her garage or cubicle to bring the next new breakthrough idea or product to market. Consequently, to get a fuller sense for what is being done in terms of American innovation, we need to take a deeper look into things and at the ongoing activities that are shaping the innovation playing field.

PATENTS PERISCOPE

As we have shown, not all patents are created equal, and just because something can be counted doesn't mean it counts. Fortunately, *Patenting Prosperity*, a paper released by the Metropolitan Policy Program (MPP) at the Brookings Institution in February 2013, enables us to get inside the numbers and make that determination.

Based upon an analysis of national and metropolitan area invention from 1980 to 2012, MPP's conclusions include the following:

- Patents are of objectively higher value now than in the recent past and more equally distributed among owners than in previous decades.

- Sixty-three percent of U.S. patents are developed by people living in just 20 metro areas that are home to 34 percent of the population.

- In recent decades, patenting is associated with higher productivity growth, lower unemployment rates and more publicly traded companies.

- Metro areas with high patent rates are significantly more likely to have graduate programs in science, especially high-ranking programs.

- Patents funded by the U.S. government tend to be of especially high quality, and federal small business R&D is associated with significantly higher metropolitan productivity growth.

The MPP findings paint a fairly rosy picture. But there are a couple of cautions. First, the MPP comments, "Still, the United States ranks just ninth in patents per capita . . . as global competition has increased." Second, "the value of invention is not evenly shared across regions because of the clustering of assets like science majors, tech sector workers and leading research universities."[9]

So there is room for innovation improvement. Meeting this need is important because, as Brookings emphasizes in the opening sentence of its paper, "Innovation is central to economic growth."

THE INNOVATION PLAYING FIELD

The Obama administration recognizes this and has always gone full throttle in its support of innovation. It released a white paper titled "A Strategy for Innovation" in September 2009.[10] The Department of Commerce has established an Office of Innovation and Entrepreneurship. In his FY 2013 budget, President Obama proposed the creation of a National Network for Manufacturing Innovation consisting of up to 15 institutes of Manufacturing Innovation nationwide funded with a one-time infusion of $1 billion. The president hit the innovation theme in his 2013 State of the Union address as well.

On January 15, 2013, the Brookings Institution convened a major event titled "Fostering Growth through Innovation." This session was the fifth of a series of forums that Brookings has held over the past three years that "have brought public and private sector leaders together with Brookings experts to examine the most promising ideas for promoting sustainable economic growth."

The event included panels on addressing fiscal challenges, U.S. manufacturing and government performance. Participants included Klaus Kleinfeld, chairman of Alcoa; Dominic Barton, managing director of McKinsey; Robert MacDonald, chairman, president and CEO of Procter & Gamble; and Phil Knight, chairman of Nike.[11]

On January 23, 2013, the Wilson Center convened a policy briefing conference call titled "Strengthening America: Inventing the Future." The call highlighted steps the United States needs to take to support R&D, improve its educational system and learn from best practices around the world.[12]

It's not just government and the think tanks. The private sector and higher education are involved as well. General Electric has opened a custom-built facility in upstate New York close to its research campus to build state-of-the-art new era batteries employing a technology their scientists developed.[13]

Doctor Robert Langer in his Langer Lab at the Massachusetts Institute of Technology (MIT) has "spun out companies whose products treat cancer, diabetes, heart disease, and schizophrenia, among other diseases, and even thicker hair."[14] MIT is also deeply involved in the development and dissemination of digital fabrication tools that individuals can use to custom design and construct everything from home furniture to living organs out of cells through a process called "additive manufacturing."[15]

There are other major trends that will impact and influence the future direction and potential of innovation. These include Big Data and Deep Learning.

Big Data is everywhere and the folks who are making a living warehousing and mining it abound. Big Data can be used to analyze web browsing patterns, tweets and transit movements; to predict behavior; and to customize messages and product offerings.

As Steve Lohr notes in a 2012 year-end column for the *New York Times* about Big Data, "I think it is a powerful tool and an unstoppable trend." Lohr cautions appropriately, however, that putting Big Data to work may take some time because of a "workforce bottleneck."

Lohr reports that the McKinsey Global Institute projected that the United States needed 140,000 to 190,000 more workers with deep analytical skills and 1.5 million more managers with the right training to use this data fully. He also stresses the need for experience and intuition to exploit the potential of this resource.[16]

The message to us from this is straightforward. Even with mounds and mounds of Big Data, human insights and innovation must come into play to matter and make a difference. Big Data. Small Minds. No Progress! Big Data. Big Brains. Breakthrough!

Deep Learning stands in contrast to Big Data. Deep Learning is the application of artificial intelligence and software programming through "neural networks" to develop machines that can do a wide variety of things including driving cars, working in factories, conversing with humans, translating speeches, recognizing and analyzing images and data patterns, and diagnosing complex operational or procedural problems.

As the *New York Times* reported in November 2012, there have been rapid advances in this field lately "made possible because of greater computer power and especially the rise of graphics processors." Deep Learning programs have recently beat humans in some head-to-head competition.[17]

Smart machines are here and they will continue to get smarter. As robots have taken over some of the jobs on the factory floor, they will take over functions in other areas of human endeavor. That's the case that Erik Brynjolfsson and Andrew McAfee make in their book *Race Against the Machine*.[18]

The real innovation challenge to us then it seems will not be to apply Deep Learning to replace humans but to use it to create new ideas, products and industries that will generate new jobs and opportunities for skilled and motivated workers. We're not certain exactly what those will be but we do know that it will demand the best in American entrepreneurship and innovation.

Getting the most out of Deep Learning will require deep thinking. That's where authentic human intelligence still trumps artificial machine intelligence. And it's what makes us optimistic about the upward movement of the American innovation curve and the potential it will bring with it.

INNOVATION OPPORTUNITIES

As we look at the evidence, it appears to us that the United States is getting back into the innovation game in a big way. Indeed, the problem may not be too little innovation but too much technological innovation, which alters delivery systems and is productivity enhancing but may not be job generating.

That's why as innovation opportunities are explored the human factor requirements must be examined as well. McAfee and Brynjolfsson provide recommendations in their book for developing practices and policies that help "people acquire the skills to be good workers in the technology intensive age." We comment further on the need to make the innovation–job skills connection later in this chapter.

At this point, it should be emphasized that the range of innovation opportunities is virtually endless. Obviously, advanced manufacturing applications stand at the front of the innovation list. The challenge and opportunity is choosing the right ones. In this regard, it is useful to reflect on Harvard Professors Gary Pisano and Willy Shih's classic 2009 *Harvard Business Review* article "Restoring America's Competitiveness," which won the McKinsey Award for that year.

In their article, Professors Pisano and Shih wrote that because of outsourcing, "many high tech products can no longer be manufactured in the United States." They identified a number of product categories that were already lost or at risk. These included semiconductors, lighting, electronic displays, energy storage, green energy production, computing and communications, and advanced materials."[19] Pisano and Shih's list warrants revisiting and updating as the nation begins its innovation trek. Based upon that analysis of that data in conjunction with the "reshoring" phenomenon, prudent investment decisions can be made based upon picking the areas in which there is the most "white space."

Although it might not technically qualify as an innovation, there also appears to be a unique opportunity to remediate America's crumbling infrastructure in an innovative fashion. In early 2013, the McKinsey Global Institute issued a new report titled *Infrastructure Productivity: How to Save $1 Trillion a Year.*

The report looked at infrastructure expenditures and needs worldwide over the past 18 years and projections for the next 18 and calculated that spending could be lowered by 40 percent or $1 trillion a year by taking three broad types of moves:

- *Optimize project portfolios*—by choosing the right combination of projects and eliminating wasteful ones
- *Streamline delivery*—by doing things such as speeding up the approval process, building incentives into contracts for time and cost savings, applying lean manufacturing techniques and adapting advanced construction techniques
- *Make the most of existing infrastructure*—by boosting asset utilization, optimizing maintenance planning and expanding the use of demand-management measures[20]

If the United States could establish an Infrastructure Bank similar to that which has been proposed in Congress for some time, or a national Industry, Infrastructure and Innovation Bank such as the one we advocate for in this chapter and in our manufacturing chapter, that institution could develop a standard template that could be used to do the type of planning required to make infrastructure projects more effective and efficient. Now that would be innovative.

INNOVATION INDUSTRY TARGETS: HEALTH CARE, GOVERNMENT AND EDUCATION

In the *Great Stagnation*, Tyler Cowen identifies health care, government and education as three of our least productive sectors and devotes a chapter to discussing their deficiencies. Similarly, Lenny Mendonca and Laura D'Andrea Tyson cite four anchors in the non-tradable sector that have acted as a drag on the economy and growth for many years: health care, education, energy and infrastructure, and government services.

Using a variety of data sources, Mendonca and Tyson found that in 2008, adjusted for population, we spent $650 billion more on health care than any developed country. Had we closed the gap between low-income students and those who were better off by 2008, GDP in that year would have been $400–$670 billion higher. If the U.S. public sector could cut in half its estimated "efficiency" gap with similar private-sector organizations, the opportunity for savings would be $100–$300 billion per year.[21]

These are some pretty heavy anchors and it will be impossible to alter the present condition and course of the country without addressing them. Put simply, productivity in the non-tradable sector stinks.

Nobel Prize–winning economist Michael Spence asserts that over the past 15 years we've significantly overdeveloped sectors such as finance and real estate, health care and government.[22] That's why Michael Lind of the New America Foundation has called for a "thoughtful supply-side investment program focusing on 'capital deepening'— improving the poor productivity in much of the U.S. service sector like health care, government and higher education by substituting technology for a lot of what is done now by labor."[23]

We don't think it's just technology. It's also process improvement. It's also streamlining and looking at "lean approaches" to operations. It's cutting unnecessary costs. The bottom line is that we need to improve the bottom line in the non-tradable sector in order to achieve the results and realize the full benefits.

That requires innovation. As Kenneth Rogoff, Harvard professor and co-author of *This Time It's for Real*, put in an article signifying on the lack of government productivity, "Today it is clear that reining in government also means finding ways to shape incentives so that innovation in government keeps pace with innovation in other service sectors."[24]

We present our pivot point recommendations on government at the end of this chapter. We presented our pivot point recommendations on education in chapter 11.

We do not have a specific recommendation on innovating in health care. But there are numerous institutions out there such as the Cleveland Clinic whose best practices should be studied, made the gold standard and universally adapted. There are also countless articles and books like the *Checklist Manifesto* by Atul Gawande, professor of surgery at Harvard Medical School, that set out methods to improve health care quality and productivity.[25]

We need to take those recommendations and make them common practice to continue to bring the health care cost curve down as we expand coverage under the Affordable Care Act. Steven Brill's groundbreaking cover article "Why Medical Bills Are Killing Us" for the March 4, 2013, issue of *Time* explains the extent and nature of this problem in detail and why it is essential for us to fix it.[26]

INNOVATION PARTNERSHIP: THE PUBLIC AND PRIVATE SECTORS

The history of innovation in the United States has always been an interdependent one between the public and the private sector. The government has provided funding and in some cases taken the lead in developing new initiatives that move the country and the economy forward. Felix Rohatyn spotlights large and transformative events that have contributed to America's growth in his book *Bold Endeavors: How Our Government Built America, and Why It Must Rebuild It Now.*[27]

These include the Louisiana Purchase, the Erie Canal, Lincoln's support of the transcontinental railroad, the Panama Canal, bringing electricity to rural America, and the interstate highway system.

Although not mentioned by Rohatyn, add to the list the WPA projects; NASA and its satellites used for weather forecasting, communication and GPS; and the internet. There are thousands of other examples across the spectrum of domestic and international programs.

The United States today is faced with the strongest international competition that it has ever seen. Mature and developing competitors like China, Brazil, India and Russia are placing a much stronger emphasis on innovation, research and economic development. China now ranks second in terms of dollars spent on R&D.

Consequently, the U.S. government needs to continue to be an investor in order for the nation to stay apace and eventually win the innovation race. Some of the priority areas for investment, as pointed out by Kent Hughes in his paper for the Wilson Center, should include science through increased funding for agencies such as the National Science Foundation, the National Institute of Standards and Technology, and the Department of Energy's Office of Science; and the Small Business Innovation Research program.

It's not just the government's role. As Hughes notes, "The U.S. innovation system depends on many parts working together, including laboratories that do basic and applied research; manufacturing facilities; a strong education system; advanced services (design, supply-chain management, and marketing); appropriate regulations; and adequate financing."[28]

In terms of financing, the private sector and public sector must share the load. In 2011, the U.S investment in R&D totaled $436 billion split roughly one-third government and two-thirds private sector. That split seems about right to us. In transitional times, when companies are tighter with their purse strings, however, the government may have to do a little more pump-priming.

The Information Technology and Innovation Foundation in its paper advocating a national network for manufacturing innovation comprised of 25 Institutes of Manufacturing Innovation (IMI) recommended that "Manufacturers should generally provide 50 percent of the resources for each IMI with federal and state (or other regional) governments comprising most of the balance." The proportional contribution can be questioned. The concept of shared responsibility and participation cannot.[29]

Bruce Katz and Mark Muro emphasize this in their Brookings white paper, *Renewing Federalism/Renewing the Economy,* in which they call for a "set of focused, astute initiatives that would at once lead the nation toward economic renewal while supporting regional and state empowerment." Katz and Muro go further declaring that "If states are the nation's laboratories of democracy, metropolitan areas are its centers of innovation—Washington should put itself in their service."[30]

Katz and his Brookings co-author Jennifer Bradley stress the importance of the metro areas in their new book *The Metropolitan Revolution: How Cities and Metros Are Fixing Our Broken Politics and Fragile Economy.*[31] In the book, they highlight success stories realized by cities and leaders in places across the country such as New York City; Portland, Oregon; and Miami by employing innovative techniques and methods to achieve positive results.

We don't know if "Washington" is willing to "put itself in the service" of the metros. We do know that we need an enhanced partnership among governments at all levels, the private sector and other institutional players in the innovation system if we want to make the United States the "creation nation" again.

MAKING AMERICA THE CREATION NATION AGAIN

You can't make a silk purse out of a sow's ear. The management consulting firm Arthur D. Little disproved this old adage in 1921 when its chemists created silk from pork by-products.[32]

Those were the good old days of U.S. innovation and, as economist Tyler Cowen points out, in the period from 1947 to 1973 because of American creativity and productivity, the inflation-adjusted median income here almost doubled. From 1973 to 2004, it rose only 22 percent, and has declined over the past ten years.[33]

This has happened for a multiplicity of reasons, including inventing it here and making it there, outsourcing pieces of the supply chain as part of the value-added assembly process, automating and/or eliminating what were once more labor-intensive processes, reducing public- and private-sector expenditures on research and development, growing the service sector and shrinking the manufacturing sector of the economy, diminishing union influence over wages and benefits, and hitting a technological plateau with no breakthrough technology to replace items such as the automobile and airplane.

Whatever the reason, it appears that when it comes to innovation that translates into economic benefits for the average citizen, the United States is now specializing in turning silk purses into sows' ears. It's time to reverse that trend and to make America the Creation Nation again.

We define "Creation Nation" as follows: *a country in which the private and public sector collaborate to develop and commercialize innovative new products and services that create new business or business opportunities that grow the economy and generate good paying value-added jobs within its boundaries.*

This definition emphasizes that innovation should be a means and not an end. The end should be increased GDP and enhanced individual economic well-being.

Ensuring that the benefits of innovation flow through to employees is essential to the future of the American economy and our system of capitalism. That's because as we noted in chapter 3 as Nobel Prize–winning economist Joseph Stiglitz observes, "No single measure can capture what is going on in a modern society, but the GDP measure fails in critical ways. We need measures that focus on how the typical individual is doing."[34]

If the pot of discretionary income available to each individual American producer and consumer becomes increasingly smaller and smaller, we can never achieve a recovery that grows the economy in a meaningful way. David Coates, Professor of Anglo-American Studies at Wake Forest University, makes a similar point contending, "the main immediate barrier to the recreation of jobs of any value here (well paid or otherwise) is not outsourcing. It is limited and uncertain consumer demand here at home."[35]

As the earlier sections in this chapter attest, America is definitely on the path to reclaiming its brand as the Creation Nation. As we follow this path, however, we need to keep our eye on the prize. We must remember the ultimate goal is not to make a silk purse out of a sow's ear but to bring home the bacon!

PIVOT POINT RECOMMENDATIONS: A "MOJO" AGENDA

That's why, as we stated in the manufacturing chapter, we need a "jobs-centric" industrial policy/agenda. We need the same jobs-oriented framing for the nation's innovation agenda—or as we prefer to call it the "Mojo" agenda.

That agenda needs to be adequately capitalized by the federal government in terms of R&D investments that stimulate private-sector participation. It should also be constructed to support the growth of what Brookings refers to in its Patenting Prosperity paper as "a strong national innovation system." To benefit regional economies and the nation as a whole, that system has to extend beyond the proposed network of 15 Institutes of Manufacturing Innovation.

With this as the overarching framework, we offer the following recommendations for inclusion in the "mojo" agenda:

- Establish a National Industry, Innovation and Infrastructure Bank
- Right-size, modernize and incentivize the federal government
- Prepare the 21st century workforce

Establish a National Industry, Innovation and Infrastructure Bank (3-I Bank)

We introduced the concept of the 3-I Bank briefly in chapter 8 of this book. We expand on the rationale for such a bank here and outline a process for its financing.

The need for a 3-I Bank comes from the fact that traditional financial institutions continue to provide inadequate capital and credit to many firms and businesses—especially the small, mid-size and start-up companies—that can play a primary role in innovation. Many banks still carry overvalued real estate assets on their books. Most banks are still primarily concerned about their own balance sheets and capitalization. This may be due to new regulations, increased governmental oversight, a natural retrenchment, return to doing business as usual and/or other investment priorities.

Whatever the reason, a substantial vacuum exists and only the government has the reach to step in and fill it in a way that will magnify the impact and benefit the national economy. Andy Grove, former head of Intel, made a persuasive case for governmental intervention and involvement in an article that he wrote for *Businessweek* on July 1, 2010.

In that article, Grove argued that based upon lessons learned from American history and studying East Asia that "job creation must be the No. 1 objective of state economic policy." He then advanced the following radical proposal, "We should develop a system of financial incentives. Levy an extra tax on the product of off-shored labor. . . . Keep that money separate. Deposit it in the coffers of what we might call the Scaling Bank of the U.S. and make these sums available to all companies that will scale their operations in America."[36]

We don't embrace Grove's proposed approach for capitalizing the Bank. But we agree absolutely on the need for such a Bank and taking it one step further to have the Bank fund start-ups and innovations. Nobel Prize–winning economist Edmund Phelps concurs with this.

Phelps says, "It makes sense to me that the U.S. government should voice support for innovation and throw its financial support into efforts to boost innovation in the economy." He advocates that the state should make an initial capital contribution to a government-sponsored enterprise and then create a system of new banks called the "Innovation Finance System" that could be loosely modeled after the U.S. Farm Credit System.

We think that the government should make a contribution to the 3-I Bank but that more importantly it should be capitalized with multiple funding streams or tranches with significant private sector participation in each. Specifically, we recommend three methods.

As the first tranche, multinationals should be allowed to repatriate their overseas profits with the caveat that they be required to invest a portion of those profits in the 3-I Bank. The repatriation process could be handled something like this:

- Firms would be allowed to repatriate all of their profits at a rate lower than the 35 percent top marginal current taxation rate.

- Repatriated profits invested in the Bank would not be taxed and would be paid interest on an established schedule for general deposits and a bonus upon completion of Bank-supported projects.

- Profits invested by a business in its own business or supply chain vendors linked to specific job creation pledges and tests also would not be taxed. If the jobs are not created, the business would pay tax plus a penalty.

- Profits invested in the U.S. treasuries and other vehicles that support government operations would be taxed at a low rate (5 to 10 percent) with the tax payment deferred over a period of three years.

- Other repatriated profits would be taxed at a modest rate—say 15 percent.

This approach would give businesses multiple options to consider. The 3-I Bank and job creation options should be the most attractive because they would have immediate and direct effects on our most critical needs today—job creation and economic growth.

A second tranche should be similar to the funding for an Infrastructure Bank proposed by Senator John Kerry and Congresswoman Rosa DeLauro in 2011. Kerry's legislation called for providing seed money to the Bank of $10 billion and then to attract private investments to large-scale infrastructure projects with the government providing no more than 50 percent of a project's costs.

This shared public-private concept should be the model not only for investment in projects but in the establishment of the Bank itself. Investors should be encouraged to hold common and preferred stock in the Bank. This could be accomplished by giving investors a tax credit on investments made in capitalizing the Bank and by establishing a reduced sliding scale "capital gains"–type tax rate on dividends paid by the Bank.

The third tranche should be a 3-I bonds program made available to individuals and institutions. These bonds should be thought of as "U.S. Jobs Bonds." The U.S. government should guarantee a modest but certain return on the bonds but that return should be tax-free. Congress has approved war bonds to be used to support the conflicts in Afghanistan and Iraq. It seems to us that the majority of U.S. citizens would be much more likely to invest in this domestic program than one related to unpopular wars.

Right Size, Modernize and Incentivize the Federal Government

The sequestration process was exactly the wrong way to reduce the size and spending of government. Cutting the agencies' budget across the board with a meat cleaver did absolutely nothing to improve governmental productivity or performance capabilities.

One of the more novel ideas that we have heard on how to make these cuts in a better way was put forward by the Brookings Institution in a paper by Paul Weinstein, Jr. That paper called for creating a bipartisan "Cut to Invest Commission" that would—operating in a manner similar to the Base Realignment and Closure Commission—identify $200 billion in low-priority spending to be eliminated with $100 billion in the savings to be redirected to high-priority investments.[37]

We absolutely agree with the need to eliminate duplication and waste. We also need to make government work leaner, better and smarter. But, as alluded to earlier in this chapter, this requires a systematic approach rather than axes and chopping blocks. We recommended such an approach with the following two steps in *Renewing the American Dream*:

1. *Have each federal government agency conduct a zero-based organizational assessment and develop a strategic blueprint to become a high-performing organization.*

2. *Implement a government-wide operational excellence initiative with maximum feasible employee involvement.*

These steps are even more relevant and necessary today as a basis for right-sizing, modernizing and incentivizing government, so we review and update them below.

1. *Have each federal government agency conduct a zero-based organizational assessment and develop a strategic blueprint to become a high-performing organization.*

Our government agencies today are confronted by budget cuts that will result in the need for reductions in force and scope of operations. These reductions can be made in an across-the-board and mindless manner or they can be designed to make these agencies into high-performing organizations.

High-performing organizations have the right strategy, the right structure, the right systems, the right employees and a laser-beam focus on the needs of their customers. That's the "right stuff" for the 21st century and managing in an era of constrained resources.

Therefore, we recommend that each federal agency create its own strategic blueprint for becoming a high-performing organization. That blueprint should be developed by conducting a comprehensive analysis of the agency's current state and defining its desired state given its new funding level. Based upon that, the agency should do a gap analysis and define the critical path to be followed to achieve the level of transformation required to achieve its desired state.

The high-performing organization strategic blueprint should be developed with the leadership of the agency's CEO championed by the COO, and directed by a performance improvement officer. Experienced organizational personnel should be involved in creating the blueprint as part of the agency's high-performance team, along with agency specialists in organizational analysis and design, human resource factors, financial analysis and information technology. The team should also have outside experts and specialists as members.

We believe that these high-performing organization blueprints are central to improving government performance in a manner that is strategic, systematic and sustainable. These new budget cuts provide an opportunity to fundamentally rethink and clarify the vision, mission and strategy of all of our governmental agencies for the 21st century. Anything else will just result in "business as usual" by smaller agencies.

2. Implement a government-wide operational excellence initiative with maximum feasible employee involvement.

After the strategic blueprints are in place, a government-wide initiative should be launched to ensure their effective implementation by building a culture of operational excellence in each agency. An organization that exhibits operational excellence has the following characteristics:

- Customer-centered
- Emphasis on quality

- Balance between efficiency and effectiveness
- Streamlined processes
- Commitment to continuous improvement
- Employees capable of and involved in problem solving
- Effective measurement and management systems
- Management decisions that are data-driven and evidence-based
- Commitment to ongoing innovation and organizational renewal

Many years ago, quality guru Ed Deming noted that up to 80 percent of the performance problems in the manufacturing environment were due to defective or imperfect processes and systems, rather than people. An organization that is committed to excellence understands this and focuses as much attention on those processes and the manner in which the work gets done as it does to defining, developing and implementing policies and programs. As Mies van der Rohe put it, "God is in the details."

An operational excellence approach can be implemented in each agency from the top down, bottom up, and managed in the middle in order to promote employee engagement and buy-in. It can build on the successes and address the failures of past governmental reform efforts such as NPR, GPRA, and PART.

Instead of throwing the baby out with the bathwater in these most difficult times, we recommend inviting everyone into the tub to play a role in discovering how the government can do more and better with less.

Prepare the 21st Century Workforce

Andrew McAfee, co-author of *Race Against the Machine,* opines that accelerating innovation and advanced technology is likely to increase inequality because it "favors more highly skilled workers over less skilled workers." McAfee points out that it is the "middle skill jobs that are shrinking" while "high skill jobs and low skill jobs" are increasing due to automation.[38]

This creates a three-part need: (1) to ensure the proper training for the new jobs that are being created, (2) to provide retraining for those today who are currently in middle-skill jobs, and, (3) to address the issue of those individuals who are working in low-pay and low-wage jobs. We provided recommendations to address parts 2 and 3 in our chapter on individual economic well-being. We address the need to prepare the "high-skill" workers here.

If its plans are accepted, the Obama administration's proposed National Network for Manufacturing Innovation (NNMI) consisting of linked Institutes for Manufacturing Innovation (IMIs) will become the primary training and development vehicle for high-skilled jobs. The Preliminary Design document for the NMMI released in January states that the IMIs will "act as 'teaching factories' to build workforce skills at multiple levels."[39]

The document indicates that in the education and training area, "An Institute will assess skills and certifications need and provide educational opportunities to improve and expand the manufacturing workforce" including K-12 programs, community colleges, university collaboration, graduate students, and postdoctoral students, "in order to impact both the technical and degreed engineering workforce."

This is a laudable, comprehensive and ambitious agenda. We recommend, however, that in order to ensure the development of the "technical workforce" in a targeted and timely manner that each IMI have a "Skilled Manufacturing Workforce Education and Training Plan."

That plan should be standards- and competency-based and developed and driven by industry input. It should identify all of the key players responsible for educating and training a skilled workforce and define and assign roles, responsibilities and performance expectations of each participant. It should also establish a specific timetable for implementation and spell out how the various players would communicate and cooperate to implement the plan.

The National Institute for Metalworking Skills (NIMS) provides an excellent model that each IMI could employ to develop customized and appropriate plans for their regions. NIMS was formed in 1995 by the metalworking trade associations to develop and maintain a globally competitive workforce. NIMS has developed national skill standards in 24 operational areas that cover the breadth of metalworking operations.

NIMS certifies individual skill against these standards. The NIMS credentialing program requires that the candidate meet both performance and theory requirements on exams that are industry designed and industry piloted.

The metalworking industry uses the credentials to recruit, hire, place and promote individual workers. Training programs use the credentials as performance measures of attainment. The credentials are often the basis for articulation among training programs.

The NIMS approach is rigorous and comprehensive. It ensures that the 21st century worker develops the cutting-edge skill and competencies required by the 21st century company.

NO MORE JOBS?

We have talked a lot about innovation but have not said much about the role and contribution of the most important person in the innovation and job creation process—the entrepreneur and innovator. That's because we saved the best for last.

Steve Jobs is an exemplar of entrepreneurship and innovativeness. The question is, when he died in 2011 did some of America's hopes, dreams and potential for future jobs pass away with him?

This need not be the case, if we can heed the key lessons that Jobs, this quintessential American, provided through his life, leadership and continuous and incredible ability to reinvent himself and his businesses.

President Obama described Jobs as "among the greatest of American innovators." Many other articles and tributes characterized Jobs as a visionary.

Indeed, Jobs was an innovator and a visionary. But we think the more accurate label for him would be that of an "evolutionary revolutionary": Evolutionary in that Jobs was a lifelong learner engaged in a personal and professional journey of exploration, discovery and growth. Revolutionary in that he was countercultural, redefining the industries he touched and transforming part of the world in accordance with his own image, likeness and preferences.

Here are some of the lessons from Steve Jobs, the evolutionary revolutionary:

- *Be Future Focused.* As those rare interviews with the extremely private and secretive Jobs revealed, he didn't live in the past and was not impressed by his own accomplishments. His life was one of becoming rather than being. He looked forward and outward, not backward and inward. He never asked, "What's been done?" He always asked—to borrow a phrase based on one of his product lines, "What is Next?"

- *Exceed Expectations.* Jobs put the "i" into phone, pod and pad. In doing so, he captured most of the buying public because that "i" was we. Jobs gave us products that delighted and dazzled and created needs that we had not even imagined. As a result, he established an emotional bond and an interdependent relationship that converted customers into technological and electronic cultists— devotees willing to stand in line to get the new product or upgrade as soon as it came out.

- *Good Enough Is Never Good Enough.* Being the first to market with a new product was not Jobs' hallmark or secret for business success. Redefining the market with the "best" product was. He accomplished this by being a detailed perfectionist and the master of intuitive and minimalist design. His mantra was simplify, simplify, simplify. As soon as the "best" new product was introduced, he and his team went to work to make it even better. On the week of Jobs' death, Apple introduced the iPhone 4s, and the 5 was in the wings.

- *Trust Your Gut.* Jobs was never a slave to the conventional wisdom. In fact, he played the game the other way. He took the unexpected and unanticipated and made them conventional ways of doing business. There is no better example of this than Jobs' success with Pixar, the computer animation studio that he bought from George Lucas in 1986 for $10 million. At that time, many in the investment community saw this move by Jobs as dalliance or a pure vanity move. Nothing could have been further from the truth. After helping to develop the next generation of computer graphics and building the Pixar brand through vehicles like *Toy Story*, he sold Pixar to The Walt Disney Co. for $7.4 billion.

- *Be Your Own Person.* Jobs was a firm and absolute believer in defining and shaping one's own destiny. Jobs' philosophy in this regard is best captured in his own words from his 2005 Stanford commencement address where he advised the graduates, "Your time is limited so don't waste it living someone else's life. Don't be trapped by dogma—which is living with the results of other people's thinking. Don't let the noise of other's opinions drown out your own inner voice."

- *Leave a Living Legacy.* Jobs' legacy is ensured by his extraordinary achievements. Walter Isaacson wrote an authorized biography of Jobs that substantiate his contributions and provide new insights into the man.[40] Jobs, however, recognized that for a legacy to survive it must be sustained, and the only way that can be done is through the ongoing efforts of others. Jobs understood that spirit and creativity are the invisible forces that move organizations and individuals and keep them vital and forever young. That is why this man who did not complete even one year of college founded Apple University to teach company executives and future leaders to think like him and to tap into their own and the company's full potential.

A few commentators have cited Jobs as an example of American exceptionalism. Some dispute the concept of American exceptionalism. No one, on the other hand, could ever dispute the fact that Steve Jobs was an extraordinary American.

This extraordinary American in his dress uniform of sneakers, faded jeans and black mock turtle neck taught his lessons through positive examples and deeds. He stands in stark contrast to pandering politicians in their mental straightjackets and buttoned-down business executives in their camouflage suits who substitute hollow rhetoric and meaningless promises for meaningful actions and problem solving.

America and the world need extraordinary Americans. Steve Jobs showed us that the future belongs to those who can envision and create it and not to those who are mired in the past and define themselves by limits rather than possibilities.

If we as Americans realize this and act upon his lessons, we will once again be able to renew our American hopes, dreams and jobs. We will be able to respond to the question, "No More Jobs?" with the answer "No! More Jobs!"

Yes. More jobs—and some of them are being brought back to the United States from India by Apple to make its Macs here. There's just nothing better, in our opinion, than an American Apple.

Pivot Point
Report Card

Instructions

This report card is provided to allow you to reflect upon and assess the progress in this pivot point area. To use the report card:

1. Review the recommendation for the area.
2. Evaluate the progress made in the area to date and assign a letter grade using the system that follows: A–excellent progress. B–substantial progress. C–some progress. D–little progress. F–no progress.
3. Describe the nature of the progress and the rationale for your rating.

We will be posting our assessment for this area on an occasional basis. To see that assessment and to provide your input and feedback on the area, visit *http://www.workingthepivotpoints.com.*

Recommendations

- A Mojo Agenda
  - A National Industry, Innovation and Infrastructure Bank
  - Right-size, Modernize and Incentivize the Federal Government
  - Prepare the 21st Century Workforce

Grade

Reason

Epilogue:
Pivot Forward

GREAT NEWS. GOOD NEWS. NEWS. BAD NEWS. SOME RAYS OF sunshine. Several clouds. Some thunder. A little rain. That was the general context for working on the pivot points that was established from Election Day 2012 to mid-2013.

In this epilogue we examine how things stack up and what factors will be influencing the pivot points going forward. We provide an analysis and a little prognostication regarding whether the United States is ready to pivot forward or pivot backward in the second half of 2013 and for the remainder of this decisive decade based upon the status at the pivot points as we wrap up writing this book.

AMERICAN EXCEPTIONALISM DEFEATS EXTREMISM

By far the brightest sunshine in this transitional period was provided by the American voters on Election Day. One of the things that makes America exceptional is the genius, common sense and levelheadedness of its people. They proved their mettle once again in this election cycle.

Immediately after the election, much of the media characterized the results as an indication that the country was divided and as a vote for the status quo. For example, The *Washington Post* observed in a

November 7 editorial, "The nation was starkly divided before, and it remains starkly divided today."[1] George Will in his column on the same day declared, "A nation vocally disgusted with the status quo has reinforced it by ratifying existing control of the executive branch and both halves of the legislative branch."[2]

Those viewpoints reflected the conventional wisdom. But, as occurs frequently, the conventional wisdom was wrong—or, at best, incomplete and inaccurate.

When we peel back the layers of the onion, drill down into the numbers and analyze the process from outside-the-Beltway-in instead of inside-the Beltway-out, we come to very different conclusions. The citizens of this nation are not nearly as divided as one would think. The national electoral vote was not for the status quo but for quo vadis (whither goest thou).

The electorate writ large unequivocally set out a mandate for moderation, goodwill, compromise and a center left–center right approach to governing this nation. Looking at the manner in which Mitt Romney's campaign for president was conducted and examining the data from a variety of perspectives explain why this is the case.[3]

During the Republican primaries in order to win the nomination, Governor Romney moved to the right of his conservative opponents such as Rick Perry, Newt Gingrich and Rick Santorum. He went Tea Party crazy for a time. His last concession to the extreme conservative wing of the party, however, was to pick Paul Ryan to be his running mate. After that Romney tacked back to the middle as quickly as he could.

He assiduously avoided Ryan's controversial budget plan and Medicare voucher proposal. Beginning from the first debate, in policy terms, Romney became virtually the mirror image of Obama on almost all issues both domestic and foreign. Their positions were so similar that in subsequent debates, if Obama answered a question first, the Governor going second could have simply responded "me too."

This movement to the middle ground continued through Romney's concession statement, which was graceful, human and authentic. In that speech Romney said, "The nation as you know is at a critical point. (*We would say a pivot point.*) At a time like this, we can't risk partisan bickering and political posturing. Our leaders have to reach across the aisle to do the people's work."[4]

Romney's words were not meant to mollify the extremist Tea Party element of the Republican Party but to acknowledge the need to bridge differences and to bring the country together to solve problems. They were a call for more civility rather than more hostility in our political discussions and negotiations

The reason for Romney's clarion call to the middle rather than a shout-out to the radical right becomes clear when you look at how the independent or moderate voters split on Election Day—about 50/50 (54 percent for Romney, 46 percent for Obama).[5] That's because after Romney's initial debate performance and in subsequent debates, he became an acceptable alternative to President Obama because he appeared mainstream, rational and reasonable and not a candidate from the conservative lunatic fringe.

Romney lost nationally by over 3 million votes, or approximately 2.5 percent of the almost 121 million votes cast.[6] Although it cannot be proven, it seems highly likely that if Romney had continued to run for president as the uber-conservative candidate who won the Republican primaries instead of as the Obama lookalike, his margin of defeat would have been considerably larger. It is not hard to imagine a defeat of the type suffered by Barry Goldwater in 1964, George McGovern in 1972 and Jimmy Carter in 1980.

So much for the divide—what we saw in the vote nationally was citizens united in their search for equanimity and balance in the manner in which they cast their ballots. We saw the same thing in some state contests where voters split their tickets to give Romney a considerable victory in the presidential race over Obama but the edge by a handy margin to the moderate Democrat in the senatorial race. Consider the following (rounded up or down to nearest whole percent):

- Indiana: Obama 44 percent. Donnelly 50 percent.
- Missouri: Obama 44 percent. McCaskill 55 percent.
- North Dakota: Obama 39 percent. Heitkamp 50 percent.

- Montana: Obama 42 percent. Tester 49 percent.
- West Virginia: Obama 36 percent. Manchin 61 percent.

This ticket splitting is evidence of what we would call the strength and power of the moderate center. This discriminating voting and ticket splitting also occurred in states such as Florida, New York, Virginia and Pennsylvania where Obama won but the Democrat for Senate ran ahead of the president in terms of the victory margin.[7]

We would be remiss if we did not comment on the special cases of the senate races in Indiana and Missouri where legitimate rape occurred. That rape was the one in which the two Republican candidates opened their mouths, inserted their feet or some other portions of their anatomies, swallowed hard, spoke profanely and, in doing so, managed to snatch smashing defeats from the jaws of certain victories. God works in mysterious ways—doesn't She?

As for this being about the status quo, forget about it. Status quo means things stay the same. In this election, the Democrats gained a net of 2 seats in the Senate and a net of 7 seats in the House. The number of female senators went to 20—an all-time high. Hispanics turned out and cast their ballots for Democrats in record numbers.[8]

As for the game of campaign money ball, time and again small money and smart money trumped big money. The U.S. Chamber of Commerce spent $24 million in 15 senate races but only backed the winner in two.[9] In spite of spending hundreds of millions of dollars on the various races, according to the *Wall Street Journal,* the Super PACs' impact appears to have been limited.[10] The following is evidence that supports that opinion.

The two super PACs that Karl Rove is affiliated with, American Crossroads (Crossroad) and Crossroads GPS (GPS), spent $170 million this election. Crossroads backed winners with just over 1 percent of the money it expended. GPS spent 13 percent of its dollars for winners. It is reported that the billionaire Koch Brothers spent $23 million on a "slew of races" but only supported three winners.[11] Last but not least, there's billionaire casino magnate Sheldon Adelson. Adelson spent $53 million this election cycle beginning with the Republican presidential primaries. On Election Day, only one Adelson-backed candidate (Dean Heller, R-NV) won.[12]

It has been widely and correctly reported that President Obama enjoyed considerable margins with African American, Hispanic, youth and women voters. His performance with the moderate and independent voters has not been stressed or analyzed enough, however. President Obama needed to get the right level of support from these voters in order to carry the swing states and win the election. He did. We now pivot forward.

In conclusion, there was a mandate this Election Day. It was a mandate for the middle road and the middle class. It was a mandate for moderation and compromise. It was a mandate for the power of the average citizens' voice in shaping America's future. It was a mandate for exceptionalism over extremism.

THE CITIZENS' MOOD—2012: REALISTIC/SKEPTICAL NOT CYNICAL

That's not to say that everyone was ecstatic at the election's outcome. Indeed, they were not.

Immediately after the election, the Pew Research Center conducted a survey through Google that found voters had a mixed reaction. The survey found that 44 percent of the voters said they were happy with the outcome; 43 percent said they were unhappy.[13]

When asked for a single word to describe their reaction, Obama voters most frequently said they were "relieved" and "happy." Many said "great," "good" and "elated."

Romney voters most frequently said they were "disappointed" or "sad." The next most frequent responses were "disgusted," "sick" and "horrified."

For nonvoters, it was a different story. The majority (55 percent) said they were neither happy nor unhappy because of the election outcome. Interestingly, 29 percent said they were "happy" as opposed to only 16 percent who said they were unhappy.[14] This is an indication that, in general, the "bystanders" were feeling supportive of the continuation of the Obama administration's work.

In another Pew Research Center survey conducted just one week after the election, the voters were more aligned with each other than divided in feeling "pessimistic about partisan cooperation" in national politics in the foreseeable future. Fully 66 percent said that relations between Republicans and Democrats would either stay the same (52 percent) or get worse (14 percent).

A broad majority of all voters wanted Barack Obama (72 percent) and the Republican leadership (67 percent) to work with the other side. In contrast, 50 percent of Republicans surveyed wanted their leaders to "stand up" to Obama and 42 percent of Democrats did not want Obama to work with the Republicans.[15]

Surveys are snapshots in time. What these survey results tell us is that the highly partisans wanted to stay partisan. But that in general the citizens were still invested in wanting to see the political process and our governance system work.

We see this as a positive sign. While they may have been "pessimistic," the average citizens were being realistic in their assessment and expectations for the future. They were skeptical rather than cynical. This is an important distinction.

Alan Gitelson, a professor of political science at Loyola University in Chicago, has been studying citizen cynicism and skepticism toward government for almost a quarter of a century. Over that period, he has found that both have increased substantially.

As Professor Gitelson explains, however, the cynicism rating is more important than the skepticism one because cynical citizens do not participate in politics.[16] Skeptical citizens might—if they can be persuaded and given the opportunity and reason to set their skepticism aside for a time—engage in what sociologists call the "willing suspension of disbelief."

The 2012 elections and their aftermath gave the American citizenry that opportunity. What happens in the political arena during 2013 will determine whether there is the reason. Later in this chapter we take a look at how people were feeling mid-year.

A LEAGUE OF THEIR OWN

One of the sources for citizen skepticism and concern about the potential for bipartisanship can be attributed to the state of the Republican Party both before and after Election Day.

If the national elections had been contested in the Republicans' political version of a fantasy football league, Barack Obama would have received 47+ percent of the vote. And they would have picked up five seats in the Senate and eight seats in the House. Just the opposite occurred.

This stunned many Republicans, whose parallel universe view had them convinced that they would not only win but dominate in the presidential and congressional election battles. Why and how did they get this so wrong? What are the implications for them and why is how this is resolved important to the future of our nation?

It's important because a vibrant two-party system makes our republic stronger. It provides the basis for compromise, forward momentum and progress on the pivot points. It builds the country up and brings us together rather than tearing us down and apart.

If the Republicans continue to play in a league of their own, they and our democracy will be worse off for it. It is from this perspective that we provide our assessment of the Republicans' current situation and prescriptions for the future.

The Reasons

There are undoubtedly many reasons for the Republicans' miscalculations this past election cycle. We want to highlight three: poor campaign execution, personal biases and—by far the most important—life within the conservative echo chamber or bubble.

Much was written immediately after the elections about the poor internal polling of the Romney campaign and its inability to get its turnout machine, ORCA, which had not been tested prior to Election Day, to work properly.[17] These performance problems certainly played a role in Romney's loss but they were not dispositive.

They were contributing factors to the doomsday scenario that transpired for the Republicans. But they were effects rather than causes. The root causes for the failures of the Republican Party in this election cycle were the mindsets of the candidates and their consultants, and the construction of a virtual reality in which many Republican politicians and avid supporters resided.

Contrary to popular opinion, no one—even the most rational and analytical among us—is a completely objective arbiter of information. We are creatures of "bounded rationality."

Each of us has filters. We examine and analyze data through those filters and discount or reinterpret that which doesn't fit our dominant paradigm.

Most of us also engage in "selection bias," in which we only search out information and associate with people who confirm our opinions.[18] When it comes to viewpoints, ideological biases can significantly constrain our objectivity and decision-making capability.

As we noted in chapter 5, political scientist Philip Tetlock discovered in his research that many experts were sometimes "blinded" by their biases and came to incorrect conclusions because of them. That caused Tetlock to label the experts "hedgehogs" because they had distorting filters through which they interpreted input. He labeled laypeople who frequently came to more accurate conclusions than the so-called experts "foxes" because they had an open mind and no preconceived positions.[19]

In this political season, in the main, the Republican candidates and consultants fell into the hedgehog category. They might have appeared foxlike when they were engaged with the Fox media machine. But the truth is they were faux foxes and soothsayers. They invented a fictional reality and forgot it was a fabrication. As a result, they were "outfoxed."

David Frum, a Republican, former speechwriter for George W. Bush and former employee of the American Enterprise Institute, described the Republican Party's condition and problems in a prescient article titled "When Did the GOP Lose Touch with Reality" that he wrote for *New York Magazine* in November 2011.[20]

In the article, Frum observed, "Over the past two decades conservatism has evolved from a political philosophy into a market segment. An industry has grown up to serve that segment and its stars have become the true thought leaders of the conservative world."

Frum also noted that, "Backed by their own wing of the book publishing industry and supported by think tanks that increasingly function as public relations agencies, conservatives have built a whole alternative knowledge system with its own facts, its own history, its own laws of economics."

If the Republicans had been able to comprehend and act upon Frum's narrative when it was written—just about one year before the election—they might have been able to reverse the course of election events. Of course, they didn't and couldn't because it didn't square with their construction of reality

Neither did Nate Silver's election projections and predictions. Silver is a statistician who has built his own model and methodology for aggregating and analyzing polls. He first came to fame in the political arena in 2008 for correctly predicting the results of the presidential elections and senate races with amazing accuracy.

He did the same thing in 2012 in his 538 blogs and columns in the *New York Times*. From the summer months through the fall, Silver showed Obama with consistent and commanding leads both nationally and in key battleground states. On the day before the election, Silver projected that there was a 91 percent chance that Obama would win the national election with a good margin and with at least 313 electoral votes. (Obama did win handily and received 332 electoral votes.)[21]

The Republicans could have relied on Silver's models and customized their strategies in response to the insights they provided state by state to try to carve out a path to victory. Instead of choosing silver, however, they chose fool's gold. They turned inward rather than outward and trusted their own pundits, pollsters and critics.

Nearly all of the Republican pundits including Peggy Noonan, Michael Barone, George Will and Glen Beck jumped on the election victory prediction bandwagon. Dick Morris, whom Hendrik Hertzberg describes as "a Fox News 'analyst' reputed to be a pollster" on election eve predicted "a landslide for Romney."[22]

The pundits were joined by the Silver scoffers of all types. Many of whom, as Jeff Bercovici noted in his article for *Forbes* on the day after the election, "seemed not to understand basic statistical concepts."[23]

The bottom line is that the Republicans missed both the narrative and the numbers. They trusted more in revelations than in reality and paid the price big time for playing in a league of their own.

The Responses

Election Day was a wake-up call for the Republican establishment. But, as might be expected, many of the responses to that call tended to be conservatively colored and ideologically oriented. They ranged from "stay the course" to "change the direction" but were definitely more "party focused" than "people focused."

Columnist Charles Krauthammer asserted, "There is no need for radical change."[24] Columnist Ryan Douthat advised, "What the party really needs much more than a better identity politics is an economic message that would appeal across demographic lines."[25] Columnist Michael Gerson cautioned, "The next Republican campaign will need to be capable of complex adjustments of ideology, policy and rhetoric."[26]

Complexity was not at the top of most Republican politicians' and donors' assessments and agendas, however. Presidential candidate Mitt Romney attributed the loss to Democratic "gifts" to different voting blocs. Vice presidential candidate Paul Ryan placed the blame on "urban areas."[27]

According to Alexander Bolton of *The Hill*, "The chief lesson GOP senators are taking away from the route is that they need to find more appealing candidates, not necessarily overhaul their policy stances."[28] The Republican governors said the failure was due to the Romney campaign's inability to "offer specifics."[29] Former Secretary of Commerce Carlos Guttierez and Republican operative Charlie Spies established a new Super PAC called "Republicans for Immigration Reform."[30]

In general, these responses indicate that many Republicans still want to play in their own league and by their own rules. If they want to compete effectively nationally, however, they will have to return to the real-world playing field with a new game plan and some new players on the team.

This requires transformation, not tweaking. Our general recommendations for accomplishing this transformation follow.

The Recommendations

In our opinion, in order to transform itself, the Republican Party and its leadership will have to make three vital shifts. They need to move from:

- Cocooning to connecting
- Base building to electorate expanding
- Lecturing and labeling to listening and learning

Politico blogger Jonathan Martin has written that there is a group of younger Republicans (under 50) who are calling for the party to "break free from a political-media cocoon that has become intellectually suffocating and self-defeating."[31] We agree completely with the need to get out of the Republican cocoon but it's not just the media that is creating it.

The cocoon is multi-layered and also comprised of rabid politicians and partisans who dominate the party's messages and agenda. This layering hermetically seals the cocoon, making it virtually impenetrable and impregnable.

The United States is a patchwork quilt nation of diverse communities. In order to win elections, it is important to connect to those communities in meaningful and authentic ways. That can't be done from inside a cocoon. It requires reaching out and touching many different types of someones in lots of different somewheres.

It demands inclusion as opposed to exclusion. The Democrats didn't win the national election because of the "47 percent." The percentages that mattered were: 90+ percent of the African American vote, 70+ percent of the Hispanic vote, 70+ percent of the Asian vote, 60 percent of the youth vote, 56 percent of the moderate independent vote, 55 percent of the female vote and approximately 41 percent of the white male vote.[32]

The Democrats also didn't win because of gifts to voters. The gifts that produced the resounding Democratic victory were not those distributed by President Obama but those he received from the Republicans. They were self-absorption and the inability to build support outside of their natural base of voters.

As we pointed out in chapter 5, according to a Pew political typology survey conducted mid-year, the Republicans began this election cycle with about 46 percent of the population as Republican or Republican leaning. The Democrats started with about 40 percent. That left 14 percent up for grabs—although some of that percentage tended to lean Democratic.[33]

The Republicans ended up with 47+ percent of the national vote, which means they only added a little more than 1 percent because of—and during—their campaign. The Democrats acquired the rest.

They did this by putting up a big tent and not a pup tent. (For more on our thoughts on the nature of these "tents," see the next section of this chapter.) The Republicans will need to do the same to defeat the Democrats and to win in the next national election cycle. They will need to shift the focus from their base and appeal beyond it in order to expand their pool of potential voters

To connect to the community and to expand the electorate, the Republicans need to become proficient at learning and listening to citizens from outside the inner sanctum of their echo chamber. The tendency, however, is to listen to the voices inside the bubble rather than those from outside it.

Eugene Robinson puts it this way, "The voices the party should ignore include those claiming that House Republicans, by retaining their majority, won some sort of mandate to continue pushing a radical conservative agenda. . . . The fog lifts. The fog descends."[34] If they stay in the fog, the Republicans will keep playing in their own league.

The old saying goes that politics is not bean bag. Nor is it played in a league of one's own. It is played in the real world in head-to-head competition.

If the Republicans have learned this lesson, we will all benefit from their new knowledge and a move toward a more bipartisan approach to governing. If they have not, we will all suffer the consequences as we remain in the grips of partisan polarization and the pivot points will be frozen in time.

POLITICAL MESSENGERS NEED NEW IDEAS

Near the beginning of 2013, former Senator Jim DeMint (R-SC), who left Congress to head the conservative Heritage Foundation, wrote an op-ed column for the *Washington Post* titled "Conservative Ideas Need a New Message."[35]

In our opinion, the conservatives' problem nationally is not a problem of messaging but one of ideas. Conservative messengers need new ideas, not new messages. And, we should add, so too do liberal messengers.

America is at a pivot point in a number of areas. We don't need tired partisan ideas from either side reframed and repackaged to address those pivot points. In fact, we don't need conservative ideas or liberal ideas at all. What we do need are fresh, good and original ideas and the willingness and ability to compromise in order to resolve the multiplicity of issues confronting us.

In his column, Senator DeMint asserted, "November's election results and exit polls suggest that a majority of Americans agree that government does too much yet still voted for more of it. The election taught conservatives that we can no longer entrust political parties to carry our message."

We're not certain what polls the senator was looking at. As far as we know, government was not on any ballot but candidates were. The citizens did not cast their votes for a government that does more or for a government that does less but for the individuals who they thought would do the best jobs in representing their interests and governing the country.

We don't understand Senator DeMint's mistrust of a political party "carrying" the message. It seems to us that since Ronald Reagan's election in 1980, The Republican Party has done an exceptional job of building its brand around the three big ideas the Gipper first articulated: smaller government, stronger defense, and lower taxes.

The question is whether those three ideas are sufficient to move the Republican Party forward and win future national elections. We don't believe they are because the Democratic Party has also embraced the smaller government/stronger defense/lower taxes mantra.

More importantly, the balance of power in national elections is shifting to the independent or "swing voter." A Pew Research Center political values study in mid-2012 reported that 38 percent of Americans identify as independents, 32 percent as Democrats and 24 percent as Republicans.

The Pew study found that the swing voters were closer to the Democrats on value issues related to "unions" and "environment," to the Republicans on issues related to the social "safety net" and "equal opportunity," and about equidistant on issues related to "government regulation of business" and "government involvement in health care." The bottom line is that the swing voters are considerably different and much more ideologically complex than either the hard-core Republican or Democrat voters.[36] (See chapter 5 for a more detailed treatment of these survey results.)

While some of the ideas from the right will resonate with them so too will some from the left. That's why today and in the future the combat for the unaffiliated voters will have to be a contest of ideas rather than rhetoric. No universal message or one-size-fits-all approach will work.

Marketing will be important and not selling. Let us explain the difference.

Selling is company-centered or in political terms party-centered. It focuses on the available product and service and tries to persuade the consumer/buyer/voter that it is perfect for them.

Marketing is customer-centered or in political terms voter-centered. It focuses on meeting the needs of the consumer/buyer/voter and tailors the product and service and message to them.

We believe that Professor Ted Levitt of Harvard was the person who originally made the distinction between marketing and selling in his classic 1960 *Harvard Business Review* article "Marketing Myopia." In his piece, Levitt posed the famous question "What business are you really in?" and argued that if the railroad executives had seen themselves as being in the transportation business instead of the railroad business they would have redefined themselves and continued to grow.[37]

We won't be presumptive enough to define the specific policy parameters for the "business" the political parties should really be in. Let us go back to the analogy, however, that we think is relevant—they can choose to be in the big tent business or the little tent business.

The big tent business is constructed based upon a broad range of ideas to appeal to a diversity of customers and to address a wide variety of needs. The little tent business is constructed based upon a few ideas to appeal to a narrow customer segment and a limited range of needs.

Ronald Reagan put the Republican Party and conservative movement nationally into the big tent business. Over the past few years, the Tea Party has shrunk the size of that tent by closing the tent flaps to many. If it continues to do so, it may eventually be in the pup tent business.

One of our favorite marketing maxims is "Be something special to someone in particular." Based upon the most recent national election, the Republicans seem to have decided that someone is primarily "conservative, white, male and older." In contrast, the Democrats seem to have decided those someones include "females, youth, minorities (African Americans, Hispanics, Asians) and independents."

Given the nation's demographics and psychographics, the Democrats appear to be in the "growth business." The Republicans need to figure out how to get there.

Those are our ideas. That's our message. We don't expect everyone to agree with us. We ask those with differing perspectives from both sides of the aisle, in the interests of goodwill and bipartisanship, please don't shoot the messengers.

DECOMPOSING CONGRESS

The national elections of 2012 put a new face on Congress and some new faces in both the House and Senate. In some cases, however, the new faces were old faces. Let's examine the results of the election cycle and how it changed the composition, if not necessarily the complexion, of Congress.

The 113th Congress' freshmen class coming into office had 94 new members. The House had 82 new members—35 Republicans and

47 Democrats. The Senate had 1 Independent, 3 Republicans and 8 Democrats. All in all, a slight tilt Democratic in both bodies.[38]

Newly elected House members included Ted Yoho (R-FL), an animal veterinarian; Kerry Bentivolio (R-MI), a reindeer farmer; and Joseph Kennedy (D-MA)—need we say more?[39] Two winners who prevailed over controversial conservative opponents were double amputee Army National Guard Iraq veteran Tammy Duckworth (D-IL), who easily beat Joe Walsh (R-IL), and construction company business owner Patrick Murphy (D-FL), who won a tightly contested race over Alan West (R-FL).

Seven House members including Alan Grayson (D-FL), Bill Foster (D-IL) and Steve Stockman (R-TX) returned to the lower chamber, having served there before.[40] It was and is still too difficult and early to say whether the new Republican members were more or less conservative than the freshmen group of the 112th Congress swept into office in the November 2010 elections.

If Dana Milbank is correct, the ideological position of the new Republicans will probably be about the same as in the 112th. The difference, as Milbank articulates in his column on the very conservative Congressman Steve Stockman titled "A House Radical Is Now in the Mainstream," is that, "his views, outlandish in the House of 1995, are more at home in the House of 2013."[41] Ben Terris reinforces Milbank's perspective in his article for the January/February 2013 edition of *The Atlantic* highlighting the fact that the Republicans hung on "to most of their 2010 additions."[42]

Terris goes on to observe, "One of the most striking aspects of the 113th Congress is its inexperience; a full 38 percent of House members have served for fewer than three years." He points out, "That's the largest percentage of rookies since the Gingrich Revolution of 1994—which, of course, resulted in a catastrophic government shutdown."

One thing that separated the 112th version of the House from the 113th early on is that members did make an overt attempt to actually do a little socializing together. In early February, some members of the freshmen class said they were going to go bowling together on February 26 to foster collaboration and working across the aisle.[43] That trip was later cancelled. So much for Congressional glasnost: No strikes. No spares. All gutter balls.

As is usually the case, the composition—if not the competition—in the Senate looked tame in comparison to that of the House. The most striking feature of the upper chamber was that the additional four women taking seats there raised the total to 20—1/5 of the Senate and a new record.

Another well-noted fact—if not celebrated by all—is that Tammy Baldwin (D-WI) is the first openly gay person to serve in the Senate. Baldwin didn't see that as a defining characteristic for her, however. She stated, "I didn't run to make history. I ran to make a difference."

Over the next two years, the nation will see what difference she and her Congressional counterparts in the 113th Congress make and what platform they establish for taking the country and its citizens forward.

CONGRESSIONAL OMENS AND INDICATORS

Coming out of the box in 2013, there were some early signs that while compromise was not going to be the order of the day for everyone, it was going to be given consideration by some.

While the can was kicked down the road with both sequestration and the debt limit, at least it was kicked. During the 112th Congress, it was virtually impossible to get anything even teed up to kick. The behavior of that Congress reminds us of Lucy in the Peanuts cartoon setting up the football for Charlie Brown and then pulling it away at precisely the moment Charlie swings his foot forward—leaving poor Charlie flat on the ground.

In this Congress, in contrast, bipartisan attempts and/or movement on a range of issues from guns to immigration to the budget—especially in the Senate—indicate a slight thawing of the frozen impasses that had characterized the prior one. Early in the year, columnists such as Ruth Marcus and Alexander Bolton were writing about the potential for pragmatic problem solving and "signs of bipartisanship" giving Obama a "narrow window" in which to move his agenda.[44]

As late as April 10, Karen Tumulty and Paul Kane, writing in *The Washington Post,* commented, "For the first time in a while, members of the two parties—at least some of them—appear to be talking about getting things done, even without the deadline of a manufactured crisis looming." Tumulty and Kane were especially complimentary to the Gang of Eight on their bipartisan draft of the immigration bill and to Joe Manchin (D-WV) and Bill Toomey (R-PA) for reaching an agreement on background checks for firearm purchases.[45]

Tumulty and Kane were quite cautious and qualified in their overall assessment, however. On guns, they noted, "If the gun measure passes the Senate, its future in the House remains uncertain." On immigration, they quoted Senator Lamar Alexander (R-TN) as follows: "The difficulty is trying to pass a comprehensive bill. Because the more things you put together, the more opponents you develop."

This quote from Senator Alexander reminded us of an argument that he made at a health care summit sponsored by NPR in February 2010 and in a follow-up interview with Ezra Klein in March of that year. Alexander said to Klein, "I've come to the conclusion that the Senate doesn't do comprehensive well. Watching the immigration bill and cap-and-trade and health care all fall beneath their own weight, I've come to the belief we need to go step-by-step. In the NPR interview that one reason not to do comprehensive is that "Our country is too big, too complicated, too decentralized."[46]

We don't necessarily agree with Senator Alexander's absolutist position on this or on the concept of "too big to do comprehensive." But we do believe that adopting a relativist approach works and that frequently doing something is better than doing nothing—especially when "doing nothing" has become the leitmotif of Congress over the past few years.

By June 2013, it started to become apparent that while there was progress being made in the Senate in terms of compromise, collaboration and cooperation, quite the opposite was the case in the House.

That's when the House unexpectedly failed to pass a farm bill. The farm bill usually sails through with bipartisan support as a matter of routine.[47]

This bill went down by a vote of 234 to 195. Only 24 Democrats voted for it because the version on the floor cut spending on food stamps for low-income families by $20.5 billion over the next ten years. Sixty-two conservative Republicans voted against it because they felt the bill didn't cut spending enough.

Even before this occurred, earlier in June, Robert Reich wrote, "Conservative Republicans in our nation's capital have managed to accomplish something they only dreamed of when Tea Partiers streamed into Congress at the start of 2011: They've basically shut Congress down."[48]

Molly Ball, in writing for *The Atlantic*, tends to agree with Reich but she astutely notes, "But the ironic thing is that, by virtue of its very do-nothingness, the do-nothing Congress got a big thing done."[49] Through the fiscal cliff deal it increased taxes on the rich and thus revenue and through the sequestration it decreased spending, resulting in a lower deficit.

Ball reports that Richard Kogan of the Center on Budget and Policy Priorities estimates that this will reduce the deficit by $3.99 trillion through 2023. She goes on to clarify, however, "That's not to say Congress did it on purpose."

So, as we look at the indicators and omens, after the first 180 days of this new Congress and the president's second administration, there are countervailing forces. Given this, our stance is that the perfect should not be made the enemy of the good. On the other hand, incremental and easily done should not be an acceptable substitute when something more complete and difficult is possible and achievable.

We are not advocating making all legislation comprehensive or making all legislation one-offs. Rather, we suggest embracing two admonitions from Albert Einstein as the overarching design principles for developing effective governmental policies and programs:

- Any intelligent fool can make things bigger, more complex, and more violent. It takes a touch of genius—and a lot of courage—to go in the other direction.
- Everything should be made as simple as possible but no simpler.

Picking up on Senator Alexander's reference to a "step-wise" approach to legislation, let us offer two other well-known thoughts: "The journey of a thousand miles begins with a single step" (Lao Tzu, Chinese philosopher). "That's one small step for man, one giant leap for mankind" (Neil Armstrong, astronaut upon setting foot on the moon).

There is crawling, first steps, baby steps, small steps, big steps, strides, leaps and long jumps. Great legislators know the size, type and/ or the number of steps required to ensure the final product that will promote America's future rather than protecting its past or themselves.

These are times and this is the decade that demands greatness. We need profiles in courage at the pivot points. We also need persistence because the level of complexity and conflict at many of these points means that change will take time.

It will not happen in one Congress or maybe even two—but it can start and be moved ahead on a positive trajectory. As we saw in chapter 1 from reviewing the historical pivot points, time is on the pivot points' side as long as there are "pivot persons" (citizens and leaders) who are committed to pursuing the policies and programs that matter for Americans and the American dream.

THE CITIZENS' MOOD—2013: CONCERNED, SKEPTICAL BUT CARING

Near the end of June 2013, *The Atlantic* released the second annual Atlantic/Aspen Institute American Values survey. The survey was conducted between May 29 and June 8, 2013. It had some encouraging and some discouraging findings.

As might be expected, there were divided opinions on social issues such as abortion and guns. On the other hand, there was strong agreement around the importance of unity (95 percent very important) and the need for greater unity (75 percent).

There was also general agreement that the drivers of unity were a commitment to factors such as "equal opportunity" and "freedom of speech" (59 percent each) rather than "social media" or "sports teams" (which received 20 percent support or less). Sixty-eight percent of the respondents—including 64 percent of Democrats—agreed that "free enterprise" unites us. A stunning 80 percent said that if we wanted to re-gain our unity we would need to shrink the gap between rich and poor.

Those were some of the encouraging elements. On the discouraging side, more than 60 percent of the respondents felt that we are more divided as a country than we were 10 years ago, and about 60 percent rated the health of our democracy as weak. An even higher percentage said America is "at least as fragmented now as it was during the Great Depression, Vietnam and Watergate."

The most disturbing part of the survey was its findings regarding the cause of our disunity. There was unity around that. According to Don Baer and Mark Penn, who wrote an article summarizing the survey results, "When asked which figures in America do the most to divide our nation, every group in America across age, gender, political party, and region said 'politicians,' choosing them at a rate of more than five to one over media figures, corporations, religious leaders and others."[50]

The most promising part of the survey were the findings that in spite of the divisive strains, we as citizens maintained our American sense of optimism regarding the need for and the potential of political problem solving. Sixty-three percent of participants said it was very important for politicians to "get unified" and 70 percent thought it is possible for citizens to come together on the issues that truly matter to America.

That's how things stood mid-2013. The public was at a pivot point and the pivot point was moving. The question is whether the unity in attitude among citizens will bring some unity in action from the politicians and other pivot persons who will have to take the lead in effectuating change.

THE PIVOT POINT CRYSTAL BALL

It is from this perspective, our analysis of the needs at the key pivot points identified herein, the progress made to date, and the potential given our preliminary summary assessment of the current status of Congress and its relation with the president that we paint three alternatives for the United States in the near term going forward (i.e., through the end of the 113th Congress): Best Case, Worst Case and Expected Case.

Before we do that let us express some reservations regarding predictions of any type. As we pointed out earlier in this chapter and originally in chapter 5, Philip Tetlock has shown that well-informed laypersons can be "foxes" and do better forecasting in many instances than the so-called experts whose personal predilections make them "hedgehogs" and allow them to get blindsided on issues where they don't keep an open mind.

Dan Gardner uses this same typology in his book *Future Babble: Why Expert Predictions Fail and Why We Believe Them Anyway*. Gardner puts the spotlight on failures by many experts, including the fact that in December 2007, *Businessweek* published a forecast in which all of the 54 economists surveyed predicted that the U.S. economy would not "sink into a recession."[51]

Nate Silver does an exceptional job of explaining why predictions go awry in his excellent book *The Signal and the Noise: Why So Many Predictions Fail—But Some Don't*. In a nutshell, what Silver, election-predictor extraordinaire, says is that the root cause of failure is a poor understanding of probability and uncertainty. Moreover, we as consumers of information tend to mistake the more confident predictions and those from more "authoritative" sources as the more accurate and reliable ones.[52]

Silver makes the case that for the United States, "Most of our strengths and weaknesses as a nation—our ingenuity and our industriousness, our arrogance and impatience—stem from the unshakeable belief in the idea we choose our own course."[53] The curative for this according to him is to make more data-driven decisions and to apply Bayesian logic in the decision-making process (i.e., think about the probability of something happening, estimate that, gather more information/data, refine and improve the prediction and estimation).

Silver humbly admits that even he—as an "expert" at avoiding the thinking traps that most "experts" make—has "made many mistakes" and his success tends to come from having "chosen my battles well."[54] Not always that well, however. He picked the 49ers to win the Super Bowl this year over the Ravens (they lost in overtime).

Nate did pick Louisville the winner of the NCAA college basketball tournament correctly giving them a 22.7 percent chance of winning the whole thing. But he incorrectly gave Indiana a 19.6 percent chance to win (lost in the Sweet Sixteen round); Florida 12.7 percent to win (lost in the Elite Eight round); and Gonzaga 9.5 percent chance to win (lost in the third round) to get to the Final Four along with Louisville.

So, for predictions, here's the deal—even with the best data/ statistics and the best process—they do not guarantee the result or outcome. They are merely estimations or approximations of what might occur in the future. We should emphasize, however, that the better the data and the more objective the analysis the greater the chance for forecasting or "guesstimating" accurately.

With that said and hoping that we have cleared our own minds of most of our prediction prejudices and are working more from verifiable facts than fantasy, let us begin our fearless "predictions" with the Expected Case.

Expected Case

Our expected case is a very modest and moderate one. In approximately four months or so, the 113th Congress has demonstrated—at least in the Senate—that it is not the 112th Congress. Thank God for small favors.

Our expected case predictions are: In spite of the Senate's rejection of the background check proposed by Senators Joe Manchin (D-WV) and Bill Toomey (R-PA) and other gun bill provisions on April 17, we still believe there could be a gun bill passed of a very limited nature with a nominal and limited background check of selected groups or individuals as its major feature. The immigration bill will be more comprehensive but the path to citizenship will be a more arduous and torturous one than many would have hoped. There will be a budget and it will have a very slight revenue enhancement component that will be achieved through some form of invisible or sin tax on goods and/or services but there will be nothing done to gore the ox of corporations or wealthy individuals.

In general, in the other pivot point areas we address in the book, such as education, innovation and manufacturing, there will be begrudging passage of single-focus item bills. There will be no legislation that is comprehensive—let alone comprehendible—in any of these areas.

We give our expected case about an 80 percent chance of occurring over the next two years. We have to admit that we didn't do a sophisticated historical statistical analysis of past votes and voting patterns to come to our estimation on this or the other two cases. They are based, however, on the research and the wealth of data that we have consumed in working on this book and the present configuration of both chambers of Congress and an assessment of the manner in which the members of the bodies were comporting themselves in addressing the key legislative issues confronting them in this new year.

Best Case

We hate to say this but we can conceive virtually no best case. Having made that confession, if we are wrong, what might be a "rosy scenario" or where could there be a "rose among the thorns"?

Overall, the best we can contemplate is that, as our expected case is accomplished, all of the leaders and members treat each other with a renewed sense of dignity and respect and that there are continuing efforts to build bipartisan bridges similar to those we saw from the Gang of Eight on the immigration bill and Senators Manchin and Toomey on the gun bill. On a particular issue, the immigration bill might exceed our expectations—although it appears the "terrorist" actions at the Boston Marathon tragedy makes this more unlikely.

There might be some substantive and substantial progress with a movement toward comprehensiveness in the manufacturing and innovation areas. We do not expect to see the strong "job centric" agendas that we advocate in both of these areas being a central part of any legislation that is passed in those areas, however.

Our estimate of the chance of the best case of the type outlined of being .05 to 1 percent. You could make a lot of money betting on this long shot if it were to occur. Our advice is to keep your checkbook in your pocket.

Worst Case

The worst case is that the initial round of civility and compromise that has characterized some of the dynamics in the first four months of the New Year disappears. There is a return to Congressional dynamics similar to those of the 112th Congress.

There is no gun bill. There is no "comprehensive" immigration bill—the highly skilled pieces pass but a meaningful path to citizenship disappears altogether or becomes such an obstacle course that only the best, brightest and bravest will be able to complete it. The approved budget is a hopeless mishmash with little to nothing that benefits ordinary folks and a strong tilt in favor of the existing power brokers (lobbyists, the wealthy, and those who retard the legislative process by controlling its topics and tempo).

The other pivot point issues will not be addressed at all or in only a symbolic manner. Any legislation that does get through on a particular pivot point—similar to what happened with the sequester—moves us backward rather than forward.

Our estimate of the chance for the worst case taking place is 19 to 20 percent. That might seem gloomy. But after the performance of the 112th Congress where the chances for the worst case taking place was 95 to 100 percent, that's a significant improvement. It's also an example of the relative deprivation theory at work. As the old song goes, "Been down so long it looks like up to me."

GREASING THE PIVOT POINTS

Numerous obstacles will have to be overcome or eliminated in order to make progress at the pivot points. Over the next two years, achieving our expected case and establishing the platform for more substantial progress in years to come will be a function of the dynamics between the administration and Congress.

The elections of 2014 will provide an opportunity to grease the pivot points to ensure forward progress. After that, sustaining progress will require changes to the rules of election, the rules of the Senate and the rules regarding the Supreme Court.

In the first quarter of 2013, President Obama took a varied and nuanced approach to his use of the presidential pulpit in an attempt to create the climate and support for passing legislation that aligned with the administration's agenda. His inaugural address in January was directed at the hearts of those in the heartland. It was criticized by many Washington pundits because it was not conciliatory and his call for a minimum wage and new spending to help those in need was not well-received by the Republicans.

What the president's address did, as we note earlier in the book, was to frame the debate and focus attention on more than just the deficit and austerity. The president reinforced this broader perspective in his February State of the Union address.

Between and immediately after those addresses the president went into full campaign mode, going around the country rallying public support for his proposals and plans such as making investments to revitalize the manufacturing sector. The president then proceeded to "make nice" by having a few dinners and engaging in a dialogue with Republican Congressional leaders. Finally, in April, the president presented his budget, which included more tax increases and a chained CPI for Social Security recipients. The budget was too conservative for many liberals and too liberal for many conservatives. It was an attempt to reach across the aisle and establish the basis for negotiation.

The importance of these presidential actions and achieving some type of "good compromise"—if not a grand deal—cannot be overstated. History has shown that the most productive years of a second-term president are the first two before he becomes a "lame duck."

Chris Lehane, a Democratic strategist who worked in the Clinton White House, describes the requirements in this situation this way, "A second-term president has to live the life of a Benjamin Button—you have to work backwards. You have a year-and-a-half, two years maximum on the domestic agenda."[55]

Time will tell what the results will be at the key pivot points over the next year and a half. The elections in November 2014 and the seating of the 114th Congress in January will provide the next chance to establish some additional momentum toward positive problem solving and policy making. It seems unlikely, however, that the 2014 elections will create a more collaborative environment in Congress.

The reasons for that are twofold. While all of the 450 house seats will be contested in this next cycle, according to the Cook Political Report, only 90 of them are in swing districts. That's a decline of about 45 percent from 164 over the past quarter century.[56]

Thirty-three senate seats are up in 2014. Democrats currently hold 20 of those seats and Republicans 13. It appears that the Republicans will hold all of those seats because they are in states that lean strongly Republican. In contrast, it appears that as many as 10 of the Democratic seats may be at risk because of the states in which they are situated.[57]

Given this, it seems likely at this point in time that the next Congress could be slightly more Republican than the current one. This will probably mean less compromise rather than more. It definitely means that for change to have a greater chance we need to make changes.

The best place to start is with the rules for election. We need to implement a national fair districting initiative and revamp the primary voting rules and processes. We provide the rationale and detailed recommendations for this in chapter 4.

We also need to reform the rules of the Senate. Many of the current rules, including the use of the filibuster, are outdated and antiquated. They put control of the body in the hands of the minority and thus inhibit majority rule. As E. J. Dionne observes, it also allows a subgroup within a party to exert tremendous influence over the party's agenda.[58]

Moreover, the Senate is not the most representative body to begin with. As Suzy Khimm points out in a January 2012 *Washington Post* article drawing on research by Alfred Stepan and Juan Linz, "In addition to having the highest number of veto players, there are four more constitutionally embedded features of the U.S. political system that, taken together, make that system even more majority constraining and, we believe, inequality inducing than any other democracy in our set . . . the principle that every state in the Union has an equal vote in the Senate . . . to compound the significance of the comparative inequality of representation of the U.S. Senate, this most mal-apportioned chamber in our set has the most comparative power in our set."[59]

We are not for changing the Senate's structure or its composition. We are in favor of bringing its rule-making processes into the 21st century and enfranchising the majority. We are also in favor of reforming the Supreme Court and bringing it into the 21st century as well.

In 2009, James MacGregor Burns, Pulitzer Prize–winning historian and political scientist, provided a brilliant and incisive indictment of the Supreme Court in his book *Packing the Court: The Rise of Judicial Power and the Coming Crisis of the Supreme Court.* In his book, Burns argues, "as the ultimate and unappealable arbiters of the Constitution, the justices have become more than the referees in constitutional disputes that the framers intended. They have gone beyond interpreting the rules—they have come to create them."[60]

We agree with Professor Burns. Think of *Bush* v. *Gore* and the Citizens United decisions as just two egregious examples of judicial overreach.

The Supreme Court has become too powerful. It is accountable to no one. As Jonathan Turley, George Washington University law professor, notes, the court is "dysfunctionally small in size."[61] Then, there's lifetime tenure. We could go on and on.

The overriding issue, however, is one of proportionality and control. Given the breakdown of the governance system on the executive and legislative side and the virtual standstill on many issues, power is ceded to the Supreme Court.

The Supreme Court is not a representative body. It is not a democratic body. But it is the body that may have the ultimate control over many of the pivot point issues while no one exercises control over it.

We believe in a strong, independent and impartial judiciary. We do not believe the judiciary should be unconstrained, however. That's un-American. No group should be above the law. We need new rules of engagement for the Supreme Court to restore the balance of powers that are essential in our democracy.

PATIENCE, PERSISTENCE AND PRINCIPLES

As we close this book, it becomes clear that working and moving forward on the pivot points is a long hard slog. It is a marathon and not a 100-yard dash. It requires patience and persistence and the ability to come back again and again after defeats.

In our opening chapter, we highlighted the fact that success at some of the more important pivot points in our history was far from instantaneous. Without the Bill of Rights, the U.S. Constitution would probably have never been ratified. Even with those Rights appended, it took three years to get the Constitution approved. The Homestead Act, which was finally signed by President Lincoln in 1862, was first passed by the House in 1852. The Sherman Antitrust Act was passed as law in1892 but not really used or enforced until President Roosevelt did so in 1902. President Franklin Roosevelt was elected to office in 1932 but the Social Security Act was not passed into law until August of 1935— about 2½ years into his presidency.

And those were relatively short time frames for gestation. Think about women getting the right to vote, civil rights and equal educational opportunity. The hands of time moved very slowly on those pivot points. But the pivot persons for those issues stayed true to their course and cause. Sometimes they had to hand off the baton to the next generation, but they did not waiver from their principles.

It should not be just about sticking to your guns (or butter for that matter). One of the core principles for those committed to working collaboratively to forge solutions at the pivot points should be the willingness and ability to change one's position when the evidence and facts do not support it. This seems to be increasingly more and more difficult to do in these confrontational and complicated times—especially in areas of "hardened beliefs." Nonetheless, it can happen.

We were heartened by an example of this that Joe Nocera of the *New York Times* provided in a column at the beginning of this year. Nocera wrote,

> Thursday night, after I got home, I had a phone conversation with Scott Rigell, a Virginia Republican who first won election in 2010 by campaigning as a modern-day fiscal conservative. That is to say, he believed, as he told me, "that we have a spending problem, not a revenue problem."
>
> But after he got to Congress, he dug deeper and came to what he calls "a data driven, analytic conclusion." Namely, spending cuts alone could not eliminate the deficit. The country needed more tax revenue as well. He showed his data to everyone he could on his side of the aisle. They nodded politely and continued to insist on not raising taxes. Rigell did not revert back, however. "We have to have the courage to critique and refine our own platform," he said. "That isn't weakness. It is intellectual honesty."

Nocera goes on to say, "I asked him if he had been punished by leadership for his courageous views. 'No', he said. Give them time, I thought."[62]

We think and say give them time, too—the pivot points and those pivot persons (citizens and leaders) who will continue to work those points until the necessary and desired outcome is achieved.

It may not be this year. It may not be the next. It may take till the end of this decade—and possibly even longer. Eventually it will be done because time is on the side of those with the patience, persistence and principles to work the pivot points to make America work again.

Acknowledgments

W E DEDICATE THIS BOOK TO OUR WIVES, DEBBIE DRIESMAN ISLAM and Sheila Smith (Crego). They share our commitment to making America work for the 100 percent.

We extend special thanks to Sheila Smith for her yeoman research efforts, referrals and recommendations that helped to shape the content and focus of this book. Thanks also to George Munoz, co-author of *Renewing the America Dream,* who blogged with us for the *Huffington Post.* Some of the blogs on which George collaborated informed sections and chapters of the book.

We also received input and feedback on the book from a number of colleagues with whom we shared certain concepts, selected chapters and in certain cases the manuscript. With deep appreciation, we acknowledge the following contributors: Karl Androes, Robert Bicknell, Allan Boscacci, John Crego, Lisa Crego, Tom Crego, Tom de Boor, Ron Gunn, Kitty Higgins, Ed Kazemek, Mark Muro, Ted Reed, Charles Smith, Jim Wall and Darryl West and Cathy Wilson.

Our research disclosed that thought leaders from across the political and social continuum are wrestling with the same issues that we consider here. This allowed us to review an enormous amount and wide range of diverse material in conducting our analysis and developing our conclusions and recommendations.

Finally, two thumbs up to those American citizens who get involved and participate in working the pivot points. We know that that work is not always easy, well recognized nor immediately rewarded. We also know, however, that it is essential for the future of America and the American dream.

We thank those unsung patriots who are toiling in democracy's vineyard. They inspire us. We hope this book can be a resource to them as they continue to work the pivot points to make America work again.

Bibliography

The books cited in the endnotes to this book are listed below.

Akerlof, George A., and Robert J. Shiller. *Animal Spirits: How Human Psychology Drives the Economy, and Why It Matters for Global Capitalism.* Princeton, NJ: Princeton University Press, 2009.

Bowen, William G., Matthew M. Chingos and Michael S. McPherson. *Crossing the Finish Line: Completing College at America's Public Universities.* Princeton, NJ: Princeton University Press, 2010. Paperback in 2011.

Bradley, Bill. *We Can All Do Better.* New York, NY: Vanguard Press, 2012.

Brynjolfsson, Erik, and Andrew McAfee. *Race Against the Machine.* Lexington, MA: Digital Frontier Press, 2012.

Burns, James MacGregor. *Packing the Court: The Rise of Judicial Power and the Coming Crisis of the Supreme Court.* New York, NY: The Penguin Press, 2009.

Bush, Jeb. *Immigration Wars: Forging an American Solution.* New York, NY: Threshold Editions, 2013.

Chinni, Dante, and James Gimpel. *Our Patchwork Nation: The Surprising Truth About the "Real" America—The 12 Community Types That Make up Our Nation.* New York, NY: Gotham Books, 2010.

Cowen, Tyler. *The Great Stagnation: How America Ate All the Low-Hanging Fruit of Modern History, Got Sick and Will (Eventually) Feel Better.* New York, NY: Dutton, 2011.

Dionne, E. J. *Our Divided Political Heart: The Battle for the American Idea in an Age of Discontent.* New York, NY: Bloomsbury, USA, 2012.

Frank, Robert H. *The Darwin Economy: Liberty, Competition and the Common Good.* Princeton, NJ: Princeton University Press, 2011.

Friedman, Thomas L., and Michael Mandelbaum. *That Used to Be Us: How America Fell Behind in the World It Invented and How We Can Come Back.* New York, NY: Farrar, Straus & Giroux, 2011.

Gardner, Dan. *Future Babble: Why Expert Predictions Fail and Why We Believe Them Anyway.* Canada: McClelland & Stewart, 2010.

Garland, James. *Saving Alma Mater: A Rescue Plan for America's Public Universities.* Chicago, IL: University of Chicago Press, 2009.

Gawande, Atul. *The Checklist Manifesto.* New York, NY: Henry Holt & Company, 2009.

Hacker, Jacob S., and Paul Pierson. *Winner Take All Politics: How Washington Made the Rich Richer—And Turned Its Back on the Middle Class.* New York, NY: Simon & Schuster Paperbacks, 2011.

Haidt, Jonathan. *The Righteous Mind: Why Good People Are Divided by Politics and Religion.* New York, NY: Pantheon Books, 2012.

Harris, William C., and Steven C. Beschloss. *Adrift: Charting Our Course Back to a Great Nation.* Amherst, NY: Prometheus Books, 2011.

Isaacson, Walter. *Steve Jobs.* New York, NY: Simon & Schuster, 2011.

Islam, Frank, George Munoz and Ed Crego. *Renewing the American Dream: A Citizen's Guide for Restoring Our Competitive Advantage.* Washington, DC: IMC Publishing, 2010.

Johnson, Dennis W. *The Laws That Shaped America: Fifteen Acts of Congress and Their Lasting Impact.* New York, NY: Routledge, 2009.

Katz, Bruche, and Jennifer Bradley. *The Metropolitan Revolution: How Cities and Metros Are Fixing Our Broken Politics and Fragile Economy.* Washington, DC: Brookings Press, 2013.

Kilian, Linda. *The Swing Vote: The Untapped Power of Independents.* New York, NY: St. Martin's Press, 2012.

Kirp, David L. *Improbable Scholars: The Rebirth of a Great American School System and a Strategy for America's Schools.* Oxford, England: Oxford University Press, 2013.

Lind, Michael. *Land of Promise.* New York, NY: HarperCollins, 2012.

Kolker, Claudia. *The Immigrant Advantage: What We Can Learn from Newcomers to America about Health, Happiness and Hope.* New York, NY: Simon & Schuster, 2011.

Krugman, Paul. *End This Depression Now.* New York, NY: W. W. Norton & Company, 2012.

Liveris, Andrew. *Make It in America: The Case for Re-Inventing the Economy.* Hoboken, NJ: John Wiley & Sons, 2011.

Mann, Thomas E., and Norman J. Ornstein, *It's Even Worse Than It Looks: How the American Constitutional System Collided with the New Politics of Extremism.* New York, NY: Basic Books, 2012.

Murray, Charles. *Coming Apart: The State of White America, 1960–2010.* New York, NY: Random House, 2012.

Rohtatyn, Felix. *Bold Endeavors: How Our Government Built America and Why It Must Rebuild It Now.* New York, NY: Simon & Shuster, 2009.

Sachs, Jeffrey D. *The Price of Civilization: Reawakening American Virtue and Prosperity.* New York, NY: Random House, 2011.

Silver, Nate. *The Signal and the Noise: Why So Many Predictions Fail—But Some Don't.* New York, NY: The Penguin Press, 2012.

Stiglitz, Joseph. *Freefall.* New York, NY: W. W. Norton & Company, 2010.

Stiglitz, Joseph E. *The Price of Inequality.* New York, NY: W. W. Norton & Company, 2012.

Terkel, Studs. *Hope Dies Last: Keeping Faith in Difficult Times.* New York, NY: The New Press, 2004.

Tetlock, Philip E. *Expert Political Judgment: How Good Is It? How Can We Know?* Princeton, NJ: Princeton University Press, 2005.

Thaler, Richard H., and Cass R. Sunstein. *Nudge: Improving Decisions about Health, Wealth and Happiness.* New York, NY: The Penguin Group, 2009.

Wadhwa, Vivek. *Why America Is Losing the Global Race to Capture Entrepreneurial Talents.* Philadelphia, PA: Wharton Digital Press, 2012.

Walker, David M. *Comeback America: Turning the Country Around and Restoring Fiscal Responsibility.* New York, NY: Random House, 2009.

West, Darryl. *Brain Gain: Rethinking U.S. Immigration Policy.* Washington, DC: The Brookings Institution, 2010.

A broad range of additional reference material was consulted in doing the research for this book. A select bibliography of those sources follows.

Acemoglu, Daron, and James A. Robinson. *Why Nations Fail: The Origins of Power, Prosperity, and Poverty.* New York, NY: Crown Business, 2012.

Ambrose, Stephen E. *To America: Personal Reflections of an Historian.* New York, NY: Simon & Schuster Paperbacks, 2002.

Clifton, Jim. *The Coming Jobs War.* New York, NY: Gallup Press, 2011.

Codevilla, Angelo. *The Ruling Class: How They Corrupted America and What We Can Do About It.* New York, NY: Beaufort Books, 2010.

Fineman, Howard. *The Thirteen Arguments: Enduring Debates That Define and Inspire Our Country.* New York, NY: Random House, 2008.

Fukuyama, Francis. *The Origins of Political Order: From Prehuman Times to the French Revolution.* New York, NY: Farrar, Straus & Giroux, 2011.

Grumwald, Michael. *The New, New Deal.* New York, NY: Simon & Schuster, 2012.

Hannan, Daniel. *The New Road to Serfdom: A Letter of Warning to America.* New York, NY: HarperCollins, 2011.

Hayek, F. A. (edited by Bruce Caldwell). *The Road to Serfdom: Text and Documents.* Routledge, London: The University of Chicago Press, 2007.

Huffington, Arianna. *Third World America: How Our Politicians Are Abandoning the Middle Class and Betraying the American Dream.* New York, NY: Crown Publishing, 2010.

Kingdon, John W. *Agendas, Alternatives and Public Policies.* New York, NY: Longman, Addison-Wesley, 2003.

Lipscomb, Todd. *Re-Made in the USA: How We Can Restore Jobs, Retool Manufacturing, and Compete with the World.* Hoboken, NJ: John Wiley & Sons, 2011.

Luce, Edward. *Time to Start Thinking: America in the Age of Descent.* New York, NY: Atlantic Monthly Press, 2012.

Morris, Dick, and Eileen McGann. *2010 Take Back America: A Battle Plan.* New York, NY: HarperCollins, 2010.

Nemerovski, Steven. *EParty.* Sheldon, KY: Wasteland Press, 2010.

Pierce, Charles. *Idiot America: How Stupidity Became a Virtue in the Land of the Free.* New York, NY: Anchor Books, 2010.

Ratigan, Dylan. *Greedy Bastards: How We Can Stop Corporate Communists, Banksters, and Other Vampires from Sucking America Dry*. New York, NY: Simon & Schuster, 2012.

Reich, Robert B. *After-Shock: The Next Economy and America's Future*. New York, NY: Alfred A. Knopf, 2010.

Reich, Robert B. *Beyond Outrage: What Has Gone Wrong with Our Economy and Democracy, and How to Fix It*. New York, NY: Vintage Books, 2012.

Rossiter, Clinton (editor). *The Federalist Papers: Hamilton, Madison, Jay*. New York, NY: New American Library, 2003.

Sabato, Larry. *A More Perfect Constitution: 23 Proposals to Revitalize Our Constitution and Make America a Fairer Country*. New York, NY: Walker & Co., 2007.

Schranger, Adam, and Rob Witwer. *The Blueprint: How the Democrats Won Colorado (and Why Republicans Everywhere Should Care)*. Golden, CO: Speaker's Corner Books, 2010.

Zingales, Luigi. *A Capitalism for the People: Recapturing the Lost Genius of American Prosperity*. New York, NY: Basic Books, 2012.

Endnotes

Preface: Pivot Points in Perspective

1 http://www.pbs.org/wgbh/americanexperience/features/primary-resources/carter-crisis/

2 http://www.pewsocialtrends.org/2012/08/22/the-lost-decade-of-the-middle-class/

3 http://www.pewsocialtrends.org/2012/09/10/a-third-of-americans-now-say-they-are-in-the-lower-classes

4 http://www.gallup.com/poll/158387/americans-feel-better-off-worse-off-financially.aspx

5 http://www.conference-board.org/press/pressdetail.cfm?pressid=4636

6 http://www.businessweek.com/ap/2012-11-01/ahead-of-the-bell-us-consumer-confidence

7 http://www.bloomberg.com/news/2012-10-24/this-election-is-all-about-health-care.html

8 This information comes from a variety of sources. The primary ones were the U.S. Census Bureau and the Bureau of Economic Analysis. Specific references include the following: http://www.census.gov/newsroom/releases/archives/income_wealth/cb12-172.html http://quickfacts.census.gov/qfd/states/00000.html http://www.bea.gov/newsreleases/glance.html http://www.indexmundi.com/g/g.aspx http://smallbiz

trends.com/2011/07/chart-job-loss-small-business.html http://articles.
washingtonpost.com/2012-06-11/business/35461572_1_median-balance-
median-income-families http://www.huffingtonpost.com/2012/09/12/
incomes-declined-in-2011_n_187723.html http://www.cbsnews.com/2102-
201_162-57317400.html http://articles.latimes.com/2012/sep/12/business/
la-fi-mo-census-income-poverty-20120912

9 http://www.rockefellerfoundation.org/news/publications/more-
americans-are-financially-insecure

10 Angus Deaton, *The Financial Crisis and the Well-being of Americans*
(Princeton, University: Center for Health and Well-being, September 2011).

11 Thomas L. Friedman and Michael Mandelbaum, *That Used to Be Us: How
America Fell Behind in the World It Invented and How We Can Come Back*
(New York, NY: Farrar, Straus & Giroux, 2011).

12 William C. Harris and Steven C. Beschloss, *Adrift: Charting Our Course
Back to a Great Nation* (Amherst, NY: Prometheus Books, 2011).

13 http://www.nytimes.com/2011/08/17/opinion/crashing-the-tea-
party.html

14 Frank Islam, George Munoz & Ed Crego, *Renewing the American Dream:
A Citizen's Guide for Restoring Our Competitive Advantage* (Washington,
DC: IMC Publishing, 2010).

15 Jeffrey D. Sachs, *The Price of Civilization: Reawakening American Virtue
and Prosperity* (New York, NY: Random House, 2011).

Chapter 1: Pivot Points in American History: The Way We Weren't

1 http://dailycaller.com/2011/01/05/original-u-s-constitution-
will-not-be-read-in-entirety-on-house-floor/

2 Dennis W. Johnson, *The Laws That Shaped America: Fifteen Acts of Congress and Their Lasting Impact* (New York, NY: Routledge, 2009).

3 Felix Rohatyn, *Bold Endeavors: How Our Government Built America and
Why It Must Rebuild It Now* (New York, NY: Simon & Shuster, 2009).

4 Friedman and Mandelbaum, op. cit., p. 46.

5 Our favorite book from a historical perspective on the manner in which
"pivot points" have influenced America is Dennis Johnson's book cited
earlier in this chapter. From a political science perspective and policy
development standpoint, we recommend John W. Kingdon, *Agendas,*

Alternatives, and Public Policies (New York, NY: Longman, 2003). From a journalistic perspective and to understand how certain pivot points are intractable, we recommend Howard Fineman, *The Thirteen American Arguments: Enduring Debates That Define and Inspire Our Country* (New York, NY: Random House, 2008).

6 http://www.archives.gov/exhibits/charters/constitution_history.html

7 http://www.archives.gov/exhibits/charters/bill_of_rights.html http://avalon.yale.edu/18th_century/rights1.aspx http://teachingamerican history.org/ratification/

8 Johnson, op. cit., pp. 75–104. http://eca.state.gov/education/engteaching/pubs/AmLnc/br27.html http://jschell.myweb.uga.edu/history/legis/morrill/htm

9 Johnson, ibid., pp. 75–104. http://www.nathankramer.com/settle/article/homestead.htm http://www.archives.gov/education/lessons/homestead-act/

10 http://www.whitehouse.gov/about/presidents/theodoreroosevelt http://www.nps.gov/history/logcabin/html/tr3.html http://www.pbs.org/wgbh/americanexperience/features/interview/tr-cooper/ http://www.let.rug.nl/usa/E/teddy/teddyxx.htm

11 Johnson, op. cit., pp. 175–202. http://www.ssa.gov/history/tally.html http://www.ssa.gov/history/fdrstmts.html

12 Johnson, ibid., pp. 202–228. http://www.gibill.va.gov/benefits/history_timeline/index.html http://docs.fdrlibrary.marist.edu/odgibill.html

Chapter 2: The Deficit and Debt Crisis: Poised on a Pivot Point

1 http://www.mainstreet.com/print/23074

2 http://www.ft.com/intl/cms/s/0/21947e50-bc5f-11e0-acb6-00144fe abdc0.html

3 http://www.pewresearch.org/2011/08/01/public-sees-budget-negotiations-as-ridiculous-disgusting-stupid/

4 David M. Walker, *Comeback America: Turning the Country Around and Restoring Fiscal Responsibility* (New York, NY: Random House, 2009).

5 Committee for a Responsible Federal Budget, *Deficit Reduction Lessons from Around the World* (September 2009).

6 The Peterson-Pew Commission on Budget Reform, "Red Ink Rising: A Call to Action to Stem the Mounting Federal Debt" (Washington,

DC: The Peterson-Pew Commission on Budget Reform, December 19, 2009). http://www.budgetreform.org

7 Paul Ryan, "Roadmap for America's Future," released on January 27, 2010. http://www.roadmap.republicans.budget.house.gov/plan

8 http://www.fiscalcommission.gov/about

9 http://www.fiscalcommission.gov/members

10 http://www.nytimes.com/2010/11/11/us/politics/11fiscal.html

11 http://www.fiscalcommission.gov/news/moment-truth-report-national-commission-fiscal-responsibility-and-reform

12 http://www.fiscalcommission.gov/news/member-statements-final-commission-report

13 http://en.wikipedia.org/wiki/United_States_House-of_Representatives_elections, 2010

14 http://online.wsj.com/article/SB100014240527487038063045762426121 72357504.html

15 http://www.cbsnews.com/8301-503544_162-20054347-503544.html

16 http://www.huffingtonpost.com/2011/04/16/obama-gop-house-budget-deficit-reduction-plan_n_850075.html

17 http://www.gallup.com/poll/147287/americans-divided-ryan-obama-deficit-plans.aspx

18 http://articles.latimes.com/print/2011/nov/21/news/la-pn-super-committee-20111121

19 http://www.huffingtonpost.com/2011/07/19/gang-of-six-unveils-debt-reduction-plan_n_902999.html

20 http://money.cnn.com/2011/07/19/news/economy/gang_of_six_budget/index.htm

21 http://www.momentoftruthproject.org

22 http://en.wikipedia.org/wiki/Cut,_Cap_and_Balance_Act http://www.huffing tonpost.com/2011/07/22/cut-cap-balance-senate-debt-ceiling_n_906531.html

23 http://www.cbsnews.com/stories/2011/07/10/ftn/main20078242.shtml http://stevenrattner.com/?s=morning+joe+charts-revenue-vs-spending+ and+tax+rates http://www.washingtonpost.com/blogs/wonkblog/wp/ 21012/0/05/the-clinton-economy-in-charts/ http://www.forbes.com/sites/ charleskadlec/2012/07/16/the-dangerous-myth-about-the-bill-clinton-tax-increase/

24 http://www.washingtonpost.com/blogs/wonkblog/wp/2012/09/05/
the-three-best-charts-on-how-clintons-surpluses-became-bush-and-
obamas-deficits/

25 http://pewresearch.org/pubs/2071/debt-limit-ceiling-tea-party-
compromise-deficit-reduction

26 This poll data was drawn from summaries on the debt ceiling and tax
increase-related polls posted by Bruce Drake to www.pollwatch.com in
July and August of 2011.

27 http://mediamatters.org/research/201109210016

Chapter 3: Attention Deficit Disorder: Show Me the Money

1 http://www.politico.com/news/stories/0712/78593.html

2 http://www.washingtonpost.com/opinions/erskine-bowles-a-deal-on-
the-deficit-now/2012/11/07/265a2854-2900-11e2-bab2-eda299503684_
story.html

3 http://www.cbo.gov/publication/43694

4 http://online.wsj.com/article/SB100014240529702039370045780762533
72633058.html

5 http://www.nytimes.com/2012/11/12/business/business-chiefs-step-
gingerly-into-the-federal-budget-fight.html?pagewanted=all

6 http://blogs.reuters.com/macroscope/2012/04/26/what-do-americans-
really-want/

7 http://swampland.time.com/2013/01/01/house-will-vote-on-senate-
passed-cliff-bill/

8 Ibid.

9 Binyamin Appelbaum and Catherine Rampell, "Bigger Tax Bite for Most
Under Senate Plan," *The New York Times*, January 2, 2103, p. B6.

10 http://swampland.time.com/2013/01/03/the-next-cliff-another-
round-of-debt-limit-brinkmanship

11 http://money.cnn.com/2013/01/01/news/economy/fiscal-cliff-deal-cbo/
index.html

12 http://www.washingtonpost.com/politics/polling/recession-recession-
countrys-economic/2013/04/05/ef3bc860-4dc0-11e2-835b-02f92c0
daa43_page.html

13 http://swampland.time.com/2013/03/01/president-obama-sequester-
will-not-happen-quote/

14 http://www.forbes.com/sites/toddganos/2013/05/11/federal-budgetse-quester-not-having-effect-on-economy-thus-far/ http://www.nbcnews.com/business/businesses-slash-jobs-sequester-impact-hits-6C9692839 http://www.inc.com/gene-marks/four-months-after-sequester-economy-improves.html http://finance.yahoo.com/blogs/the-exchange/remember-sequester-finally-dinging-economy-191320555.html

15 http://www.nonprofitquarterly.org/policysocial-context/22391-economic-policy-institute-federal-sequester-s-effect-on-state-budgets.html

16 http://thehill.com/blogs/floor-action/house/289521-house-approves-ryan-budget/

17 http://thehill.com/blogs/floor-action/senate/289747-senate-rejects-ryan-budget-on-40-59-vote/

18 http://nbcpolitics.nbcnews.com/_news/2013/03/23/17426960-senate-passes-budget-with-1-trillion-tax-hike/

19 http://www.decodedscience.com/the-paul-ryan-and-patty-murrary-budget-plans-a-comparison/27974

20 http://www.washingtonpost.com/wp-srv/special/politics/presidential-budget-2014/ http://www.upi.com/Top_News/US/2013/04/14/The-Issue-Plenty-to-love-loathe-in-Obamas-2014-budget/UPI-50651365928200/ http://swampland.time.com/2013/04/10/president-obamas-2014-budget-remarks-transcript/

21 http://thehill.com/blogs/on-the-money/economy/278291-house-sets-stage-for-wednesday-debt-ceiling-debate/

22 http://www.washingtonpost.com/business/economy/house-republicans-plant-to-keep-debt-limit-but-suspend-it-until-may/2013/01/22/14bc4f3e-64ae-11e2-85f5-a8a9228e55e7_story

23 http://thehill.com/homenews/news/293503-president-and-gop-senators-agree-to-swap-papers-on-deficit-reduction-despite-muted-expectations/

24 http://thehill.com/blogs/on-the-money/budget/293315-white-house-backs-budget-conference-as-path-forward-on-debt

25 http://www.cbo.gov/publication/44324

26 http://www.politico.com/story/2013/06/government-shutdown-debt-ceiling-92546.html

27 http://www.bloomberg.com/news/2013-06-09/next-debt-ceiling-histrionics-could-do-real-harm.html

28 http://www.businessweek.com/ap/2013-06-25/stocks-bounce-higher-on-strong-economic-reports

29 http://www.nytimes.com/2013/06/16/business/economy/even-pessimists-feel-optimistic-over-economy.html?pagewanted=all&_r=

30 David Stockman, "Sundown America," *Sunday Review, The New York Times* (March 31, 2013), pp. 1, 6.

31 http://articles.washingtonpost.com/2013-03-28/opinions/38097465_1_free-market-subsidy-financial-firms

32 "Free Exchange: Where Did Everyone Go?" *The Economist*, March 23, 2013, p. 82.

33 http://www.heraldtribune.com/article/20130622/ARTICLE/306229997

34 http://www.nytimes.com/2013/06/27/business/gdp-estimate-is-cut-for-first-quarter-to-1-8.html

35 http://www.thefiscaltimes.com/Articles/2011/06/22/WP-Obama-Announces-Plan-to-Bring-Home-33000-Troops-from-Afghanistan.aspx#page1

36 http://www.huffingtonpost.com/2012/05/04/mitt-romney-unemployment-rate-_n_1477979.html

37 Daniel Gross, "Myth of Decline: U.S. Is Stronger and Faster Than Anywhere Else," *Newsweek*, May 7, 2012.

38 Paul Krugman, *End This Depression Now* (New York, NY: W. W. Norton & Company, 2012).

39 Islam, Munoz, and Crego, op. cit., pp. 14–15.

40 http://economix.blogs.nytimes.com/2011/07/29/jobs-deficit-investment-deficit-fiscal-deficit/

41 http://www.washingtonpost.com/politics/republicans-try-a-softer-focus/2013/02/05/4a90cbbc-6fcb-11e2-aa58-243de81040ba_story.html

42 http://www.huffingtonpost.com/2013/01/30/shrinking-gdp-recession_n_2581713.html

43 http://thehill.com/blogs/floor-action/house/281173-members-propose-new-calculation-to-reflect-true-unemployment-rate

44 http://www.nytimes.com/2013/01/13/sunday-review/americas-productivity-climbs-but-wages-stagnate.html?_r=0

45 Ibid.

46 http://www.nytimes.com/2013/02/04/opinion/a-million-jobs-at-stake-with-sequester.html

47 http://www.pewstates.org/research/data-visualizations/federal-grants-to-states-subject-to-sequester-vary-widely-across-program-areas-85899448245

48 http://www.politifact.com/rhode-island/statements/2012/apr/22/mitt-romney/mitt-romney-says-annual-new-business-startups-have/

49 http://articles.washingtonpost.com/2012-12-07/business/35673031_1_surepayroll-business-owners-small-firms

50 http://construction.about.com/od/New-Construction/a/Construction-Forecast-2013.htm

51 http://www.constructionexec.com/Issues/January_2013/Economic_Outlook.aspx

52 http://www.economist.com/news/briefing/21569381-idea-innovation-and-new-technology-have-stopped-driving-growth-getting-increasing

53 http://www.nber.org/papers/w18315

54 Michael Porter and Jan Rivkin, "Choosing the United States," *Harvard Business Review,* Vol. 90, No. 3 (March 2012), p. 84.

55 http://www.theatlantic.com/business/archive/2012/06/hey-that-famous-skills-shortage-you've-heard-about-it's-a-myth/258207

56 http://business.time.com/2012/06/04/the-skills-gap-myth-why-companies-can't-find-good-people/

57 http://www.bls.gov/bdm/us_age_naics_00_table5.txt

58 http://www.census.gov/newsroom/releases/archives/income_wealth/cb12-108.html

59 http://www.businessinsider.com/underwater-mortgages-decline-2012-7

60 "Points of Light," *The Economist,* July 14–20, 2012.

61 http://www.huffingtonpost.com/thomas-kochan/jobs-crisis-national-emergency_b_165475

Chapter 4: Congressional Dysfunction: Beltway Blues

1 http://washingtonpost.com/blogs/wonkblog/wp/2013/01/04/goodbye-and-good-riddance-112th-congress/

2 http://www.washingtontimes.com/news/2013/jan/9/captol-hill-least-productive-congress-ever-112th-/page=all

3 http://www.foreignpolicy.com/articles/2011/07/19/worst_congress_ever

4 http://www.foreignpolicy.com/articles/2011/07/27/super_bad

5 http://theweek.com/article/index/238354/10-insulting-labels-for-outgoing-112th-congress

6 http://washingtonpost.com/blogs/wonkblog/wp/2013/01/04/goodbye-and-good-riddance-112th-congress/

7 http://www.newyorker.com/arts/critics/atlarge/2011/01/17/110117crat_atlarge_lepore

8 http://www.nytimes.com/2011/11/02/us/house-of-representatives-affirms-in-god-we-trust-motto.html?_r=0

9 Sachs, op. cit. See especially chapter 1, pp. 3–11 and chapter 7, pp. 106–131.

10 George Packer, "The Broken Contract," *Foreign Affairs* (Volume 90, Number 6, November/December 2011), pp. 30–31.

11 http://www.people-press.org/2010/04/18/distrust-discontent-anger-and-partisan-rancor/

12 http://www.gallup.com/poll/155357/americans-confidence-banks-falls-record-low.aspx

13 Tyler Cowen, "Broken Trust Takes Time to Mend," *Sunday Money, The New York Times* (June 17, 2012), p. 6.

14 Maureen Dowd, "Moral Dystopia," *Sunday Review, The New York Times* (June 17, 2012), pp. 1–6.

15 http://thehill.com/blogs/blog-briefing-room/news/276121-poll-congress-less-popular-than-colonoscopies-root-canals-nickleback

16 http://articles.washingtonpost.com/2013-01-03/opinions/36210807_1_middle-class-tax-cuts-president-obama-tax-rates

17 http://www.realclearpolitics.com/video/2013/01/06/bob_schieffer_washington_once_home_to_bipartisan_giants.html

18 http://www.abebooks.com/Honorable-Profession-Tribute-Robert-Kennedy-Hardcover/6108943357/bd

19 http://www.nytimes.com/2013/01/09/us/richard-ben-cramer-writer-on-large-topics-dies-at-62.html?_r=0

20 http://www.theodore-roosevelt.com/trsorbonnespeech.html

21 http://www.colorado.edu/conflict/peace/example/fish7513.htm

22 http://articles.washingtonpost.com/2012-09-19/world/35495262_1_sequestration-budget-cuts-bush-tax-cuts

23 http://articles.washingtonpost.com/2012-10-31/opinions/35500859_1_
republican-george-allen-democrat-tim-kaine-richard-mourdock

24 http://www.newyorker.com/online/blogs/hendrikhertzberg/2012/05/
mann-and-ornstein.html

25 http://www.nolabels.org/12-ways-help

26 http://www.cbsnews.com/8301-18560_162-57544861/is-the-u.s-senate-
broken/

27 http://www.huffingtonpost.com/garethprice/secession-petitions_b_
2152763.html

28 http://www.newyorker.com/online/blogs/backissues/2012/11/secession-
stories.html

29 http://www.washingtonpost.com/politics/decision2012/house-
republicans-poised-to-hold-majority-democrats-declare-end-of-
the-tea-party/2012/11/06/f5767e92-27b3-11e2-b2a0-ae18d6159439_
story.html

30 http://www.washingtonpost.com/opinions/wiping-out-partisan-bias-
in-us-house-elections/2012/11/15/bb8279be-2d2d-11e2-a99d-
5c4203af7b7a_story.html http://www.washingtonpost.com/opinions/
harold-meyerson-gops-gerrymandered-advantages/2012/11/13/4785e4d6-
2d2f-11e2-a99d-5c4203af7b7a_story.html

31 http://www.huffingtonpost.com/george-munoz-frank-islam-and-
ed-crego/the-politics-of-division-_b_1609323.html http://www.people-
press.org/2012/06/01/trend-in-party-identification-1939-2012/

32 http://www.nytimes.com/2012/11/23/us/politics/one-party-control-
opens-states-to-partisan-rush.html

33 http://thehill.com/opinion/columnists/juan-williams/267227-opinion-
california-leading-the-way-to-a-more-functional-congress

34 http://www.abcactionnews.com/dpp/news/political/fair-districts-a-
factor-in-florida-election-results-in-2012

35 Lorelie Kelly, *Congress' Wicked Problem: Seeking Knowledge Inside the
Information Tsunami* (Washington, DC: New America Foundation, Open
Technology Institute, December, 2012).

36 Islam, Munoz and Crego, *Renewing the American Dream,* op. cit., pp. 169,
290–291.

37 http://www.theweek.com/article/index/222880/the-growing-wealth-gap-
between-congress-and-consituents-by-the-numbers#

38 http://articles.washingtonpost.com/2011-12-26/business/35287703_
1_disclosures-wealth-representatives

39 http://www.nytimes.com/2011/12/27/us/politics/economic-slide-took-a-
detour-at-capitol-hill.html?pagewanted=all&_r=0

40 http://articles.washingtonpost.com/2011-12-26/business/35287703_
1_disclosures-wealth-representatives

41 Kelly, op. cit., p. 3.

42 Peter J. Boyer, "Congress Is Getting Rich Off Wall Street and Peter Schweizer Won't Stop Until Everyone Knows It," *Newsweek*, November 21,
2011, pp. 34–38.

43 http://www.nytimes.com/2011/12/27/us/politics/economic-slide-took-a-
detour-at-capitol-hill.html?pagewanted=all&_r=0

Chapter 5: Citizenship Dysfunction: Coming Together or Coming Apart?

1 Pew Research Center for the People & the Press, "Partisan Polarization
Surges in Bush, Obama Years: Trends in American Values, 1987" (http://
www.people-press.org), pp. 1–11

2 Ibid. pp. 93–102.

3 Linda Killian, *The Swing Vote: The Untapped Power of Independents* (New
York, NY: St. Martin's Press, 2012).

4 David Brooks, "What Moderation Means," *The New York Times*
(October 26, 2012), p. A27.

5 Ross Douthat, "Sympathy for the Undecided," *The New York Times*
(October 21, 2012), p. SR 12.

6 Pew Research Center for the People & the Press, "Beyond Red vs. Blue:
The Political Typology" (www.people-press.org), pp. 1–8.

7 Jonathan Haidt, *The Righteous Mind: Why Good People Are Divided by
Politics and Religion* (New York, NY: Random House, 2012).

8 http://www.npr.org/2012/08/30/160357612/transcript-mitt-romneys-
acceptance-speech

9 http://dyn.politico.com/printstory.cfm?uuid=975C4EDO-D2E7-
513C-9D2659881038BEAE

10 http://www.monticello.org/site/research-and-collections/jeffersons-
religious-beliefs

11 http://www.huffingtonpost.com/dorian-de-wind/democrats-god_b_ 1867764.html

12 http://www.nytimes.com/interactive/2012/09/06/us/politics/convention-word-counts.html

13 Ashley Parker, "In Romney's Hands, Pledge of Allegiance Is Framework for Criticism," *The New York Times* (September 9, 2012), p. 12.

14 http://www.thenation.com/print/article/reason-why

15 Time/CNN/ORC poll conducted by telephone with 814 adults on January 14–15, 2013. Results presented in "Your Brain Under Fire," *Time*, January 28, 2013, pp. 37–41.

16 http://www.people-press.org/2012/12/14/public-attitudes-toward-gun-control/

17 http://www.people-press.org/2013/01/14/in-gun-control-debate-several-options-draw-majority-support/

18 http://www.huffingtonpost.com/geoffrey-r-stone/guns-put-up-or-shut-up_b_2413562.html

19 Milton Rokeach was a very influential social psychologist. His best-known works were *The Open and Closed Mind* (1960), *Beliefs, Attitudes and Values: A Theory of Organizational Change* (1968) and *The Nature of Human Values* (1973). He developed the Rokeach Values Survey, a tool used to measure people's relative ranking of values and then to predict a wide variety of factors, including party affiliation and religious belief.

20 William Hart and Dolores Albarracin, et al., "Feeling Validated Versus Being Correct: A Meta-Analysis of Selective Exposure to Information," *Psychological Bulletin*, Vol. 135, No. 4 (2009), pp. 558–588.

21 Philip E. Tetlock, *Expert Political Judgment: How Good Is It? How Can We Know?* (Princeton, NJ: Princeton University Press, 2005).

22 George A. Akerlof and Robert J. Shiller, *Animal Spirits: How Human Psychology Drives the Economy, and Why It Matters for Global Capitalism* (Princeton, NJ: Princeton University Press, 2009). Although not specifically focused on the market meltdown of 2008, Sunstein and Thaler in their excellent book *Nudge* provide examples of flawed decision making and of humans and provide recommendations to move our decision making in the right direction on issues that matter to us as individuals. See Richard H. Thaler and Cass R. Sunstein, *Nudge: Improving Decisions About Health, Wealth and Happiness* (New York, NY: The Penguin Group, 2009).

23 Islam, Munoz, and Crego, op. cit., pp. 38–39.

24 The material in this subsection was drawn from a presentation developed by Ed Crego for the Our American Voice Facilitators Workshop sponsored by the Barat Education Foundation for groups of facilitators, in 2010, 2011 and 2012.

25 The Founders' Constitution. Chapter 18, Document 26, The University of Chicago Press. Noah Webster. *A Collection of Essay and Fugitive Writings on Moral, Historical, Political and Literary Subjects. Boston, 1790.* http://press-pubs.uchicago.edu/founders/documents/v1ch18s26.html

26 http://newdeal.feri.org/er/er19.htm

27 On January 10, 2012, the White House held a special event and released two new papers: an Education Department Report, "Civic Learning and Engagement in Democracy: A Road Map and Call to Action" and the final report by the National Task Force on Civic Learning and Democratic Engagement, "A Crucible Moment: College Learning and Democracy's Future," http://www.ed.gov/civic-learning. Their earlier reports and studies have come from groups such as the Center for Civic Education, The National Assessment of Educational Progress Civics Test, and the Center for Information and Research on Civic Learning and Engagement and the American Youth Policy Forum.

28 http://www.npr.org/2012/09/06/160713941/transcript-president-obamas-convention-speech

29 http://www.npr.org/2012/08/30/160357612/transcript-mitt-romneys-acceptance-speech

30 http://www.nytimes.com/2012/08/31/opinion/party-of-strivers.html

31 David Brooks, "Why Democrats Lead," *The New York Times* (September 7, 2012), p. A27.

32 E. J. Dionne, Our *Divided Political Heart: The Battle for the American Idea in an Age of Discontent* (New York, NY: Bloomsbury, USA, 2012).

33 We first presented this definition along with additional thoughts on citizenship in our book, *Renewing the American Dream.* Islam, Munoz, and Crego, op. cit., pp. 44–46.

34 http://www.jstor.org/discover/10.2307/4181903?uid=3739600&uid=2129&uid=2&uid=70

35 Bill Bradley, *We Can All Do Better* (New York, NY: Vanguard Press, 2012), p. 161.

36 Seth Schiesel, "Former Justice Promotes Web-Based Civics Lessons," *The New York Times* (June 9, 2008). http://www.nytimes.com/2008/06/09/arts/09sand.html

37 Islam, Munoz and Crego, op. cit., p. 207.

38 http://www.humanitiescommission.org/_pdf/HSS_Report.pdf

39 http://thehill.com/video/house/283387-rangel-to-introduce-legislation-to-reinstating-the-draft-

40 http://www.nytimes.com/roomfordebate/2012/03/20/would-a-draft-reduce-the-number-of-post-traumatic-stress-cases/a-draft-would-force-us-to-face-reality   http://articles.washingtonpost.com/2012-04-19/opinions/35452589_1_military-draft-ground-war-world-war-ii

41 http://articles.washingtonpost.com/2013-02-21/opinions/37222144_1_military-draft-military-recruits-volunteer http://articles.washingtonpost.com/2012-04-27/opinions/35451946_1_civil-war-world-war-military-conscription

42 Islam, Munoz and Crego, op. cit., pp. 226–227.

43 http://www.clipsandcomment.com/2008/09/11/transcript-servicenation-presidential-forum-at-columbia-university/

44 http://www.news.harvard.edu/gazette/2006/06.15/09-lehrer.html

45 http://www.nationalservice.gov/about/serveamerica/index.asp

46 http://newdeal.feri.org/er/er19.htm

47 http://www.news.harvard.edu/gazette/2006/06.15/09-lehrer.html

48 http://www.time.com/time/magazine/article/0,9171,2145991,00.html

49 Bill Marsh, "Getting to Vote Is Getting Harder," *The New York Times* (October 21, 2012), p. 7.

50 http://www.huffingtonpost.com/rev-bob-edgar/a-good-start-on-voting-re_b_2687693.html

51 Adam Liptak, "Lost Votes, Problem Ballots, Long Waits? Flaws Are Widespread, Study Finds," *The New York Times* (February 6, 2013), p. A17.

52 Islam, Munoz and Crego, op. cit., p. 203.

53 Ibid., p. 208.

54 http://articles.washingtonpost.com/2013-06-25/politics/40186313_1_voting-rights-act-voting-laws-congress

55 http://www.huffingtonpost.com/2013/07/02/north-carolina-republicans_n_3533550.html?utm_hp_ref=politics

56 http://www.huffingtonpost.com/george-munoz-frank-islam-and-ed-crego/interdependence-day-celeb_b_701016.html

Chapter 6: Individual Economic Well-Being: The 100 Percent

1 David Leonhardt, "Income Inequality," *The New York Times*, January 18, 2011. Read also the paper by Thomas Piketty and Emmanuel Saez, "The Evolution of Top Incomes: A Historical and International Perspective" (supported by NSF grant and the MacArthur Foundation).

2 http://www.billmoyers.com/2013/02/22/in-this-recovery-the-rich-get-richer/

3 http://www.cbpp.org/cms/?fa=view&id=3697

4 http://www.brookings.edu/opinions/2012/0410_99_percent_winship.aspx

5 http://economix.blogs.nytimes.com/2012/09/20/new-york-state-leads-in-income-inequality/

6 http://www.nytimes.com/2012/04/17/business/for-economists-saez-and-piketty-the-buffett-rule-is-just-a-start.html?pagewanted=all

7 Charles Blow, "America's Exploding Pipe Dream," *The New York Times* (October 29, 2011), p. A17. Charles Blow, "Inconvenient Income Inequality," *The New York Times* (December 17, 2011), p. A25.

8 Sabrina Tavernise, "For Americans Under 50, Stark Findings on Health," *The New York Times* (January 10, 2013), p. A3.

9 http://articles.washingtonpost.com/2013-01-16/opinions/36384458_1_life-expectancy-health-care-affordable-care-act

10 Annie Lowrey and Catherine Rampell, "Jobless and Hopeless in America," *The New York Times* (November 2, 2012), p. B1.

11 http://js.washingtonpost.com/opinions/weak-job-creation-has-become-the-norm/2013/02/13/40a7d0f0-6f1c-11e2-8b8d-e0b59a1b8e2a_story_1.html

12 Economic Policy Institute, *The State of Working America 12th Edition* (Washington, DC: EPI, 2012).

13 http://articles.washingtonpost.com/2012-12-09/opinions/35721589_1_higher-unemployment-rates-young-workers-labor-market

14 Annie Lowrey, "Younger Generations Lag Parents in Wealth Building," *The New York Times* (March 15, 2013), p. B1. Charles M. Blow,

"A Dangerous 'New Normal' in College Debt," *The New York Times* (March 9, 2013), p. A17.

15 Floyd Norris, "By Gender and by Age, an Unequal Recovery," *The New York Times* (February 9, 2013), p. B3.

16 Phillip Longman, "The Hole in the Bucket," *Washington Monthly*, Vol. 44, No. 7/8 (July/August 2012), pp. 13–17.

17 www.pewsocialtrends.org/2012/08/22/the-lost-decade-of-the-middle-class/

18 http://www.brookings.edu/research/papers/2012/09/20-pathways-middle-class-sawhill-winship/

19 http://www.nationofchange.org/more-evidence-our-middle-class-sliding-toward-third-world-1372686156

20 http://articles.washingtonpost.com/2013-02-13/business/37070931_1_job-creation-growth-drives-recoveries

21 http://www.census.gov/newsroom/releases/archives/income_wealth/cb11-157.html

22 http://www.huffingtonpost.com/dean-baker/poverty-the-new-growth-in_b_1833158.html

23 David Leonhardt, "Better Colleges Failing to Lure Poorer Strivers," *The New York Times* (March 17, 2013), p. 1.

24 Rich Morin and Seth Motel, "A Third of Americans Now Say They Are in the Lower Classes," (http://www.pewsocialtrends.org).

25 http://campaignstops.blogs.nytimes.com/2012/01/26/don't-mind-the-gap/

26 http://www.people-press.org/2012/02/02/lower-income-republicans-say-government-does-too-little

27 Charles Murray, *Coming Apart: The State of White America, 1960–2010* (New York, NY: Random House, 2012).

28 Jacob S. Hacker and Paul Pierson, *Winner Take All Politics: How Washington Made the Rich Richer—And Turned Its Back on the Middle Class* (New York, NY: Simon & Schuster Paperbacks, 2011).

29 Robert H. Frank, *The Darwin Economy: Liberty, Competition and the Common Good* (Princeton, NJ: Princeton University Press, 2011).

30 Dante Chinni and James Gimpel, *Our Patchwork Nation: The Surprising Truth About the "Real" America—The 12 Community Types That Make up Our Nation* (New York, NY: Gotham Books, 2010).

31 Murray, op. cit., p. 22.

32 http://takingnote.blogs.nytimes.com/2012/09/19/the-redistribution-of-wealth/

33 http://articles.washingtonpost.com/2012-09-25/opinions/35495014_1_tax-code-income-rate-on-capital-gains

34 Michael Grunwald, "One Nation on Welfare. Living Your Life on the Dole," *Time* (September 17, 2012), pp. 31–37.

35 http://www.huffingtonpost.com/jared-bernstein/makers-takers-and-yoyos_b_1899709.html

36 http://www.washingtonpost.com/blogs/wonkblog/post/the-biggest-driver-of-income-inequality-capital-gains/2012/01/02/gIQA181EWP_blog.html

37 http://www.huffingtonpost.com/2012/09/12/incomes-declined-in-2011_n_1877323.html

38 David Kocieniewski, "280 Big Public Firms Paid Little U.S. Tax, Study Says," *The New York Times* (November 3, 2011), p. B1.

39 Robert Semple, "Where the Trough Is Overflowing," *The New York Times* (June 3, 2012) SR, p. 12.

40 http://taxfoundation.org/article/federal-spending-received-dollar-taxes-paid-state-2005   http://articles.washingtonpost.com/2011-05-17/opinions/35232047_1_federal-income-taxes-average-income-new-taxes

41 http://thehill.com/opinion/columnists/juan-williams/276787-opinion-the-perils-of-political-paralysis

42 http://thehill.com/blogs/floor-action/house/277379-50-billion-sandy-bill-splits-gop-but-clears-the-house

43 Bruce Stokes, *Public Attitudes Toward the Next Social Contract* (Washington, DC: The New America Foundation, 2013).

44 Ibid., p. 12.

45 http://www.huffingtonpost.com/jared-bernstein/union-membership-rate_b_2535602.html

46 http://data.bls.gov/cgi-bin/print.pl/news.release/union2.nr0.htm

47 We did these calculations working with data posted at Unionstats.com. The site is maintained by Barry T. Hirsch and David A. Macpherson (http://www.unionstats.com)

48 http://www.salon.com/2012/08/29/scott_walker_radical_chic

49 Steven Greenhouse, "Caterpillar Workers Ratify Deal They Dislike," *The New York Times* (August 18, 2012), p. B1.

50 Eugene L. Meyer, "A Campus Built by Labor Is Going on the Block," *The New York Times* (August 1, 2012), p. B6.

51 http://www.nytimes.com/2012/08/19/opinion/sunday/bruni-teachers-on-the-defensive.html

52 Eduardo Porter, "Unions' Past May Hold Key to Their Future," *The New York Times* (July 18, 2012), p. B1.

53 http://www.huffingtonpost.com/jared-bernstein/union-membership-rate_b_2535602.html

54 http://thehill.com/blogs/blog-briefing-room/news/282981-ralph-nader-pans-obama-call-for-higher-minimum-wage http://thehill.com/homenews/house/285413-liberals-press-for-1010-minimum-wage-more-than-obama-requested http://articles.washingtonpost.com/2013-04-09/opinions/38401502_1_roger-hickey-social-security-medicare

55 http://articles.washingtonpost.com/2013-02-18/opinions/37159077_1_wage-william-wascher-economists-david-neumark

56 John Schmitt, *Why Does the Minimum Wage Have No Discernible Effect on Employment* (Washington, DC: Center for Economic and Policy Research, February 2013). Jared Bernstein, "An Inequality Debate Heats Up," *Huffington Post Blog*, January 18, 2013.

57 Catherine Rampell, "Majority of Jobs Added in the Recovery Pay Low Wages, Study Finds," *The New York Times* (August 31, 2012), p. B1.

58 Reid Cramer, "The Asset Agenda," *Washington Monthly*, Vol. 44, No. 7/8 (July/August 2012).

59 Center on Budget and Policy Priorities, "Policy Basics: The Earned Income Tax Credit" (updated February 2013) http://www.cbpp.org/index.cfm?fa=view&id=2505#

60 http://www.usa.gov/shopping/realestate/mortgages/mortgages.shtml http://portal.hud.gov/hudportal/HUD?src=/topics/avoiding_foreclosure http://www.whitehouse.gov/the-press-office/2012/03/06/fact-sheet-president-obama-announces-new-steps-provide-housing-relief-ve

61 Robert Greenstein Letter to the Editor, "Invitation to a Dialogue: Fighting Poverty," *The New York Times* (February 6, 2013), p. A22.

62 Joseph E. Stiglitz, *The Price of Inequality* (New York, NY: W. W. Norton & Company, 2012).

63 Joseph E. Stiglitz, "Inequality Is Holding Back the Recovery," *The New York Times* (January 20, 2013), SR, p. 1.

64 Jerry Z. Muller, "Capitalism and Inequality: What the Right and the Left Get Wrong," *Foreign Affairs,* Vol. 92, No. 2 (March/April 2013), p. 50.

65 Anant A. Thaker and Elizabeth C. Williamson, "Unequal and Unstable: The Relationship Between Inequality and Financial Crises" (Washington, DC: New America Foundation, 2012).

66 Studs Terkel, *Hope Dies Last: Keeping Faith in Difficult Times* (New York, NY: The New Press, 2004).

67 http://www.guardian.co.uk/theobserver/2004/aug/22/society.studsterkel

68 Islam, Munoz, and Crego, op. cit., p. 35.

Chapter 7: Global Competition: Up Against the BRIC Wall

1 World Economic Forum, *The Global Competitiveness Report 2012–2013* (World Economic Forum, 2012).

2 Ibid., pp. 1–9.

3 Ibid., pp. 13–14.

4 Ibid., pp. 16–17.

5 Ibid., pp. 18–19.

6 Ibid., p. 20.

7 Ibid., pp. 116–117 and analysis.

8 Ibid., pp. 304–305 and analysis.

9 Ibid., pp. 198–199 and analysis.

10 Ibid., pp. 138–139 and analysis.

11 Ibid., pp. 360–361 and analysis.

12 Ruchir Sharma, "Broken BRICs," *Foreign Affairs* (Foreign Affairs, November/December 2012, pp. 2–7. See also Robert J. Samuelson, "The BRIC Rescue That Wasn't," *The Washington Post* (October 14, 2012). http://articles.washingtonpost.com/2012-10-14/opinions/35502245_1_bric-countries-ruchir-sharma-breakout-nations

13 World Economic Forum, op. cit., pp. 49–55.

14 Ibid., pp. 56–60.

15 http://www.wto.org/english/news_e/pres12_e/pr676_e.htm

16 United Nations Conference on Trade and Development, *Trade and Development Report, 2012* (New York, NY: United Nations, 2012).

17 http://www.washingtonpost.com/opinions/what-will-replace-the-globalization-model/2012/10/16/57cf62da-0e6d-11e2-bd1a-b868e65d57eb_print.html

18 http://articles.washingtonpost.com/2012-12-30/opinions/36071260_1_production-workers-capital-flows-cost-advantage

19 "High on Economy, CEOs Wary of Hiring," *Sarasota Herald Tribune* (March 14, 2013), p. 1D.

20 http://www.whitehouse.gov/administration/advisory-boards/jobs-council

21 Council on Competitiveness, *A Clarion Call for Competitiveness* (Washington, DC: Council on Competitiveness, 2012).

22 http://www.economist.com/news/21566352-michael-porter-and-jan-rivkin-co-leaders-harvard-business-schools-united-states

23 Ibid.

24 "An America That Works," *The Economist,* March 18, 2013.

25 "Declinism Resurgent," *The Economist,* May 12, 2012.

26 The most positive analysis of the U.S. position and future possibilities comes from Daniel Gross. He first provided it in his lead *Newsweek* article of May 7, 2012, pp. 22–28. Other articles casting things for the United States in a positive light going forward include Rana Foroohar, "Go Glocal," *Time* (August 20, 2012), pp. 27–32 and Sherle R. Schwenninger and Samuel Sherraden, *The Promise of (and Obstacles to) America's Emerging Growth Story* (Washington, DC: New America Foundation, 2012).

Chapter 8: Manufacturing: Slip, Sliding, Away?

1 http://m.theatlanticcities.com/jobs-and-economy/2013/02/sorry-mr-president-manufacturing-will-not-save-us/4656/

2 http://growth.newamerica.net/publications/policy/what_the_president_should_have_said

3 http://www.whitehouse.gov/the-press-office/2012/07/17/fact-sheet-white-house-advanced-manufacturing-initiatives-drive-innovati

4 http://www.politifact.com/truth-o-meter/statements/2013/feb/12/barack-obama/barack-obama-says-us-has-created-half-million-manu/

5 Rana Foroohar and Bill Saparito, "Made in America," *Time* (April 22, 2013), pp. 22–29.

6 http://www.theatlantic.com/magazine/archive/2012/12/the-insourcing-boom/309166?

7 "Reshoring Manufacturing," Special Report on Outsourcing and Offshoring, *The Economist* (January 19–25, 2013), pp. 6–13.

8 The Institute for Supply Management issues monthly reports. For the most recent report and to compare it to the status of manufacturing at the time this chapter of the book was written in early 2013 go to http://www.ism.ws/ISMReport/MfgROB.cfm?

9 This data comes from an Institute of Supply Management press release published by www.prnewswire.com on December 11, 2012.

10 http://www.heraldtribune.com/article/20130702/ARCHIVES/30702 1039/-1/search10?p=2&tc=pg

11 Foroohar and Saparito, op. cit. See also http://www.washingtonpost.com/blogs/wonkblog/wp/2012/11/19/American-manufacturing/

12 http://www.heraldtribune.com/article/20130702/ARCHIVES/3070210 39/-1/search10?p=2&tc=pg

13 Bureau of Labor Statistics, "Industry Employment and Output Projections to 2020," *Monthly Labor Review*, January 2012.

14 http://www.mckinsey.com/insights/employment_and_growth/an_economy_that_works_for_us_job_creation

15 http://www.manufacturing.gov/nnmi.html

16 http://www.industryweek.com/research-amp-development/sherrod-brown-pushes-manufacturing-teaching-hospitals

17 http://www.brown.senate.gov/newsroom/press/release/sens-brown-and-kirk-introduce-national-manufacturing-strategy-act

18 http://washingtonpost.com/blog/2chambers/post/house-democrats-re-launch-make-it-in-america-manufacturing-jobs-agenda/2011/05/04/AFy0ylqF_blog.html

19 http://dc.streetsblog.org/2011/03/15/sen-kerry-introduces-new-infrastructure-bank-bill/

20 Andrew Liveris, *Make It in America: The Case for Re-Inventing the Economy* (Hoboken, NJ: John Wiley & Sons, 2011).

21 http://www.whitehouse.gov/the-press-office/2012/07/17/fact-sheet-white-house-advanced-manufacturing-initiatives-drive-innovati

22 http://www.brookings.edu/research/papers/2013/01/14-federalism-series-race-to-the-shop-katz http://www.brookings.edu/research/papers/2013/01/14-federalism-series-advanced-industries-hubs http://www.brookings.edu/research/papers/2013/01/14-federalism-series-manufacturing-universities

23 David M. Hart, Stephen J. Ezell and Robert D. Atkinson, *Why America Needs a National Network for Manufacturing Innovation* (Washington, DC: The Information Technology & Innovation Foundation, December 2012).

24 Frank Islam and Ed Crego prepared a White Paper titled *Working the Pivot Points: Renewing Manufacturing to Renew the American Dream* in July 2011. That unpublished 81-page paper was shared with various congressional leaders and subject matter experts. It provides a detailed assessment of performance on the manufacturing renewal recommendations from *Renewing the American Dream* and an examination of the state of manufacturing and manufacturing legislation at the time of its preparation.

25 John F. Sargent Jr., *The Obama Administration's Proposal to Establish a National Network for Manufacturing Innovation* (Washington DC: Congressional Research Service, August 28, 2012). CRS Report for Congress. R42625. Summary, p. 1.

26 http://www.whitehouse.gov/sites/default/files/microsites/ostp/pcast-advanced-manufacturing-june2011.pdf

27 http://www.mckinsey.com/insights/mgi/research/labor_markets/an_economy_that_works_for_us_job_creation

28 http://www.mckinsey.com/insights/mgi/research/productivity_competitiveness_and_growth/the_future_of_manufacturing

29 Islam and Crego, op. cit., p. 8.

30 Ibid., p. 8.

31 Foroohar and Saparito, op. cit., p. 29.

Chapter 9: Entrepreneurs: I Have a Dream

1 https://www.wellsfargo.com/press/2013/20130124_WellsFargoSBI

2 http://www.nfib.com/press-media/press-media-item?cmsid=62013

3 http://www.nfib.com/research-foundation/surveys/small-business-economic-trends

4 http://www.gallup.com/poll/160199/small-businesses-cutting-workers-hiring.aspx

5 http://www.nytimes.com/2013/02/14/business/smallbusiness/small-businesses-struggle-impeding-a-recovery.html?_r=0

6 http://www.nytimes.com/2013/03/04/business/economy/corporate-profits-soar-as-worker-income-limps.html?hp&_r=1&

7 http://www.bloomberg.com/news/2013-01-14/small-firms-to-remain-missing-link-in-u-s-expansion-economy.html

8 http://www.sba.gov/sites/default/files/files/Small_Business_Economy_2012(2).pdf

9 http://stevenrattner.com/interview/msnbcs-morning-joe-startups-and-job-creation/

10 Citi Research, *Empirical and Thematic Perspectives—Does Size Really Matter? The Evolving Role of Small Firms in the U.S. Economy* (Citi Research, December 10, 2012), p. 1. (http://www.citivelocity.com)

11 Dane Stangler, "The Economic Future Just Happened," *Ewing Marion Kauffman Foundation Report* (June 9, 2009).

12 Ewing Marion Kauffman Foundation, "2013 State of Entrepreneurship Address," February 5, 2013, p. 1.

13 Islam, Munoz and Crego, op. cit., pp. 106–109. These pages address activities in 2008 and during the first year of the Obama administration.

14 http://www.sba.gov/content/sba-applauds-stimulus-bill-planning-underway-broadest-quickest-small-business-impact http://www.sba.gov/content/small-business-jobs-act-2010 http://www.gpo.gov/fdsys/pkg/BILLS-112hr3606enr/pdf/BILLS-112hr3606enr.pdf

15 http://www.businessweek.com/articles/2013-02-11/how-did-karen-mills-the-departing-sba-chief-do

16 http://www.sba.gov/administrator/7585/3215

17 http://www.entrepreneur.com/article/225433#

18 http://www.washingtonpost.com/blogs/wonkblog/wp/2013/02/05/the-cbos-new-budget-outlook-in-six-charts/

19 http://articles.washingtonpost.com/2013-02-15/business/37117216_1_boehner-spokesman-michael-steel-government-shutdown-cuts-and-reforms

20 http://www.whitehouse.gov/the-press-office/2013/02/08/fact-sheet-examples-how-sequester-would-impact-middle-class-families-job

21 http://www.kauffman.org/newsroom/high-growth-firms-account-for-disproportionate-share-of-job-creation-according-to-kauffman-foundation-study.aspx

22 Karen Mills Guest Post for the Kauffman Foundation on February 5, 2013. http://blogs.forbes.com/kauffman http://www.forbes.com/sites/kauffman/2013/02/05/fueling-economic-expansion-through-investment-in-entrepreneurs/

23 Ewing Marion Kauffman Foundation, "2013 State of Entrepreneurship Address," February 5, 2013.

24 http://dealbook.nytimes.com/2013/02/07/helping-start-ups-with-local-support-and-national-networks/

25 http://articles.washingtonpost.com/2012-08-03/business/35490714_1_small-business-jobs http://www.cnn.com/2012/07/13/politics/small-business-btn

26 http://boss.blogs.nytimes.com/2010/03/10/why-wont-the-s-b-a-loan-directly-to-small-businesses/?_r=0

27 http://www.businessweek.com/articles/2013-02-01/three-months-after-sandy-a-report-card-on-small-business-relief

28 Citi Research, *Empirical and Thematic Perspectives—Does Size Really Matter? The Evolving Role of Small Firms in the U.S. Economy* (Citi Research, December 10, 2012), p. 1. (http://www.citivelocity.com)

29 http://www.nytimes.com/2011/10/24/opinion/small-businesses-arent-key-to-the-economic-recovery.html For a more technical discussion on this also read Jared Bernstein's post, http://www.huffingtonpost.com/jared-bernstein/small-business-job-creation_b_1685869.html

Chapter 10: Immigration: Don't Fence Me In

1 http://www.immigrationupdate.wordpress.com/famous-american-immigrants/

2 Darryl West, *Brain Gain: Rethinking U.S. Immigration Policy* (Washington, DC: The Brookings Institution, 2010), p. x.

3 Ibid., pp. x–xi.

4 http://www.democracyjournal.org/21/our-best-imports-keeping-immigrant-innovators-here.php?page=all

5 West, op. cit. See chapter 1 for detailed list and discussion of costs and benefits of immigration.

6 Claudia Kolker, *The Immigrant Advantage: What We Can Learn from Newcomers to America about Health, Happiness and Hope* (New York, NY: Simon & Schuster, 2011).

7 http://www.kauffman.org/newsroom/immigrant-entrepreneurship-has-stalled-for-the-first-time-in-decades-kauffman-foundation-study-shows.aspx

8 Vivek Wadhwa, *Why America Is Losing the Global Race to Capture Entrepreneurial Talents* (Philadelphia, Wharton Digital Press, 2012).

9 West, op. cit., pp. 30–32.

10 http://www.pewhispanic.org/2012/04/23/net-migration-from-mexico-falls-to-zero-and-perhaps-less/

11 http://articles.washingtonpost.com/2013-01-25/politics/36540737_1_immigration-reform-immigration-laws-immigration-status

12 http://www.christianpost.com/news/obama-lends-support-to-gang-of-eight-immigration-reform-plan-89107/

13 Kate Nocera and Manu Raju, "Immigration Reform: Senate Stuck on Lower-Skilled Workers," *Politico.com*, March 5, 2013.

14 Ashley Parker, "Visas Are Urged for Lower-Skilled Work," *The New York Times* (February 22, 2013), p. A16.

15 http://www.policymic.com/articles/35671/immigration-reform-2013-gang-of-8-plan-released-here-is-what-is-in-it

16 http://articles.washingtonpost.com/2013-01-30/opinions/36647247_1_immigration-reform-immigration-speech-immigration-system

17 http://thehill.com/homenews/senate/308307-senate-approves-immigration-bill-in-68-32-vote

18 http://www.nytimes.com/2013/06/19/us/politics/boehner-says-he-wont-push-through-an-immigration-bill.html?pagewanted=all&_r=0

19 http://thehill.com/homenews/senate/308307-senate-approves-immigration-bill-in-68-32-vote

20 http://www.nytimes.com/2013/02/13/business/tech-companies-and-immigrant-advocates-join-forces.html/

21 Parker, op. cit., p. A16.

22 http://www.huffingtonpost.com/huff-wires/20130208/us-immigration-bipartisan-group/

23 Jeb Bush, *Immigration Wars: Forging an American Solution* (New York, NY: Threshold Editions, 2013).

24 Ken Thomas, "Immigration Stance Cost Romney Votes, Jeb Bush Says," *Sarasota Herald Tribune* (March 5, 2013), p. 5B.

25 Michael D. Shear, "Bush Makes Bid to Explain Views on Immigration," *Sarasota Herald Tribune* (March 6, 2013), p. 6A.

26 This meeting was widely reported. This discussion is drawn from a blog posting at blog.pe.com on March 3, 2013.

27 Jake Sherman and Kate Nocera, "Immigration Talks Gain Momentum," *Politico.com* (March 5, 2013).

28 http://www.politico.com/story/2013/04/house-immigration-reform-bob-goodlatte-90632.html

29 http://thehill.com/homenews/house/308217-boehner-immigration-bill-needs-majority-in-both-parties

30 http://thehill.com/homenews/house/308097-timing-of-legalization-becomes-key-to-reform-chances

31 http://www.nytimes.com/2013/06/26/us/politics/gop-in-house-leaves-immigration-bill-in-doubt.html?pagewanted=all

32 http://www.brookings.edu/blogs/the-avenue/posts/2012/11/16-immigration-singer

33 http://www.theatlanticcities.com/politics/2012/10/why-we-should-worry-about-drop-immigrant-led-start-ups/3577/ http://www.theatlantic.com/international/archive/2012/10/why-do-brazil-china-and-india-get-all-the-entrepreneurs-these-days/263140/

34 West, op. cit., pp. 129–152.

35 http://www.nytimes.com/2013/02/08/opinion/americas-genius-glut.html

36 Annie Lowery, "Struggling to Measure an Economic Impact," *The New York Times* (June 27, 2013), p. A22.

37 Raul Hinjosa-Ojeda, "The Economic Benefits of Comprehensive Immigration Reform," *Cato Journal,* Vol. 32, No. 1 (Winter 2012), pp. 175–199.

38 Congressional Budget Office Cost Estimate, "Senate Amendment 1150 to S. 1348, the Comprehensive Immigration Reform Act of 2007," June 4, 2007.

39 http://www.brookings.edu/research/papers/2013/04/11-worker-shortage-immigration-west

40 http://www.brookings.edu/blogs/up-front/posts/2013/01/29-immigration-greenstone-looney

41 http://www.washingtonpost.com/blogs/wonkblog/wp/2013/01/29/five-things-economists-know-about-immigration

42 http://www.huffingtonpost.com/jared-bernstein/economics-of-immigration_b_2584509.html

43 http://business.time.com/2013/01/30/the-economics-of-immigration-who-wins-who-loses-and-why

44 Eduardo Porter, "Immigration Reform Issue: The Effect on the Budget," *The New York Times* (February 6, 2013), p. B1.

Chapter 11: Education: Up in the Error

1 http://www.huffingtonpost.com/2012/08/05/mooc-massive-open-online-courses_n_1744430.html

2 http://articles.washingtonpost.com/2012-06-29/politics/35459154_1_student-loan-loan-rates-republicans-plan

3 http://www.consumerfinance.gov/pressreleases/consumer-financial-protection-bureau-and-u-s-department-of-education-joint-report-finds-a-cycle-of-boom-and-bust-in-private-student-loan-market/

4 http://harkin.senate.gov/help/forprofitcolleges.cfm

5 http://www.nytimes.com/2012/07/30/education/harkin-report-condemns-for-profit-colleges.html?pagewanted=all&_r=0

6 http://www.apscu.org. Press release of July 29, 2012, and Harkin Report Backgrounder that accompanies release.

7 http://www.heraldtribune.com/article/20130702/ARCHIVES/307021057/-1/search10?Title=STUDENT-LOANS-Analysts-fear-it-may-ultimately-hurt-the-entire-housing-market

8 http://www.onewisconsinnow.org/press/institute-new-national-research-shows-trillion-dollar-student-loan-debt-crisis-a-clear-and-present-d.html

9 http://www.acenet.edu Press release of October 17, 2011.

10 http://www.nytimes.com/2012/05/13/business/student-loans-weighing-down-a-generation-with-heavy-debt.html?pagewanted=all

11 Paul E. Lingerfelter, "The National Commission on Accountability in Higher Education" (Washington, DC: American Council on Education, February 15, 2005).

12 National Commission on Higher Education Attainment, "An Open Letter to College and University Leaders: College Completion Must Be Our Priority" (Washington, DC: American College on Education, January 2013).

13 http://www.insidhigher.com/news/2013/01/24/national-commission-higher-education-attainment-releases-final-report

14 http://www.nytimes.com/2013/03/09/opinion/blow-a-dangerous-new-normal-in-college-debt.html

15 http://chronicle.com/article/StudentsStates-Near-a/137709/

16 http://money.cnn.com/2012/09/17/pf/college/college-costs-obama/index.html

17 U.S. Department of Education/Federal Student Aid, *Federal Student Aid Strategic Plan FY 2012–2016* (Washington, DC: U.S. Department of Education, December 2011), p. 6. http://federalstudentaid.ed.gov/about/performance.html

18 http://www.forbes.com/sites/michaelnoer/2012/08/01/americas-top-colleges-2/

19 http://www.insidehighered.com/news/2009/10/23/garland

20 http://www.businessweek.com/articles/2012-04-09/why-college-isnt-for-everyone

21 Harkin Report, op cit., Executive Summary, p. 1.

22 Kevin Carey and Andrew P. Kelly, *The Truth Behind Higher Education Disclosure Laws* (Washington, DC: American Enterprise Institute, Education Sector, 2011).

23 http://online.wsj.com/article/SB10001424052748703822404575019082819966538.html

24 http://pewresearch.org/pubs/2261/college-university-education-costs-student-debt

25 http://www.businessweek.com/articles/2012-04-09/why-college-isnt-for-everyone

26 http://centerforcollegeaffordability.org/archives/8408

27 Andrew Hacker, "Is Algebra Necessary," *The New York Times* (July 29, 2012), p. SR1.

28 Federal Student Aid, op. cit., pp. 11–12.

29 Harkin Report, op. cit., Executive Summary, p. 1.

30 David Deming, Claudia Goldin and Lawrence F. Katz, "The For-Profit Postsecondary School Sector: Nimble Critters or Agile Predator" (Center for Analysis of Postsecondary Education and Employment, February 2012). Also in winter issue of *Journal of Economic Perspectives*, Vol. 26, No. 1 (2012), pp. 139–164. Visit http://capseecenter.org

31 Jennifer Medina, "Teacher Training Termed Mediocre," *The New York Times* (October 22, 2009). http://www.nytimes.com/2009/10/23/education/23teachers.html

32 http://www.nctq.org/dmsStage/Teacher_Prep_Review_2013_Report

33 Federal Student Aid, op. cit., p. 12.

34 U.S. Department of Education, Office of Planning, Evaluation and Policy Development, "Evaluation of Evidence-Based Practices in Online Learning: A Meta-Analysis and Review of Online Learning Studies" (Washington, DC: U.S. Department of Education, September 2010). http://www.ed.gov/about/offices/list/opepd/ppss/reports.html

35 http://www.edweek.org/ew/issues/technology-in-education/

36 Arne Duncan, "Harness the Power of Technology," *Learning and Leading with Technology* (ISTE: International Society for Technology in Education, June/July 2011).

37 http://www.edweek.org/ew/isssues/no-child-left-behind/

38 http://www.ed.gov/news/press-releases/26-more-states-and-dc-seek-flexibility-nclb-drive-education-reforms-second-round

39 Hacker, op. cit., p. SR1.

40 http://www.nytimes.com/2012/05/15/business/colleges-begin-to-confront-higher-costs-and-students-debt.html?pagewanted=all&_r=0

41 http://www.nytimes.com/2012/06/26/opinion/fixing-college-through-lower-costs-and-better-technology.html

42 James Garland, *Saving Alma: A Rescue Plan for America's Public Universities* (Chicago, IL: University of Chicago Press, 2009).

43 William G. Bowen, Matthew M. Chingos and Michael S. McPherson, *Crossing the Finish Line: Completing College at America's Public Universities* (Princeton, NJ: Princeton University Press, 2010). Paperback in 2011.

44 Editors, "2012 College Rankings," *Washington Monthly* (September/October 2012). http://www.washingtonmonthly.com/college_guide/feature/_introduction_jobs_are_not.php

45 http://capseecenter.org/for-profit-nimble-critters/

46 http://www.huffingtonpost.com/dr-kevin-manning/higher-education-career-advice_b_1747861.html

47 http://www.usnews.com/opinion/blos/economic-intelligence/2012/07/20/community-colleges-prepare-next-generation-of-workers

48 Richard Perez Pena, "The New Community College Try," *The New York Times* (July 22, 2012), Education Life, pp. 18–21.

49 http://www.gatesfoundation.org/college-ready-education

50 Al Baker, "Certifying Teachers, More by How They Teach Than How They Test," *The New York Times* (July 30, 2012), p. 3A. For information on Stanford Center director visit https://ed.stanford.edu/faculty/pecheone.

51 http://connectededucators.org/cem/about

52 http://learning.blogs.nytimes.com/2012/08/01/for-connected-educator-month-tips-from-33-educators-we-admire/?_r=0

53 http://www.corestandards.org/the-standards

54 Letters to the Editor, "Sunday Dialogue: Improving Our Schools, Will a New Set of Standards and More Tests Help Students?" *The New York Times* (July 22, 2012), SR p. 2.

55 http://www.nytimes.com/2012/05/15/business/colleges-begin-to-confront-higher-costs-and-students-debt.html?pagewanted=all&_r=0

56 http://www.newamerica.net/events/2013/skills_beyond_school_oecd

57 http://www.nytimes.com/2012/06/26/opinion/fixing-college-through-lower-costs-and-better-technology.htm

58 http://www.huffingtonpost.com/2012/12/11/international-tests-show-_n_2273134.html

59 Bracey's quotes are drawn from a paper by Valerie Strauss, "Do International Test Comparisons Make Sense," posted the day before the PISA results were reported for 2012.

60 Brown Center on Education Policy at Brookings, *The 2012 Brown Center Report on American Education: How Well Are American Students Learning?* (Washington, DC: The Brookings Institution, 2012), p. 5. For a more detailed discussion, read pp. 25–31.

61 http://www.huffingtonpost.com/2012/12/11/international-tests-show-_n_2273134.html

62   Brown Center on Education Policy at Brookings, op. cit., pp. 17–24.

63   Misty Lacour and Laura D. Tissington, "The Effects of Poverty on Academic Achievement," *Educational Research and Reviews,* Vol. 6, No. 7 (July 2011), pp. 522–527 (Academic Journals, July 2011). http://www.academic-journals.org/err/pdf/pdf%202011/july/lacour%20and%20tissington.pdf

64   Salvatore Saporito, "Mapping Educational Inequality: Concentrations of Poverty among Poor and Minority Students in Public Schools," *Oxford Journal* (University of North Carolina Press, 2007). http://sf.oxfordjournals.org/content/85/3/1227. ISSN 1534-7605

65   Nina Rees, Letter to Editor, "Inside the World of Charter Schools," *The New York Times* (March 4, 2013), p. A20.

66   http://articles.washingtonpost.com/2013-03-01/opinions/37373713_1_kipp-students-kipp-schools-traditional-public-schools

67   http://schoolfinance101.wordpress.com/2013/03/01/the-non-reformy-lessons-of-kipp/

68   http://www.huffingtonpost.com/2013/01/31/charter-schools-stanford-report_n_2586231.html

69   Center for Research on Education Outcomes, *Charter School Growth and Replication Executive Summary* (Stanford University, CREDO, January 30, 2013), pp. 1–10.

70   http://credo.stanford.edu/documents/UNEMBARGOED%20National%20Charter%20Study%20Press%20Release.pdf

71   http://www.brookings.edu/blogs/brown-center-chalkboard/posts/2013/07/03-charter-schools-loveless

72   Motoko Rich, "Grants Back Public-Charter Cooperation," *The New York Times* (December 5, 2012), p. A20.

73   "Value Added Remodeling," "Special Report: America's Competitiveness," *The Economist* (March 16–22, 2013), pp. 8–16.

74   Motoko Rich, "12 States Get Failing Grades on Public School Policies from Advocacy Group," *The New York Times* (January 7, 2013), p. A10.

75   David L. Kirp, *Improbable Scholars: The Rebirth of a Great American School System and a Strategy for America's Schools* (Oxford: Oxford University Press, 2013).

76   David L. Kirp, "The Secret to Fixing Bad Schools," *The New York Times* (February 10, 2013), SR p. 5.

77 http://articles.washingtonpost.com/2013-02-14/politics/37087821_1_childhood-education-preschool-expansion-graduation-rates

78 Motoko Rich, "Few States Look to Extend Preschool to All 4-Year-Olds," *The New York Times* (February 14, 2013), p. A15.

Chapter 12: Innovation: Progress Is Our Most Important Product

1   Tyler Cowen, *The Great Stagnation: How America Ate All the Low-Hanging Fruit of Modern History, Got Sick, and Will (Eventually) Feel Better* (New York, NY: Dutton, 2011).

2   See also Tyler Cowen, "Innovation Is Doing Little for Incomes," *The New York Times* (January 30, 2011), BU, p.4.

3   http://www.nber.org/papers/w18315.pdf

4   For two good articles addressing and discussing Cowen and Gordon's findings read "Has the Ideas Machine Broken Down?" *The Economist* (January 12, 2013), pp. 21–24 and Martin Wolf, "Is Unlimited Growth a Thing of the Past?" *Financial Times*, October 2, 2012. http://www.ft.com/intl/cms/s/0/78e883fa-0bef-11e2-8032-00144feabdc0.html

5   http://www.govtech.com/newsletters/Question-of-the-Day-for-081911.html

6   http://articles.cnn.com/2011-09-16/politcs/obama.patent-reform_1_patent-office-first-to-file

7   http://www.nytimes.com/2013/02/09/opinion/nocera-innovation-nation-at-war.html

8   http://www.reuters.com/assets/print?aid=USBRE91E03320130215

9   Jonathan Rothwell, Jose Lobo, Deborah Strumsky and Mark Muro, "Patenting Prosperity: Invention and Economic Performance in the United States and Its Metropolitan Areas" (Metropolitan Policy Program at Brookings, Brookings Institution, February 2013). http://www.brookings.edu/metro

10 http://www.whitehouse.gov/the-press-office/president-obama-lays-out-strategy-american-innovation

11 http://www.brookings.edu/events/2013/01/15-growth-innovation

12 http://www.wilsoncenter.org/publication/strengthening-america-inventing-the-future

13 http://www.nytimes.com/2012/12/14/business/companies-see-high-tech-factories-as-fonts-of-ideas.html

14 http://www.nytimes.com/2012/11/25/business/mit-lab-hatches-ideas-and-companies-by-the-dozens.html

15 http://www.foreignaffairs.com/articles/138154/neil-gershenfeld/how-to-make-almost-anything

16 Steve Lohr, "Sure, Big Date Is Great. But So Is Intuition," *The New York Times* (December 30, 2012), BU, p. 3.

17 John Markoff, "Learning Curve: No Longer Just a Human Trait," *The New York Times* (November 24, 2012), p. A1.

18 Erik Brynjolffson and Andrew McAfee, *Race Against the Machine* (Lexington, MA: Digital Frontier Press, 2012).

19 Gary Pisano and Willy Shih, "Restoring American Competitiveness," *Harvard Business Review* (July/August 2009), pp. 114–122.

20 http://www.mckinsey.com/insights/mgi/research/urbanization/infrastructure_productivity

21 http://www.mckinsey.com/insights/americas/reducing_the_drag_on_the_american_economy

22 ww.gsb.stanford.edu/news/bmag/sbsm1201/spence_jobs.html

23 Michael Lind has authored numerous papers and articles focused on restructuring the American social contract and the American economy. In 2012, he authored an important economic history of the United States, *Land of Promise* (New York, NY: HarperCollins, 2012).

24 http://www.nationofchange.org/unstarvable-beast-1357143641

25 Atul Gawande, *The Checklist Manifesto* (New York, NY: Henry Holt & Company, 2009).

26 Steven Brill, "Why Medical Bills Are Killing Us," *Time* (March 4, 2013).

27 Rohatyn, op. cit.

28 http://www.wilsoncenter.org/publication/strengthening-america-inventing-the-future

29 Information and Technology Innovation Foundation, op. cit.

30 http://www.brookings.edu/research/papers/2012/11/13-federalism-budget-economy

31 Bruce Katz and Jennifer Bradley, *The Metropolitan Revolution* (Washington, DC: Brookings Institution Press, 2013).

32 http://libraries.mit.edu/archives/exhibits/purse

33 Tyler Cowen, "Innovation Is Doing Little for Incomes," *The New York Times* (January 30, 2011), BU, p. 4.

34 Joseph Stiglitz, *Freefall* (New York, NY: W. W. Norton & Company, 2010), pp. 284–285.

35 http://www.huffingtonpost.com/david-coates/going-beyond the presiden_b_2757999.html

36 http://www.huffingtonpost.com/george-munoz-frank-islam-and-ed-crego/its-time-to-play-in-the-3_b_944885.html

37 Paul Weinstein, Jr., "Cut to Invest" (Brookings Metropolitan Policy Program, November 2012).

38 http://news.yahoo.com/blogs/lookout/american-workers-race-against-machine-165318939.html See also http://www.nytimes.com/2011/10/24/technology/economists-see-more-jobs-for-machines-not-people.html?_r=0&gwh=B5975790CBBE84DBFBD428785DF5C697

39 Executive Office of the President National Science and Technology Council Advanced Manufacturing National Program Office, "National Network for Manufacturing Innovation a Preliminary Design" (January 2013). http://www.manufacturing.gov. anmpo@nist.gov

40 Walter Isaacson, *Steve Jobs* (New York, NY: Simon & Schuster, 2011).

Epilogue: Pivot Forward

1 http://www.washingtonpost.com/opinions/congress-can-now-move-past-partisan-gridlock-at-last/2012/11/07/84122bf0-2918-11e2-96b6-8e6a7524553f_story.html

2 http://www.washingtonpost.com/opinions/george-will-the-winner-is-the-status-quo/2012/11/07/719280e0-28fc-11e2-bab2-eda299503684_story.html

3 Numerous analyses have been done on the Romney campaign. One of the best that we saw was published in the *New York Times Election* 2012 special insert, pp. P1-P20, published on November 8, 2012.

4 http://www.washingtonpost.com/politics/decision2012/mitt-romneys-concession-speech-full-transcript/2012/11/07/99f9c98c-28a0-11e2-96b6-8e6a7524553f_story.html

5 http://www.people-press.org/2012/11/07/changing-face-of-america-helps-assure-obama-victory/

6 http://www.cbsnews.com/election-results-2012/

7 Ibid.

8 http://www.usatoday.com/story/news/politics/2012/11/07/democrats-pick-up-seats-in-senate-despite-odds/1690359/ http://www.politico.com/news/stories/1112/83501.html http://pewresearch.org/pubs/2412/pew-research-exit-poll-analysis-2012-obama-reelection

9 http://www.democraticunderground.com/1014297576

10 http://online.wsj.com/article/SB10001424127887324073504578105371839771426.html

11 http://reporting.sunlightfoundation.com/2012/Return-on-investment-story/

12 http://www.forbes.com/sites/stevenbertoni/2012/11/08/why-sheldon-adelsons-election-donations-were-millions-well-spent/

13 http://www.people-press.org/2012/11/07/no-consensus-view-on-election-outcome/

14 http://www.people-press.org/2012/11/07/no-consensus-view-on-election-outcome/

15 http://www.people-press.org/2012/11/15/low-marks-for-the-2012-election/

16 Professor Alan Gittelson has lectured extensively on this topic. He draws upon a variety of sources for the data used in his lectures, including Gallup, Pew, the University of Michigan Survey Research Center and the National Opinion Research Center at the University of Chicago. His favorite print resources include Garry Wills, *A Necessary Evil: A History of Distrust of Government* (New York, NY: Simon & Schuster, 1999); Joseph S. Nye et al., eds., *Why People Don't Trust Government* (Boston, MA: Harvard University Press, 1997); E. J. Dionne, Jr., *Why Americans Hate Politics* (New York, NY: Simon & Schuster, 1991).

17 http://www.washingtonpost.com/opinions/marc-thiessen-how-obama-trumped-romney-with-big-data/2012/11/12/6fa599da-2cd4-11e2-89d4-040c9330702a_story.html

18 http://www.news.illinois.edu/news/09/0701listening.html

19 http://www.newyorker.com/archive/2005/12/05/051205crbo_books1

20 http://nymag.com/news/politics/conservatives-david-frum-2011-11/

21 http://www.huffingtonpost.com/2012/11/07/nate-silver-obama-reelection_n_2086556.html

22 http://www.newyorker.com/talk/comment/2012/12/03/121203taco_talk_hertzberg

23 http://www.forbes.com/sites/johnmcquaid/2012/11/07/three-lessons-from-the-nate-silver-controversy/

24 http://www.washingtonpost.com/opinions/charles-krauthammer-the-way-forward/2012/11/08/6592e302-29d8-11e2-96b6-8e6a7524553f_story.html

25 http://www.nytimes.com/2012/11/11/opinion/sunday/douthat-the-gops-demographic-excuse.html?_r=0

26 http://www.washingtonpost.com/opinions/michael-gerson-renewing-the-republican-party/2012/11/08/4d3f6294-29d8-11e2-96b6-8e6a7524553f_story.html

27 http://thecaucus.blogs.nytimes.com/2012/11/14/romney-blames-loss-on-obamas-gifts-to-minorities-and-young-voters/ http://www.nytimes.com/2012/11/14/us/politics/ryan-sees-urban-vote-as-reason-gop-lost.html

28 http://thehill.com/homenews/senate/268099-senate-republicans-election-lesson-is-to-work-on-fielding-better-candidates

29 http://www.huffingtonpost.com/2012/11/15/mitt-romney-republicans_n_2135967.html

30 http://www.motherjones.com/politics/2012/11/super-pac-republican-party-immigration-gay-marriage

31 http://www.politico.com/news/stories/1112/83704.html

32 http://www.csmonitor.com/USA/DC-Decoder/Decoder-Wire/2012/1107/Election-results-2012-Who-won-it-for-Obama-video (Asian and White vote) http://www.huffingtonpost.com/2012/11/07/gender-gap-2012-election-obama_n_2086004.html (women vote) http://sweetness-light.com/archive/wp-fact-checker-independents-not-important#.UL9oTeTAeYU (Independent vote) http://abcnews.go.com/blogs/politics/2012/11/a-draw-on-the-economy-a-win-on-empathy-and-the-face-of-a-changing-nation/ http://www.independent.co.uk/news/world/americas/us-elections/swings-and-roundabouts-how-a-divided-nation-voted-8294799.html

33 http://www.people-press.org/typology/

34 http://www.washingtonpost.com/opinions/eugene-robinson-republicans-dont-heed-lessons-of-the-election/2012/11/15/09dbf1a0-2f5c-11e2-9f50-0308e1e75445_story.html

35 http://articles.washingtonpost.com/2013-01-10/opinions/36272177_1_welfare-reform-conservative-ideas-missile-defense

36 http://www.people-press.org/2012/06/04/

37 http://hbr.org/2004/07/marketing-myopia/

38 Jeremy W. Peters, "113th Congress: This Time, It's Out with New," *The New York Times* (December 10, 2012), p. 1.

39 http://thehill.com/capital-living/275309-portrait-of-the-113th-congress-40

40 Peters, op. cit., p. 1.

41 http://articles.washingtonpost.com/2013-01-15/opinions/36384848_
    1_gun-control-gun-free-steve-stockman

42 Ben Terris, "Animal House," *The Atlantic* (January/February 2013),
    pp. 24–25.

43 http://thehill.com/capital-living/cover-stories/281303-bowling-down-
    the-aisle

44 http://thehill.com/homenews/administration/282151-an-end-to-
    gridlock-well-maybe-a-respite http://articles.washingtonpost.com/2013-
    01-29/opinions/36616407_1_house-republicans-immigration-reform-
    immigration-plan

45 http://articles.washingtonpost.com/2013-04-10/politics/38434930_1_
    senate-republicans-immigration-overhaul-president-obama

46 http://voices.washingtonpost.com/ezra-klein/2010/02/alexander_
    draft.html

47 http://www.washingtonpost.com/blogs/wonkblog/wp/2013/06/20/
    the-house-farm-bill-unexpectedly-fails-195-234-so-what-happens-next/

48 http://www.huffingtonpost.com/robert-reich/the-quiet-closing-of-
    washington_b_3412675.html

49 http://www.theatlantic.com/magazine/archive/2013/07/the-do-nothing-
    congress-has-done-a-lot/309378/

50 http://www.theatlantic.com/national/archive/2013/06/one-nation-
    divisible/277286/

51 Dan Gardner, *Future Babble: Why Expert Predictions Fail and Why We
    Believe Them Anyway* (Canada: McClelland & Stewart, 2010).

52 Nate Silver, *The Signal and the Noise: Why So Many Predictions Fail—But
    Some Don't* (New York, NY: The Penguin Press, 2012).

53 Ibid., p. 10.

54 Ibid. Read the Introduction to the book (pp. 1–17) to get a good orienta-
    tion to Silver's top-line perspective on the prediction process and how to
    professionalize it to make it more "perfect."

55 http://thehill.com/homenews/administration/283333-obama-and-the-endless-campaign

56 http://www.washingtonpost.com/politics/washington-confronts-still-divided-america/2013/04/12/3b5167e4-a386-11e2-82bc-511538ae90a4_print.html

57 www.senate.gov/galleries/pdcl/reelection2014.html http://www.Usconservatives.about.com/od/campaignselections/a/Democratics-Senate-Seats-Up-for-Re-Election-In-2014.html/

58 http://www.washingtonpost.com/blogs/plum-line/wp/2013/04/08/the-morning-plum-revisit-filibuster-reform-harry-reid

59 http://www.washingtonpost.com/blogs/wonkblog/post/does-the-structure-of-the-us-senate-promote-inequality/2012/01/12/gIQA9IxNtP_blog.html

60 James MacGregor Burns, *Packing The Court: The Rise of Judicial Power and the Coming Crisis of the Supreme Court* (New York, NY: The Penguin Press, 2009). http://www.nytimes.com/2009/07/26/books/review/Liptak-t.html?_r=0&gwh=5B608452281E715DE9A1D0FDE0AA768A http://www.slate.com/articles/arts/books/2009/07/the_supreme_court_on_trial.html

61 http://www.startribune.com/opinion/160128835.html

62 Joe Nocera, "Over the Cliff and Back," *The New York Times* (January 5, 2013), p. A.15.

Index